THE
HONEY
GATHERERS

THE
HONEY
GATHERERS

Travels with the Bauls: the wandering
minstrels of rural India

Mimlu Sen

RIDER

LONDON SYDNEY AUCKLAND JOHANNESBURG

To Rati Bartholomew: my English teacher and friend;
To my children: Krishna, Diya and, last but not least, Duniya;
To my grandchildren: Aniya, Arthur and Iskandar.

1 3 5 7 9 10 8 6 4 2

This edition first published in 2010 by Rider, an imprint of
Ebury Publishing
A Random House Group Company

First published in 2009 in India as *Baulsphere* by Random House India

The Random House Group Limited Reg. No. 954009

Addresses for companies within the Random House Group can be found at
www.rbooks.co.uk

A CIP catalogue record for this book is available from the British Library

The Random House Group Limited supports The Forest Stewardship
Council (FSC), the leading international forest certification organisation.
All our titles that are printed on Greenpeace approved FSC certified paper
carry the FSC logo. Our paper procurement policy can be found at
www.rbooks.co.uk/environment

Mixed Sources
Product group from well-managed
forests and other controlled sources
www.fsc.org   Cert no. TT-COC-2139
FSC   © 1996 Forest Stewardship Council

Printed and bound in Great Britain by Clays Ltd, St Ives plc

ISBN 9781846041891

Copies are available at special rates for bulk orders. Contact the sales
development team on 020 7840 8487 or visit www.booksforpromotions.co.uk
for more information.

To buy books by your favourite authors and register for offers visit
www.rbooks.co.uk

Note from the author: the line illustrations are based on sketches drawn by
Hari Goshain in the author's 'little green Chinese notebook' in 1991, when
the guru was visiting a literary festival in Aix en Provence. The author and
publishers are also grateful to quote from the translation of Shakti
Chattopadhyay's 'Abani, Tumi Bari Aachho?' copyright © Arunava Sinha.

Contents

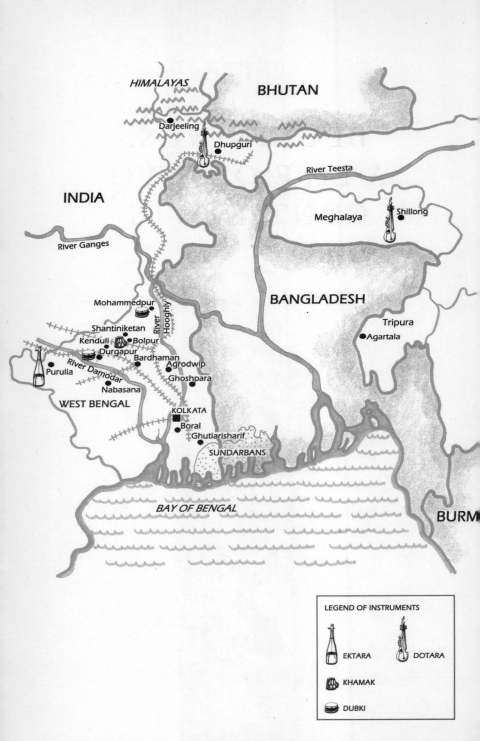

I

BEGINNINGS: A LIFE ON TWO CONTINENTS

Illustration overleaf: The Vault of Existence No 1. The Vault of Existence No 1 and the Vault of Existence No 2 (see page 235) describe the human condition. This first Vault represents a human being in a state of unawareness, feeding on honey from a beehive, unconscious of the bees buzzing around, ready to sting him. The man is framed by two chequered pillars of time, which represent the span of his life. A white rat, Day, and a black rat, Night, nibble at these pillars. Our man keeps feeding on honey, ignorant of the snake which has opened its jaws wide to swallow him and blind to the tiger which waits for him on an upper branch to devour him.

I SAT AWAKE at the barred window of my prison cell after lock-up, my mind buzzing with a thousand thoughts. It was hard for me to go to sleep with the lights on, but this was the rule in Presidency Jail, Kolkata. There was no breeze and the June night was sweltering hot.

Crickets chirped steadily in the darkness outside. Occasionally I could hear the high-pitched whistle of a mole scurrying across the floor to feast on the remains of food on our plates, stacked by the cell door. The two other female prisoners who shared the cell with me, still young girls, lay sleeping peacefully, shrouded mysteriously in their white prison saris and blankets, resembling giant root vegetables.

This prison was nothing more than a replica of the society I'd left behind me in the city. The Female Ward was a jail within a jail. And the Political Ward was a jail within a jail within a jail ... here I was thrice removed from freedom. Outside the barred window an austere phalanx of prison guards separated us from the city, segregating us from the world of men. A bright clear moon covered all with silver.

Close by, hardly a mile from where I sat, the bass siren of a giant trawler on the River Hooghly blared a heraldic note as it left the Kidderpore Docks for the Andaman Sea. How I wished I were on one of those ships, sailing that river, to the great waters.

Nearby roared the caged Royal Bengal tigers in Alipur Zoo, just across the road from Presidency Jail. Behind my cell, the general ward hummed with the night sounds of women, coughs, curses, wails, moaning and mourning. I longed for silence.

Then miraculously, at midnight, a mellow contralto feminine voice rose slowly in song, loud, proud, clear and melodious. Suddenly all other noises faded out. A dancing lilting percussion played on a pitcher, sounding like giant drops of falling water, and a drone instrument, its single note played repetitively on a single string, spread aerophonic vibrations in a great spiral web, accompanying the arias, rising and falling like the waves of a deep and tranquil sea.

> On the banks of this river of life,
> My heart swings and my life swings,
> I drown and gulp in the currents
> Beyond the reach of grand thought
> My heart swings and my life swings ...
> No one will stay with you for ever,
> We will all go down the same path
> Old or young.
> Who are we? Where are we from?
> Where will we go to?
> We deceive ourselves, Bhaba the madman says,
> Exulting in moments of laughter, tears and play.
> We'll drown in endless waters
> Caught in this earthy mandala of illusion and desire.
> My heart swings and my spirit swings. [1]

The words of the song, premonitory, prophetic, calmed me down at this moment of utter despair. It was as though a cooling fluid coursed through my veins as my body surrendered to the music.

I knew that I was listening to a Baul melody. I had some idea of such songs from my mother, a passionate singer and music lover, and I was obsessed by a Baul track on an album called *Indian Street Music*, which had been published in America two years earlier, in 1970, and played often on the radio. It was sung by Lakhon Das, brother of the famous Purna Das Baul.

> O mon amar,
> Shajo Prakriti
> Prakritir shobhab dhoro, sadhan koro
> Dekhbi urdho hobe deher goti
> Mon amar shajo Prakriti ...

> O my spirit, dress like nature,
> Learn to be a woman,
> Acquire spiritual knowledge,
> You'll find that the pace of your body
> Will quicken again,
> O my spirit, dress like nature.

My mother had told me that the Bauls were wandering bards who travelled by foot from village to village, to fairs and to festivals. The word 'baul' derived from the word 'vatula', meaning one who is possessed by the wind; it referred to the windblown, errant character of a Baul. The Bauls sang in buses and trains. Their melodies were poignant, their texts enigmatic. Clothed in long, flowing, multi-coloured robes called alkhallas, often living in pairs, they played their frenetic rhythms on strange, handmade instruments of wood and clay, miming the contradictory moods of nature and of passion.

To the poor, they offered the wealth of the human spirit; to the blind, the divine light of inner vision; to the sick and the ageing, they gave the comfort of faith and cured them with songs, natural medicine and yogic practice. The rich and the arrogant, the selfish and the mercenary, were all subject to their provocative mockery. To women, they offered parity in sexual relations, the possibility of exploring their own bodies, and of leading men to a greater knowledge of theirs. They decried the male-dominated society around them, caught in the shackles of the caste system, and exposed the fanatic parochialism of the mullah and the pundit. These were men and women after my own heart.

Here, in the female ward of Presidency Jail, Kolkata, the haunting Baul melody spoke to me of a freedom that could not be curtailed. Liberty, in fact, was power over the self and not over others. The body could be shackled but not the spirit.

Every night, after lock-up, other voices would lift in song too. I never found out who all those women singers were, voices from among the prisoners in the common ward. Some were prostitutes from Kalighat, some petty criminals, pickpockets, rice smugglers, bird catchers and snake trappers. Their songs were lively, direct and full of spirit, unlike those of the political prisoners who stood in a row every evening resolutely to sing the 'Internationale' and the 'Red Lantern', treating their fellow prisoners with contempt, calling them the 'lumpen proletariat'. They did not talk to me because I chatted with everyone, class enemy or not, especially Bijoya, the formidable warder, who wielded her stick hard and free on everyone, but who came to sit by me each night after lock-up, smoking her chillum, coughing and spluttering, and narrating stories and fables: of Bon Bibi, the forest mother and how she had killed a tiger, of Manik Pir, the Sufi saint and how he had met the Hindu god of artisans, Viswakarma, on his way to the Haj.

I had always hoped for a just and egalitarian Indian society and my experiences had already confirmed for me that rural India desperately needed to be transformed. It had been my impulse to meet the leaders of the banned communist Naxalite party that had led to my arrest at the age of twenty-two in June 1972, and to my year in jail.

Ironically, by the time I was imprisoned, I knew that the Naxalites were not the group for me. I had found their leaders to be misguided, power hungry, caste conscious, sexist, suspicious and insecure, advocating terrorism when their party was banned to maintain their power over the young people, who were raring for change. More inspired by the romanticised guerrilla ideals of Che Guevara and Django (a popular spaghetti western) than by Marx and Lenin, these young people were taking to guns and knives, fabricating homemade bombs, fighting the police in the streets and reciting to each other parrot-like from their new Bible, the Little Red Book of Mao Tse Tung.

When I was arrested, I had declared to the Special Branch police on Lord Sinha Road who had interrogated me that I was a Marxist, of the Harpo tendency, influenced by the Situationists of May 1968 in Paris. (Harpo, after all, was a kind of a Christic figure, a fool and clown, an inspired madman rather like the Baul singers. Only the Bauls had ancient method in their madness.)

As I sat listening to the last verse of the Baul song fade into the prison night air, I knew I was still searching for the right path.

*

I was born a bawling baby with a rebel heart, in 1949, in Shillong, in the crater of a long dormant volcano which rumbled under us from time to time, like a slumbering old dragon. My mother, to calm my tempestuous spirit, sent me to school at the age of three, to a Catholic convent run by Irish nuns. On weekends, she would send me to my grandmother Aasmani, who tied my ankle to a bedpost to prevent me from climbing all over her house. Because of my non-stop chatter my grandmother called me Kathar Sagar, which meant literally 'a sea of words' (the *Katha Sarit Sagar* being an ancient collection of stories). At home, my mother tamed my restlessness by training me to sing devotional songs, and took on a dance master to teach me an acrobatic dance form which mingled masculine and feminine movements.

Outside school hours, she let me run wild and free on our estate, which spanned an entire hill. She taught me to sniff the perfume of the raat ki rani, a flower which bloomed only at night, to watch a myriad stars in the clear night skies once the monsoon rains were over, to read fables – she told me endless stories: the *Mahabharata* and the *Ramayana*, Oscar Wilde and Bernard Shaw. She had a circle of literary friends and, like all of them, read widely. My father, a patriarch, came from the plains of Sylhet, now in Bangladesh. He doted on me and would try to discipline me like any other girl from the Sen family, but to no avail – I was a tomboy, preferred trousers to dresses, and kept my hair short. I would run away, out of his earshot, into the hills and forests above our Tudor-style bungalow, scaling trees and launching my catapult, clambering over the rocks in the mountain stream which cascaded down to the valley below.

When I reached puberty, I ran away from home for good. However, this lasted only a day, because a Marwari family, merchants from Rajasthan, picked me up at a petrol pump on the main road out of Shillong and informed the police, who had received a call from my alarmed father about his missing daughter

In 1967, at the age of eighteen, an adult at last, I left my parents, who had moved to Kolkata. I dropped out of my English Literature course, finding it hard to concentrate on studying Shelley's 'pathetic fallacy' in the great colonial classrooms with their groaning fans swirling slowly high above our heads, while just next to us crowds shouted slogans and tear gas bombs sizzled and fumed on College Street, as a massive student movement gained momentum.

I left my parents to do voluntary social work for victims of famine in the village of Kowaikala in the drought-stricken Bodhgaya district in Bihar. With the exception of myself, all the volunteers were British and American, some of the Americans draft resisters from the war raging in Vietnam. I heard news of the world through them, and all the new music coming out of America and Britain: Otis, Janis, Creedence Clearwater Revival. I would return home on the Gaya Mail from time to time, covered in dust and soot, and tell my mother my own stories: about the lack of food and water, the shocking violence of the caste system in Bihar, the villagers shackled to this age-old system, the beauty of the Buddhist temples in Bodhgaya, the magenta and purple sunsets, the Tibetan monks who droned 'Om Mani Padme Hum' in their deep bass voices, and of course stories about my new friends in Bihar: Steve Minkin of the Peace Corps who wandered the Bihari countryside like a latter-day prophet, Jill Buxton, the half-crazed English lady who carried medicine to remote villages in her Land Rover, the dying writer Mulk Raj Anand and the fervent Gandhian Dwarko Sundarani, who led the relief projects in the area from the Samanvaya Ashram where I was based.

I pleaded with Mother to join me. But arthritis had pinned her to her bed, and it seemed that she was overpowered by the city. She would not come with me, and I could not drag her away from her sedentary, oppressive city life. She would listen to me in excitement and encourage me to be independent, all the while warning me of dangers which might befall me if I was on my own.

Father was baffled. Had I gone off my head? To pacify him, Mother pleaded with me to return to college, so I did, this time to Indraprastha College in Delhi. After my year of hanging off trains and walking about remote, impoverished Bihari villages, it was difficult to adapt to the regimented life of an undergraduate in residence.

So, about a year later, when the opportunity came to join an expedition of British students returning to London along with a dozen Delhi University students – travelling mostly by land across the Middle East, in a long, most unusual journey through Europe – I jumped at it. At last, the world would be mine. En route, we had to fly over Pakistan and join the cavalcade of buses in Kabul, driving on to Herat, Meshed, Tehran in Iran, to Erzurum in Turkey; to Trabzon on the Black Sea over the Zo Digli mountain passes, on to Ankara and Istanbul; through Thessalonica in Greece to Zagreb, Belgrade, Salzburg, Munich, Bruges and finally on to London.

After two months in England, I ran away from the group of student delegates who were representing India, aided and abetted by two friends: one gave me her overcoat, and the other stole my passport from the group leader for me, accompanying me to Waterloo, from where I caught a train and ferry to Paris, with five pounds in my pocket. It was a Paris still on a high, on the last bubble of effervescence left by the student revolt of May 1968. My Air India return ticket was valid for twelve months; I stayed on that whole glorious year.

Jean Claude Fortot and Leo Jalais, French social workers I'd met in Bihar, gave me a roof over my head till I found a room as an au pair, and introduced me to Jharna Bose, who befriended me and took me to visit the painter Paritosh Sen and his wife Jayasree. All three took care of me, provided me with the occasional meal and a sympathetic ear.

It was the Paris of sex and drugs and rock and roll, of Eldridge Cleaver lecturing at Maubert Mutualité and of the Black Panthers discovering their African Islamic roots, The Who breaking their guitars on stage; the Paris also of feminism, psychoanalysis and existentialism. I would stay up all night, going from café to café, meeting the architects of the revolt, philosophers, painters and film makers.

When I finally returned to Kolkata in October 1970, Mother was terminally ill and it appeared that parts of India were in the throes of a Maoist revolution led by the Naxalites. It was then that I became entangled in politics and imprisoned.

Once I was released, I spent a year on parole in Kolkata, having signed a bond that obliged me to stay at Father's house there. As soon as parole was lifted, I left for New Delhi, where my friend

Renee from Shillong welcomed me into her apartment in Nizamuddin. Then I found an apartment of my own in Nizamuddin West, near the tomb of the Sufi saint Nizamuddin Auliya, and would spend evenings listening to qawwalis, Sufi devotional music.

Working for a year in New Delhi as a journalist, I tried to come to terms with what I'd lived through these past few years. Father encouraged me to return to Paris in November 1975, when I was twenty-seven, knowing I was completely unadapted to life in Kolkata. He bought me a one-way Air France ticket to Paris. This time, I left with the stipulated five hundred dollars in my pocket.

Some years passed. I was thirty-three. In Paris, I now lived in a ménage à trois. Not like the Mormons, rather like children of the post-Woodstock era. I lived with Terai and his wife, Katoun. Terai is French, born in Papeete, in the middle of the great Pacific Ocean. He was brought up by his father, a French judge of de Gaulle's *force libre*, who subsequently became a dissident theosophist in south India. I had met him when we'd been students of Delhi University. Katoun was his childhood sweetheart, an exquisitely beautiful, upright, uptight French Catholic with a big heart and a *feu au cul* as she bluntly put it. We were dear friends.

Terai was soft, compassionate and tender, and radiantly handsome, knew my adventurous past and loved my rebel heart. Result: I fell desperately in love with him. We were in a fix. I proposed that there was an alternative to forcing Terai and Katoun to separate; all three of us would live together, happily ever after. And after some initial dithering, they both gave in to my quixotic logic. Katoun became the mother of one, and I became the mother of two of Terai's children. Katoun and I squabbled and screeched at each other. We shared our beds with each other, as well as our responsibility for the children.

All three of us were great music lovers. We never missed Bob Marley, the Rolling Stones or Bob Dylan when they came to Paris. Katoun introduced me to Boris Vian, Jacques Brel, Edith Piaf and Georges Brassens. Terai worked in a travel agency and visited India frequently, bringing back albums of Kishori Amonkar, Gangubai Hangal and SD Burman for me. Whenever I was homesick for India, I'd put on those albums, wrap a sari around myself, village style as I'd learnt in jail, light a joint, and stare at my mother's smiling face, a portrait on my wall, as I hummed the songs of Sachin Karta, as SD Burman was known in Shillong.

> Ooo jani mohua keno matal hoyna
> Ooo jani bhromor keno katha koyna ...
>
> (I know why the mohua flower is never drunk,
> I know why the droning bee never says a word ...)

Terai and Katoun tolerated my nostalgia. We were a family. When, one September day in 1982, I read out a flyer for a concert of Indian music at Alliance Française on Boulevard Raspail in Paris, Terai instantly agreed to accompany me. Katoun would stay at home and look after the children; I'd done my share of babysitting that week, while they had been at the opera with Katoun's father, Clym, a Wagner critic and an enthusiastic supporter of our unusual lifestyle.

I usually avoided going to Indian cultural performances in Paris, but this time I decided to make an exception to my rule. The flyer that had slipped through the slat in the middle of our front door had announced a Baul concert.

> Eight rooms
> Nine doors
> No locks.
> It's a house on three floors,
> On top, courts and tribunals,
> In the middle, merchants,
> On the ground floor,
> Clerks who meditate
> On the room of the spirit,
> It's a house on three floors. [2]

I was still haunted by the songs I had heard from within the confines of my prison cell ten years earlier. It was as if those figures, silhouetted behind the bars of their cells in the Female Ward, beckoned to me perpetually, refusing to let me forget them. I had caught a glimpse of the profoundly intelligent souls belonging to women who lived below the bottom tier of society and who possessed a vast female inherited repertoire of songs, stories and earthy bodily wisdom. My heart yearned to return to them.

Then, in 1979, a documentary by Georges Luneau, *Le Chant des Fous*, had given me another glimpse of these itinerant singers of Bengal. Broadcast on French television, Luneau's film showed a quasi-mythical world of mystic minstrels and ecstatic song; a pastoral world of rice fields, banyan groves and forests of teak by the sides of great river valleys, and of monasteries marked by incredible peace and harmony. Here, among a people who tilled the soil and battled with inclement weather, these bards of rural Bengal created joyous, miraculous music. Wild and free, they raised their clamour in the mansions of the rich, and roared in gaiety in the courtyards of the poor.

The concert was like nothing I'd witnessed before. Dressed in saffron robes and patchwork jackets, three Baul singers played the simplest of instruments. The first carried a one-stringed drone; the second strode in cockily, a khamak plucking drum slung in a bandoulière over his shoulder; while the third came tripping in, jingling a tambourine. Each singer had a remarkable face. Sitting in an open circle on the stage, they invoked their ancestors. Their voices sounded so familiar, I felt I knew them already.

Subal Das, the first, and the eldest, sat in the middle, his hair tied in a traditional Vaishnava chignon on top of a fine, tough Mongol face. He bent his head to tune his drone, and then, tilting it back, cried out:

> O guru, pierce through the unbroken mandala,
> Take mercy on me, show me the light.
> (Akhanda mandale he guru nash koro,
> Aamarey kripa korey aalo dekhao!)
>
> O guru! Put the salve of knowledge in my eyes!
> (Gyana anjana nayaney dao!)

The two singers on each side of him joined in the refrain:

> Gyana anjana nayaney dao!
> Gyana anjana nayaney dao!

The second singer, Gour Khepa, a handsome man in his thirties, playfully snatched the phrases from Subal's lips. In contrast to the smile on his face, his voice expressed utter grief and distress:

> I am a blighted being,
> Blundering about in a life of barren domesticity,
> Meaning eludes me.

The two others joined in the refrain:

> Gyana anjana nayaney dao!
> Gyana anjana nayaney dao!

The third singer, Paban Das Baul, graceful, lithe and radiant, came vocally pattering up front, bringing softness, a pleading quality, to the invocation.

> I kill myself wandering, my feet are heavy,
> Take mercy on me, show me the light.

His peers took up the refrain:

> Gyana anjana nayaney dao!
> Gyana anjana nayaney dao!

Small, slim and fine, Subal began to dance, as though suspended on an invisible thread, his gestures like those of an imperious lover. His voice, polished like brass, took me down the muddy waters of the great rivers of my ancestral land: the Ganga, the Padma and the Brahmaputra.

> O boatman, I've not found the beginning
> Nor the end of this river.

The urgent push of these waters was palpable in each phrase of his song, warning me of dangerous currents eddying inside me. I was to learn, over time, that Subal was irascible, bulimic, acid, profound – a shrunken sage – and that he had watched his family die in the Bengal famine of 1943.

Even more disturbing and irresistible was Gour Khepa. Mocking, teasing, he sent out a charge of energy through his instrument, electrifying the entire audience. His companions receded into the background as he took over the stage, his khamak howling in rage, his strident voice rising in decibels to a point where it became unbearable, crushing all feelings with the sheer weight of its dissonance. Grinning and grimacing, he had the defiant, paranoiac posture of someone in a constant state of challenge, playing games with anyone whose eyes met his.

I didn't even notice Paban at first, next to these two more forceful figures. Feminine, pliant, with a head of curly locks, he had an innocent face, his bright eyes laughing. He hung about in the background, poking his index finger into his left nostril to clean it, unaware that the French public in the auditorium were chuckling because they imagined his gesture was part of the show. He rose, swirling gracefully around Subal and Gour, striking his tambourine softly at first, then building up, little by little, to a crescendo of thundering rhythm, till at last he began to sing. Transported by the spell of his deep, bass voice and his insistent, steady tempo, the two older singers leaned and swayed, then leapt up to join him in a dance. The three formed an ensemble, turning, dancing, jumping; they began to whirl, commanding space like a cyclone.

They reminded me of a pillar of dust I had seen while driving through the drought-stricken Bodhgaya district of Bihar in 1967, crossing the horizon at its own pace, uprooting electric poles and trees, making cows fly.

The magicians on stage charged each other with energy like lightning conductors. Each passed his current to the other, creating sonic waves with their instruments, which transformed into birds: clay-bellied babblers and bamboo-nosed warblers, wood-eared and copper-beaked, gut-eyed and silk-voiced, humming, droning, jingling.

I sat, enthralled, wanting to cry out to them, wanting to break the stunned silence of those who sat around me. The shadowy figures of the women who I'd heard singing in prison were no longer with me. The sorrow I'd felt in being removed from the lands of my origin and in being torn from my beloved mother suddenly left me, like a breath held for too long.

When the concert was over, I walked up to the stage. Paban was seated there alone, looking morose. His face expressed surprise and awe when I addressed him in Bengali. He rushed off in search of Deepak Majumdar, a bearded, bespectacled Bengali intellectual with the traditional jhola bag slung across his shoulder, and the leader of their group. With his consent, we made a date for dinner at my home the next evening.

The next evening, we dined together in the little basement kitchen of our home on the Rue du Moulin des Prés. Deepak and the Bauls seemed as delighted to meet me as I was to meet them, and even more so when they saw what I'd cooked for them: a simple Bengali supper of rice, dal, fried aubergines and some catfish picked up in Chinatown nearby and cooked into a light, watery curry spiked with kalonji, chilli and coriander.

Paban cried out. 'Hari bol! Hari bol!' (Take the name of Hari!)

'Magur macher jhol!' (A catfish curry!) rhymed Gour Khepa, grinning from ear to ear.

'Ghor jubotir kol!' (The lap of a young woman!) Subal Das took up the rhyme *sotto voce*, his thin lips curling slightly on his inscrutable face.

We were old soulmates although we'd only just met, and I chatted with Deepak happily.

Terai and Katoun disappeared after dinner. They had to be at work at nine the next morning, and lived by the rigid Parisian clock. My own clock was more flexible. I had a part-time job as a translator, and often worked from home. So I stayed up with the Bauls till dawn, entranced, listening to them play and record their songs on my little tape player, and chatting with Deepak, who turned out to be a cult Kolkata poet.

He also had an encyclopaedic knowledge about the Bauls, as well as the life and struggles of the famous poet Rabindranath Tagore. Tagore, who had first introduced the Bauls to the West, he told me, was ostracised by a strand of puritanical Bengali society because of his friendship with the disorderly, barrel-voiced, hemp-smoking Bauls who flocked to his side in the small town of Shantiniketan in West Bengal, and disturbed the peace of the genteel, anglicised middle-class folk at his newly founded University of Visva-bharati. The very same society received him with adulation when he won the Nobel Prize.

Forgotten things, buried in myself, floated to the surface as I listened to these stories. The texts of the songs that the Bauls sang for me took me back to places I'd almost forgotten. I felt released from the obscurity of the years separating me from a childhood spent with my mother in the northeastern hills of India. At dawn, in winter, we would walk uphill towards the Tripura Castle. We would stand on a stone ledge, below which lay a secret rose garden and a goldfish pond. If the sky was clear, we would glimpse through the mist the snowcapped peaks of the eastern Himalayas. She would sing to me then, songs from the plains of Bengal which lay some-where in between those peaks and the ones we stood on.

So I knew every word of the song Subal now sang to me. It was a song my mother had taught me:

> I've gone mad seeing the beauty of Gour!
> Medicines have no effect on me.
> Come, friend, let's go to the river!
> The thorn of Gour is terrible

If it pierces you, you'll be destroyed!
Gourango transformed into a serpent
Has pierced my body
Come friend, let's go to the river! 3

I felt hit in the guts, in the centre of the solar plexus, the manipur chakra, stung by a stealthy serpent. I'd held my breath for too long.

Paban helped me clear up in the basement and load the dishwasher while Deepak, Subal and Gour Khepa smoked their last chillum of ganja, arguing with each other vociferously in the living room upstairs. Wild and abandoned on stage, reincarnating a veritable bhairava baba – a divine lord of the forest – Paban was quiet off stage, seeming overpowered by his articulate, bullying elders. He was twenty-six years old but looked like a stripling, and fell easily into the role of a younger brother, calling me didi – sister. He invited me to visit the Baul Mela, the festival of Kenduli in mid-January, on the day of the new moon, Makar Sankranti. Mela, in local parlance I learnt, meant 'plenty'. It also meant a fair.

Makar, Paban told me, was a crocodile, but when he attempted a sketch on my kitchen wall with a pencil, it looked more like a dragon. I made a mental note to wipe it off before Katoun woke up, as I told Paban I'd try to make it. We stood at the window for a while, as dawn broke over the poplars in our triangular patch of back garden. A blackbird sang on the laurel tree, announcing the sunrise. Like the Magi, the three Baul singers and their guide, Deepak, loaded me with invisible treasures and left to catch a train to Marseilles and La Ciotat.

The house was in a shambles, dishes piled in the sink in the basement and cigarette butts strewn all over the floor of the sitting room. I was past sleeping; I made myself some coffee and began to clean up. At seven, I woke the children; Terai shaved and left for the office; Katoun ran to catch her bus to the school where she worked part-time as a monitor. No one knew about the cyclone that was spiralling inside me, about to carry me off far away from this life.

I spent the morning running through my household chores, listening to my recordings of the night before with the volume turned up. The Bauls' voices – jazzy, mischievous, emotional – inhabited me, squatting like refugees from some third world. They had broken into my house and left with the goods.

Paban's voice bellowed at me through the tape recorder:

> If you want to conquer your spirit,
> Form a gang of bandits
> Use devotion as your pivot,
> And break into the house of dharma.
> Ram Chandra says:
> The day has passed by
> I must dress like a thief now
> The art of robbery is worthwhile
> If you don't get caught. [4]

Feeling like a thief, I telephoned Deepak upon his return from Marseilles. He invited me to watch *Carmen* at Peter Brook's theatre at the Bouffes du Nord, with him and the Bauls.

After the performance, we were invited to break bread with the cast. I sat on one side of the table with Subal, Gour and Paban, while the eminent Mr Brook sat opposite us with Deepak Majumdar and Georges Luneau, who monopolised his attention, not bothering to introduce me or to include the Bauls in the conversation. Gour, restless, itching for a fight, tried to break through the monumental pyramid of words Deepak inevitably built up to explain the smallest little detail. He raised his ogre's voice and began hurling insults at Deepak in Bengali, obviously hating not being the centre of attention. Subal sat by him with a crooked smile on his face. Meanwhile, Paban handed me his paper napkin, on which he'd drawn an ektara (a round-bottomed, thin-necked instrument) with a pair of eyes and a nose and mouth, P – A – B – A – N written under it in squiggly English letters: his first love note to me.

No sooner had I accepted Paban's gift than Gour Khepa flicked my spoon and sent its contents flying in the air, splashing the three men opposite us with milky green watercress soup. I would have stayed on to watch this scene play out, but I had to leave as it was time for the last metro train. I turned back to wave at Paban, who followed me with his eyes while the others continued to argue with each other, hardly noticing my departure.

A couple of months went by. I listened to the Bauls' recordings over and over again. Their voices beckoned to me more and more strongly. If Terai and Katoun were struck by my obsession, they had no notion of its singularity. To them, it must have seemed an aspect of what they knew to be my temperamental nature. But this fascination was too important for me not to share.

My old friend Jharna and her husband Deben, who lived nearby, on Rue Lepic in Montmartre, became my allies. I'd met Jharna on my first walkabout in Paris in the winter of 1969, without a centime in my pocket and with a head full of dreams. She fed me, called me Srikanto, a runaway character in a nineteenth-century Bengali novel, and became my guardian angel.

Jharna had come to Paris to write her doctoral thesis on the influence of French symbolism in Bengali literature. She had stayed on when she met the great Deben Bhattacharya, a trailblazing, self-styled ethnomusicologist who moved to Paris in the seventies. He had been the first to point out to the world that the gypsies had originally travelled from Rajasthan across the Middle East, to fan out to Europe and North Africa. Deben had showed me his beautiful photographs of a procession of gypsies in the famous village of Santa Maria de la Mer, in the south of France. He had entered the procession disguised as a gypsy, holding an altar in his hands in which he had cleverly insinuated a tape recorder.

I confided in Deben and Jharna about my desire to explore the world of the Bauls, to begin with a visit to the festival in Kenduli, and indeed to return to India for a while.

Terai, Katoun and I had been drifting apart since the summer. Passion had scurried out of what had become our practical, established routine of life and love in Paris. There was no space for dream and play. And I was yearning for a deep, familiar breath of India, to share it with my children. I needed them to be known and loved by my family in India, however dangerous and irrational it might be to prise them away from the French École Communale. I needed to mourn my beloved mother, who had died over a decade earlier. I needed to settle accounts with my father, who wanted me to take some responsibility for his affairs in Shillong and in Kolkata, as he had retired from business. Many things had been left unsaid between us since my mother's death, and I felt ready to return to them now.

Deben cheered me on in this impulsive enterprise while Jharna, more sober, advised me to live in Shantiniketan; here my intentions were more likely to be understood than in Kolkata. She handed me the keys of her flat on Southern Avenue, in Kolkata, to use as a transit point. Deben lent me his marvellous book of translations of Baul songs, *Mirror in the Sky*.

The text was accompanied by haunting black-and-white photographs taken by Richard Lannoy of the great Nabani Khepa, an exemplary Baul singer and friend of Tagore, with his sons, the great Purna Das and Lakhon Das Baul, whose song had so haunted me. It was this modest little volume which had brought Allen Ginsberg to Shantiniketan in the sixties, a journey which was to lead to another one. Purna and Lakhon went on to travel to New York, and were befriended by Sally and Albert Grossman, who got them an album deal with EMI. Baul singers entered the annals of modern music history; Purna Das Baul was immortalised on the album cover of Bob Dylan's *John Wesley Harding*.

Terai and Katoun didn't say much when I told them of my decision to leave for Kolkata, and eventually make a base for myself and the children in the university town of Shantiniketan, as Jharna had recommended. They knew me well enough by now. I was stubborn, individualistic, cussed, self-willed and restless. My departure felt to them like the end of our relationship although I swore eternal friendship and love to them. We finally agreed that I would leave with Duniya, who was just a little over two years old. Krishna, who was older, would come and join me later, once I'd settled down and had a place of my own.

Terai went upstairs, avoiding my eyes. I switched on the radio. One of Bach's fugues was playing. Katoun and I looked at each other and laughed; the word *fugue* in French meant the sudden disappearance of an individual from where they lived. It was time for me to disappear.

December 1982. We woke up inside mosquito nets in my father's house on Jhautalla Road, south Kolkata. Duniya was amazed to find her cousins, Rahul and Kunal, sleeping like sardines next to her. Maya, a very young maid, not more than twelve, came in with a cup of Darjeeling tea for me, specially brewed for me by my brother, Gautam. I sipped it pleasurably, listening to the morning sounds which penetrated the thick walls of the old mansion. The grinding of trams on Amir Ali Avenue, the high-pitched bells of the rickshaw, and clanging of prayer gongs in the house next door, cawing crows, chirping sparrows, and the cries of 'kabadi wallaaaaaa ... ' – the call of the tin can man, who bought old newspapers, empty bottles and cans – pierced through the distant roar of traffic on the main road. I heard the rattling of a dugduggi, a kettle drum; Maya came rushing in: 'Didi! Didi! Bandorwala!'

It was the monkey man. He led in a pair of monkeys on a leash, and settled down on the porch. The she-monkey was wearing a miniskirt and a blouse, and a thin red scarf wound around her head. The he-monkey wore an embroidered skull cap and tight black drill trousers.

'Chak a chak!' said the monkey man, rattling his drum.

The two monkeys faced each other, raised and lowered their eyebrows comically.

'Dhak a dhak!' cried the monkey man. 'Kama Sutra dekho!' (Come watch the Kama Sutra!)

The he-monkey mounted the she-monkey and they somersaulted over each other in a perfect wheel. The children laughed and clapped their hands. Then Father entered with a bag stuffed with provisions from the market, handed them out, and chased the monkey man off. The children were distracted by the gifts he'd brought back: a clay pot piggy bank painted in red, white and green, and some crunchy peanut brittle.

The telephone rang. It was Deepak, returning my call. He proposed that we try to meet at the Kenduli Baul festival, which Paban had told me about in Paris. It was in mid-January, three weeks from now. But I had no idea how to get in touch with the Baul singers, as I told Deepak.

Deepak told me I would find Subal Baba with his wife Sundari Ma in his ashram in Aranghata, in the district of Nadia, and that Gour Khepa could be found with his khepi Hari Dasi in the vicinity of Bolpur station. Listening to him, I remembered that Bauls often use the title 'khepa' at the end of their names, which describes those who are endowed with frenetic energy (literally meaning 'the enraged one'). Khepi is the feminine of khepa and a Baul's consort such as Hari Dasi is called his khepi.

Deepak added that he'd spotted Paban 'hanging about' the TV station in Tollygunge in Kolkata. I flared up, finding him unjustly disparaging. 'You've been telling everyone that each Baul is a walking radio station, haven't you? Is it surprising that Paban should wish to outdo his peers? He's younger, more modern than Gour and Subal. Why are you big machos always after Paban's blood?'

Deepak was delighted with my reaction, and told me conspiratorially, much to my irritation, that Paban knew I had arrived in the city and that he had already given him my address. It didn't take long for the young Baul to ring the bell of my father's house.

He was dressed in a plain cotton kurta and trousers, and looked like any other city kid except for the length of his hair, which hung in ringlets over his forehead, and a snaky earring on his earlobe. Instead of lounging on a cane chair in the hallway under the cool breeze of the fan, as any of my friends would have, he stood petrified in a corner, his small head bowed when he noticed Father. My father lifted his own patrician head, took a good look at him, barked 'Ki he?' – So, sir? – and returned to his Sunday morning paper. I came to Paban's rescue and ushered him into my room. I knew that he came from a world that didn't sit on chairs.

My room was bare except for a mattress on the floor. Duniya lay on a dhurrie, sprawled out amidst her toys. My things were spread out on the floor. Papers, pencils, crayons, books and cassettes were strewn carelessly on a low table. Duniya turned to Paban and studied his face gravely, then silently handed him her fluffy brown bear. Paban breathed a sigh of relief, took his shoes off carefully, and placed them outside the door. Settling down on the dhurrie, he began to turn the cassettes over.

I switched the tape recorder on to play him my recordings from Paris. Subal's voice blared out. Paban listened for a minute, and then switched it off. He picked up his small tambourine and began to sing. Duniya clambered on to my lap. We kept time and listened to him, spellbound.

> Raise the sail, boatman, don't delay,
> Untie the rope, boatman,
> Let's go to Medina
> Prophets of the world have come
> To this scintillating house of maya and meena
> When they weep, a thousand diamonds,
> When they laugh, a shower of pearls!
> O Compassionate One,
> He who has the Murshid as his companion
> Has no fear of crossing the waters,
> The Kabaa is in his heart
> And Medina is in his eyes
> O the light of Noor has illuminated the world,
> The lamp of Noor burns bright in each house in Medina. 5

Paban's song was an invitation to set off on a journey to wondrous shores. I was enchanted, at once bristling with anticipation, impervious to the world outside.

Father's leonine head appeared above us, just then. He stood at the door of my room and questioned Paban, from across the threshold. 'Where do you come from?'

'Mohammedpur in Murshidabad district,' Paban replied.

'Oh, so you are a Mussulman?' my father asked. It was surely Paban's choice of song which had led to this question. My hackles rose.

Paban's tone was low and humble, but firm and proud, as he responded. 'No, sir, my family is Vaishnava. I sing Baul songs. We Bauls make no difference between Hindu and Mussulman.'

Although Father had refused to look at me, he breathed a distinct sigh of relief. 'We are Vaishnavites too,' he said then, surprising me. [6]

Turning to me, Father said warningly, 'Listen, my dear, you know the rules. If you want to do things your way, you must do it on your own, and if you live under my roof, you must abide by my rules.'

'Yes, Father! I'm leaving soon. I've decided to live in Shantiniketan for a while,' I told him. He knew me well.

This had been the golden rule between us since I'd first left home at seventeen, and it allowed us to interact as equals, much to the surprise and jealousy of other members of the family whom my father crushed with his aristocratic glare. But I had learnt to glare back early in life and take on the aspect of Ranachandi, which was his pet name for me, Chandi being the warlike form of the energetic goddess Kali.

Anyone who sets foot in Kolkata quickly comes to know that it is through strict segregation that a status quo is maintained between the village and the city. There was no exception to this rule in our high caste, Westernised, urban family, which depended on a support system of servants; villagers who'd come to the city to find work when they'd been starved out of their villages. This had been going on in Bengal for three centuries, and will probably go on for another three.

As a member of the low caste village world, Paban's presence in my room was an aberration and a shock to the household. His voice, which carried a mile or two in open fields, was an instant magnet, and his instrument, a simple wooden tambourine with two sets of metal clappers, rumbled like distant thunder, annulling the possibility of a private rendition. However, since I had the reputation of being a headstrong rebel with a sharp tongue who had lived licentiously in Paris, as well as that of being Father's favourite, no one complained.

The news of Paban's subsequent visits would spread like wildfire through the neighbourhood, however. Firstly, through the network of housemaids and servants and drivers who systematically spied on everyone and reported back to the saabs and memsaabs about the goings-on in the area; and, secondly, more importantly for me, because Father, on his way back from the market every morning, roared news about his spoilt, wilful daughter to all and sundry. It was his way of placing his umbrella over my head; Bengali culture is oral, and the spoken word invariably carries the most weight.

Paban stayed for lunch. He sat at our immense Queen Anne dining table looking pretty woebegone, especially when Father began to question him about his presence in Kolkata. He explained timorously that he had formed a band with his brother Swapan and some village musicians, and that they were about to leave for New Delhi for a TV show on a national network. He would be back in a few days, with Swapan and the other members of his band, and they were then to go together to the Kenduli Baul mela.

Paban told us that it was in Kenduli that Baul singers drew up their calendar of engagements for the season. All the local producers of Baul music, usually from the coal and iron belt of the Damodar Valley area and from the hinterland of Durgapur, poets and intellectuals from Kolkata, and often small producers of cassettes and 'little' magazines which tried to perpetuate the Baul tradition by printing contemporary repertories, would all converge at Kenduli. Paban and his band were sought-after and extremely popular there.

I invited Paban to lunch with us again on his way back from New Delhi. We could then go together to Kenduli. Father shot me a baleful glance, which I ignored.

He had accepted my life in Paris without giving me too much trouble. When I had been expecting my son Krishna five years previously, I'd written to him making a clean breast of my life with Terai and Katoun. That was another rule between us since Mother's death; to tell each other the stark, naked truth, even if it hurt. He had read my letter out to my elder brother Gautam in a grave voice and bought himself a ticket to Paris to visit us. When he arrived, Krishna was seven months old and Diya, Katoun's daughter, just two months old. Katoun told him she felt like she had been pregnant for fourteen months, which cheered him up instantly. He got on well with Katoun and her father, Clym, after this. We all went on a marvellous trip to visit friends in Bayonne, in the southwest of France. The local ironmonger in the village of Mirepeix in the Basque country still remembers my father as the Indian raja who bought all his bronze lanterns. They now shine in Kolkata at night, during the frequent power cuts.

But this was different. 'So why now remigrate to the world of the Bauls? You are an uzbok! A dolt!' he said, the minute Paban left.

He was closer to the truth than he knew. The Bauls had emerged from the mingling of early Sahajiya Buddhist and Vaishnava philosophy and practices with Sufism, which arrived in India down the silk route from the Middle East with the advent of Islam in India. 'So Uzbekistan is probably close to where it all started,' I told Father triumphantly.

My father snorted at me impatiently as I explained all this to him, and focused on Duniya, taking her off to nap with him as she always did, sprawled on his big belly.

I had the afternoon to myself. I looked out of the window at the mango tree outside, in our neighbour Ahmed Ali's garden. A kokil warbled, reminding me of the dawn my mother had left us. February 1971, when I'd just turned twenty-one.

'Turn the house around so that I can go out the other side.' So she had instructed me in this very room, as though the house was a Lazy Susan. As she was carried out on a stretcher to the St John's ambulance, she asked for music. She'd long ago chosen the music she wanted to leave the world to, irritating me with her fatalism: 'The Blue Danube', of all things.

'O Danube divine, pam pam pam pam. Such rapture is mine, I ne'er can tell.'

The end was terrible, pipes and catheters thrust into her struggling body. Just before she lost consciousness, she murmured: 'I think I'm falling into a gorge.'

Her eyes opened for a second, and she looked straight at me as she waltzed into the depths, the clouds lying low, into the fog and the rain of her beloved Khasi and Jaintia Hills; to a heavenly ball-room filled with twirling dancers, finally a star of the silver screen.

In the absence of a feminine presence at home, Father had no option but to ask my aunt to reason with me. My aunt had lived with us in Shillong when I was a child. Unlike my mother, she was a conservative, traditional Bengali housewife.

To reassure Father, I went to visit her before setting out for Kenduli with Paban. I sat for lunch with her husband and his brothers, while she served us. She would eat only once the men had eaten, abiding by laws made by the ancient king Manu some two thousand years ago. Afterwards, we sat on her terrace in Lake Gardens, as she put out bottles of salted lime to pickle in the sun. She looked preoccupied, a sharp little worry furrow on her forehead.

'Whatever you do, mona meye, never take a diksha mantram,' she told me.

'Of course not!' I prevaricated, a little put out at the suddenness of her remark. Taking a diksha mantram meant being initiated by a guru through the transmission of secret words. However, I was moved by her term of endearment, mona meye – sweetie pie; she had used it with me on very special occasions, when I was a child.

'Mona meye, let me tell you a story,' she began. 'My great-aunt, your great-great-aunt, Borthakurma, was widowed in the forties. Your grandfather, as her nephew and the eldest brother in the family, gave her shelter in our joint family home in Sylhet. He ruled the family roost with an iron hand. Your grandmother suffered from asthma and badly needed rest. Borthakurma took over the reins of the kitchen from her, proving herself to be no less of a dictator than her draconian grand-nephew. She ran the kitchen like a factory, which functioned full steam from dawn to dusk. She was always hot and foul-tempered, wiping her face and neck with the end of her sari as streams of perspiration ran down her face. We children were terrified of her lashing tongue and fist, and never went into the kitchen when she was around.

'Every evening, Borthakurma would prepare a big bowl of rice pudding and a mountain of flatbreads, and carry them to your grandfather when he returned from court. He would run through his evening meal in a matter of minutes. Aunt and nephew would then sit solemnly waiting for the four beeps which announced the evening news on the radio. Afterwards, she would plan the next day's menus and the shopping for the family, which often extended to a hundred-odd people.

'Borthakurma also fed fools, beggars and madmen. A true blue Baidya family will always serve sadhus, gurus and Vaishnavas. And so, one day, a sage, wearing saffron robes, with a noble face and streaming white locks, came into the compound. Borthakurma served him with her own hands, in the courtyard in front of the kitchen. We children noticed from our perch in the mango tree that he whispered something into her ear when she bent to serve him. To our amazement, we saw a beatific smile spread over her face. Her angry, lined countenance softened and became smooth.

'The next morning, the household awoke to a bloodcurdling wail, and a terrific clamour from the direction of the kitchen. Borthakurma was kicking cooking pots and pans over, and they clattered and spun like tops on the kitchen floor. When she saw her nephew approaching her, she careered off the track that led out of the compound, mourning and wailing. Your grandma brought her back into the inner courtyard, asking, "What on earth is the matter?"

'Borthakurma looked blank, muttering continuously under her breath: "Siddhi guru! Siddhi guru! Siddhi guru! Siddhi guru!"

'It was a while before we children could take in the enormity of what had happened. Borthakurma had been given a diksha, an initiatory mantram, by the old sadhu. She went to sleep repeating the mantram, but when she awoke she'd retained only half of it. She rushed downstairs only to find that the old sadhu had disappeared. There was no knowing where he had gone. From that day on, she flailed about the compound like a headless chicken, her post in the kitchen forgotten, with that half mantram a constant drone on her lips.

'Your grandfather was devastated. Borthakurma was his favourite aunt and ally. He would break down in tears when he returned from court in the evenings to see if she had still not returned to normality. The family, moreover, was deprived of her delectable cooking and her formidable organisation of the kitchen. Little by little, the sad woman lost her grip on the world. She withdrew from the kitchen, forgot to bathe, comb her hair or change her clothes and stopped eating, constantly muttering the mantram; before finally descending into a deep, catatonic trance. After a couple of years of unbearable suffering, she passed away in her sleep.

'After the cremation, the entire family congregated for festivities orchestrated by your grandfather. Mourners sang, weeping and rolling on the floor. Hundreds of visitors arrived. Food was cooked according to the strict rules of the funeral rites: mung bean dal was soaked in water overnight and served with freshly grated coconut and sugar in the mornings; milk was turned into curds and whey; fine-grained pearly atap rice was steamed with mung beans; fresh vegetables were served with ghee for the midday meal. In the afternoon, the younger women and children chattered in the courtyard, cutting reams of white foolscap paper into paper chains and domes and lustres to decorate the courtyard, till it was dusk and time for tea. Calm descended on the family, freed, at last, of a troubled soul.

'But at twilight, Uma, the youngest among us, came running into the courtyard, shivering and sobbing. "Borthakurma is alive! I heard her in the toilet!"

'Your grandfather had been reading his evening paper as usual with his legs stretched wide apart on the wooden slats of his easy chair. He looked at us unbelievingly for a few moments, then ordered for torches to be lit. The toilet cabin was at the edge of the compound under a giant mango tree. Your grandfather headed in that direction while the servants held up the torches to light his passage. We children trailed behind, terrified. A voice could be heard distinctly from the direction of the toilet.

'"Siddhi guru! Siddhi guru! Siddhi guru! Siddhi guru!"

'The servants drew back fearfully. Your grandfather snatched a torch and held it high. On a high branch of a fig tree which overhung the cabin sat a pair of blinking mynahs, chattering Borthakurma's refrain.

'"Siddhi guru! Siddhi guru! Siddhi guru! Siddhi guru!"

'The black birds, disturbed, squawked and flew into our faces. We leapt back in fright. Your grandfather and all the elders, bewildered at first, burst out laughing. A pair of mynah birds had made their nest in the tree above the toilet. They had learnt my great-aunt's mantram while she dropped her turd every day. Hearing your aunt Uma enter the cabin at the very same hour as Borthakurma would have done, they had started screeching her half mantram in greeting!'

Through her story my aunt was transmitting several messages to me. She was warning me, astutely, that no good would come of my truck with Bauls and fakirs. We were a high caste Baidya family. Traditionally, the Baidyas practised ayurvedic medicine and rarely married outside their caste in order to preserve their knowledge of herbal lore and cures. However, Paban was a Baul singer, and the inevitable intimacy which travelling with him to the world of the Bauls was sure to entail, represented a kind of dangerous openness; a loosening of caste bonds and a rupture with family rules, the customs of our Hindu society.

But I was in no mood to listen.

'People will always give you advice. Listen to what they say but do what you really want to. Trust yourself.' So Mother had counselled me early in life. Thank God for Ma!

The next morning, after breakfast, I strapped my rucksack to my back and filled our water bottles. Duniya, who was in my father's arms, watched me with worried eyes, straining to return to me. She did not want to be left behind! We waved goodbye to my father through the window of the black and yellow taxi in which Paban waited for us, and left for Howrah station, to catch a train from Kolkata to Durgapur. Father looked very sad.

Leaving the city was a long and difficult process. Masses of humanity struggled to enter the city and here we were, longing to be free of it. Everywhere around us were cries of alarm, incessant honking of horns, fumes of diesel from motorbikes and scooters which wound their way through the maze of stationary trucks and buses, bullock carts loaded with merchandise; masses of people pulled in by a terrific, magnetic force. Earth city, city of Kolkata, cursed city, city of refuse, city of refusal.

We waited in the taxi, in the middle of choked traffic on Howrah Bridge, watching the swiftly moving brown sludge of the Hooghly River below. Paban plucked the strings of his dotara, a small lute-like instrument, and sang softly, 'Sarbonaisha Padma nodi tor ki ache sudhhai.'

> O Padma, river of disaster, I beseech you,
> Tell me, are you endless?
> I'd hoped to reach the shore quickly,
> But six boatmen have cheated me,
> They've axed down my boat
> And now I have no hope of reaching the shore. 7

Duniya, impatient, moved from my lap to Paban's. Just a few weeks ago I'd walked with Krishna and Duniya on the banks of the Seine, eating candyfloss and visiting the apiary in the Jardin des Plantes. It seemed so far away, and so long ago.

I looked over and noticed that Paban seemed uneasy. We were on shifting sands now. Paban, years younger than me, was already more mature than I was. It is only now, looking back, that I realise that he was possibly already aware of our impending union and its dangers. I, on the contrary, was quite oblivious to the fact that we were going to develop a life-long relationship. For the moment he was just a young friend with rare, magical qualities who would guide me into the world of Baul songs.

Suddenly, miraculously, the traffic cleared. We entered the giant railway station at Howrah, and soon left behind the huge mass of steel and concrete that was the industrial suburbs of Kolkata. Duniya had fallen fast asleep in my arms, and Paban was dozing. I took stock of my surroundings as the train plunged us into mile after mile of field and village, dark, heavy clouds hanging overhead, signalling pollution.

To see Kolkata, the economist Ashok Mitra had said, you had to get out of it.

From the window of the train, the story of Bengal was written in unmistakable letters: on the immense junkyards and dilapidated shantytowns which bordered the railway line.

There had been immense technological development here in the early part of the twentieth century, as the Indian Railways transformed life in the Indian subcontinent. The machine goods industry of Howrah serviced the Indian Railways, bringing tea and jute, primary cash crops, to the port of Kolkata.

But the final partition of Bengal in 1947 led to a slump in development. The rich hinterlands, which had provided the industrial belt with raw materials and nourishment, remained in East Pakistan, present day Bangladesh, whilst the factories and technology were located in West Bengal. The three main resources of the state – tea, jute and the machine goods industry – collapsed because of technological decline. Next, the collapse of these industries led to massive unemployment. In this acute situation, politicians of the extreme left became active and joined up with international protest movements. Very aware of the need for change, I had felt compelled to make contact with these movements and to try to meet their leaders, which had resulted in my arrest a decade earlier and the year I spent in Kolkata's Presidency Jail.

Kolkata soon shrank from its international stature to a mere provincial city. In 1970, a Pan Am flight transporting GIs to Vietnam was besieged on the runway of Dum Dum airport by crowds demonstrating against the Vietnam War. Overnight, Pan Am, along with several major international airline companies, rerouted their flights through Bombay and Bangkok. Suddenly, money abandoned the megapolis. Strikes and lockouts continued to paralyse industry. This led to a flight of capital to labour-safe areas such as Delhi in the north and Bangalore in the south. In the meanwhile, after the war of 1971 and the formation of Bangladesh, the number of people in the city increased to frightening proportions, as massive populations drifted towards Kolkata.

The Bauls and the Vaishnavas, the tantrics, worshippers of Shiva and Shakti, the village yogis, and the fakirs – indeed the entire itinerant world of popular folk tradition – joined this migration. Whereas the Bauls and the Vaishnavas are known for their mendicant and, to some degree, itinerant ways, the tantrics are viewed as being perhaps more esoteric; practising hatha yoga and often devotees of Kali, they carry out rites viewed by other sections of society as repulsive, such as meditating on dead bodies and using skulls for their rituals. The fakirs, on the other hand, are mystics of Sufi origins who sing marfati, Islamic devotional songs, which distinguish between the way of knowledge and the way of law.

These practitioners of folk music, arts and crafts were caught between the devil and the deep blue sea. Disillusioned with the anarchy and superficiality of life in the city, they retreated deep into the impoverished countryside, living on the edges of the villages and small towns. Somewhere in between these two closed worlds they lived, constantly on the move. The traditional support systems were disappearing. Religious barriers were hardening. The villagers who patronised the Bauls lived themselves in dire poverty and conflict.

The rich, rustic world that was the fount of their inspiration was drying up, as well. The Bauls were essentially rural bards; how were they to survive if that very world was in decay? Paban's attempt to move out of this deadlock was to create a modern band which played traditional Baul music. But not all Bauls managed to do so. Tinkori Chakraborty, who joined us on the train, described their situation well. Tinkori was a thin, wiry man, with fine features and straggling hair, a beard and an intense, ascetic face, topped with an elaborately embroidered fakiri cap. He had left his home and his Brahmin father to follow the Bauls as a young man. He was a brilliant percussionist who played the dubki, similar to a tambourine. When he sang he never knew when to stop, but he knew how to tell stories.

'A Baul singer was going on his round of madhukuri, collecting alms in the villages adjoining his ashram. The villagers who were themselves impoverished gave him no alms. At midday, hot, tired and dejected, our Baul took shelter under a tree. A bird sang on the tree and the Baul went into a state of pure ecstasy, listening to the song of the bird.

'Hare Krishna Radha! Hare Krishna Radha! Hare Krishna Radha!

' "In this world which has forgotten the divine magic of lovers, here is a bird who remembers the sacred names," thought the Baul to himself.

'A fakir was passing by. He saw the Baul sitting under the tree, illuminated and joyous.

' "O brother Baul," the fakir said to the Baul singer, "pray share with me the reason of your joy! In this dismal world of poverty, your face shines like a new coin."

' "O brother fakir," the Baul replied, "listen to this bird. In a world which has forgotten the holy names here is a bird who chants Hare Krishna Radha!"

'The fakir turned his ear to listen to the song of the bird. "O brother Baul," he said, "I do not hear the bird say the names you speak of!"

' "What do you hear?" the Baul retorted.

' "I hear the bird say: Allah Rasool Khuda! Allah Rasool Khuda!" insisted the fakir. "Holy messenger of God!"

'They began to argue vociferously. A vegetable vendor who was passing by saw the two wise men quarrelling.

' "O my fathers!" he declared. "Pray what is the reason of your dispute? If you holy men fight each other, what shall we ordinary mortals do?"

'The two men elaborated the reason for their dispute to the vegetable vendor.

'The vendor, in his turn, turned his ear to the song of the bird. "O my fathers!" he exclaimed. "I do not hear what you hear."

' "What do you hear?" asked the Baul and the fakir.

' "I hear the bird sing of what's in my basket: Piyaj roshoon aada! Piyaj roshoon aada." Onions, ginger and garlic! Onions, ginger and garlic!'

Laughing, we reached Bardhaman Junction, ninety kilometres north of Kolkata, and stopped for a few minutes before the train sped into the countryside. The hinterland looked tired and over-used, like an old crone. Skeletal cows grazed in fields empty of vegetation. Hardly any forests anywhere and mile after mile of barren land. The ponds and water bodies next to the railway line glistened with the rainbow colours of grease and pollution.

Gazing at the scenery, I reflected for a moment on the signifi-cance of madhukuri, which Tinkori had mentioned in his story. The word refers to the rounds Bauls make in order to receive alms in return for their singing. It literally means 'honey gathering', and has a ritual and sacred significance. When the song of a Baul penetrates the ear, flowers bloom in an inner tree, the kalpabriksha, and honey rises along the stamen to the pistils of these blossoms. It is in exchange for this intangible gift that villagers give alms of rice and lentils, fresh fruit, vegetables and oil to the Bauls.

I woke out of my daydream as the train filled with an older, poorer population. Paban whispered in my ear that I should be careful now because there were, around us, the beggar, the inevitable pickpocket, the conman, the chhintai parties, the snatchers. Vendors ferried their wares up and down the aisles crying out in loud nasal voices, 'Chai! Chai!'

Duniya stood up on her seat and looked around her with great interest. We bought slices of cucumber, muri – puffed rice – tea, boiled eggs, a squeaky plastic doll, a nail cutter, some tiny red boxes of Chinese tiger balm and a cheap edition of Bengali folk tales. Paban listened, enchanted, as I read stories from *Khonar Bocchon* or *The Wise Words of Khona*, and *Malanchamala, the Garden Beauty*, two exemplary heroines. Khona is a vac siddha, one whose power over words is such that whatever she says comes true. Her father-in-law, who fears her powers, cuts her tongue off.

Malanchamala is a stable girl who looks after a winged mare, Harikali. She is forced to marry Chandramanik, an infant prince, only twelve days old. Together, this incongruous couple are banished to life in the forest, to make friends with Bagh, the tiger, and his wife, Baghini, and their little cubs. Under the watchful eye of Malini, the garden keeper's wife, they live through many adventures. Chandramanik imagines that Malanchamala is his mother. Together, they live through countless episodes which will take them through two cycles of twelve years before he realises that she is his wife, and not his mother!

I had no idea that Paban and I would be living out a similar scenario, soon. Sages, after all, write prophetic tales so that we ordinary mortals can discover the meaning of our lives. Paban told me that the very same story existed as a piece of musical theatre written by the famous saint Shiraj Shah, the guru of the most renowned Baul poet Lallan Fakir, who had deeply influenced Rabindranath Tagore and was the subject of Allen Ginsberg's famous poem, 'After Lalon'. Called *Roop Bhan Jatra*, it was a different version in which Malanchamala was called Roop Bhan and Chandramanik Rahim.

Meanwhile, the landscape began to change outside our train window. Factories and townships gave way to fields in cultivation; shimmering ponds encircled with giant palmyras; small, snaking rivers, and clumps of trees which marked off village settlements. We were heading below the poverty line, the line that separates the world of the urban gentlemen, the babus, to which I belonged, from the world of the Bauls, the world of Paban.

II

DURGAPUR: CAMPFIRES, WITCHES AND SHANTYTOWNS

Illustration overleaf: Madan, the god of desire, with his bow and arrow. Madana is a reincarnation of Krishna and the equivalent of the Roman god Cupid. The Bauls believe that desire is one of five arrows, corresponding to the five senses, which lead to enlightenment.

WE GOT OFF the train at Durgapur station to call on Paban's family for a couple of days, en route to the Kenduli festival. Paban also needed to gather together all the members of his band for their performances in Kenduli. The band included his brother Swapan; Naba Kumar, a flautist and farmer who lived in a village about ten kilometres from Durgapur; and Madhusudhan Ganguly, a tabla player who would join us later as his village was on the way to Kenduli.

Durgapur, the second largest city of West Bengal, was an inflamed nerve centre. The morning papers on the train had stated that brick-bats and bombs were being used in gang fights between factions of militia organised by party bosses. The city, in the stranglehold of a war between unions and management, straddled, like a dying colossus, a huge expanse of what was once cultivable land. In the early part of the century, outlying villages had been literally uprooted by the mining of coal and iron. The land was now chequered, divided into colonies and housing estates.

Paban's family had settled here, on the edge of the city, in Deshbondhunagar Colony. They had left their original village, Mohammedpur, which lay to the north of Kolkata, when he was a child of six. I'd expected to find that he lived in a monastery among the Bauls, and was surprised to see a makeshift shanty township appear on the horizon, and to discover that he was a kid from the slums, just like those grimy boys with frayed trousers found in railway stations all over India.

As we approached the colony in a cycle rickshaw, we stopped at a level crossing for the passage of a train. A small boy, about six or seven years old, panting and out of breath, appeared alongside us. Paban pulled him up onto the rickshaw. It was his nephew, Bakul.

Over the years, I was to see Paban repeat this gesture again and again, reaching out to his impoverished family, lifting them out of dire straits, calming their unending anguish with his songs; trying, unceasingly, to pull them across the poverty line.

Wordlessly, Bakul pointed towards the railway line, where two village women, shrouded from head to foot in cotton saris, were being led away by two massive policemen, dressed in traditional white dhotis, half-sleeved shirts and black shoes. The men shouted curses and showered blows on the women with their lathis as the strange procession advanced, Indian file, along the railway line.

Duniya looked at my face and sensed that I was upset. She was about to burst into tears, but was distracted by the train which roared past us, whistling: whoo ooo ooooo! The gate reopened at the level crossing. The rickshaw puller pedalled strenuously over the bumpy railway lines, carrying us past the rail gates and over a dirt road. We entered the colony of red-tiled shacks and shanties, built on the edge of a canal, and stopped in front of a cluster of huts, nestled on top of a hillock.

Paban's entire family had congregated at the very top of the hillock, above the huts. All eyes were fixed on the two women who had been apprehended. They hardly noticed our arrival. The railway station lay to the left of where we stood. We had a clear view of the passing trains; unused wagons lay in the railway yard near the station. In the distance, we saw the dwindling figures of the two women and the two policemen, who were still raining blows on them with their batons.

I looked in the opposite direction. Beyond the canal lay a vista of dried-out fields. It was late morning and the sky was sparkling blue, the sun strong although we were in the middle of winter. Paban pointed to the horizon; the Kenduli Baul festival, in the village of Kenduli, lay just beyond.

Mukul, another nephew of Paban, came running up from behind us just then, through the shrubbery that bordered the canal. He had a bulging jute sack in his hands. Through a tear in the sack gleamed jet-black chunks of coal. His face, hands and feet were covered with soot, and his eyes were bright with laughter.

Paban's eldest brother, Amulya, winked at me conspiratorially and turned to Mukul. 'Rajar chheley, koylawala!' (The coalman, song of a king!) he declared ruefully.

This was normal practice in this part of the world; begging and stealing were a way of life here.

'Hide the sack before the cops come back. We can't keep it in the house,' Amulya told Mukul. Mukul disappeared down the hillock towards the canal with his loot.

It was part of everyday life for the women in the colony to pilfer coal from the trains. They ground it into powder and mixed it with cowdung to make gul, balls of fuel for their cooking fires. One day, quite soon after we'd arrived, I was to join the women as they foraged with an akushi – a long stick with a curved blade on top, usually used to pick fruit – to rake out pieces of coal from the wagons of passing trains going from the collieries in the Asansol and Dhanbad regions to Kolkata. We returned home to the colony, grimy and dusty but full of energy.

But the two housewives whom we had just seen had been arrested because they hadn't had the money to pay off the policemen when they had been caught. Like many women in the colony, they were the thieving mothers of children who would later learn to become thieves themselves.

Paban was the one that got away. He had learnt how to climb out of the basket of crabs. Using his voice as his akushi, he picked out songs from the vast repertory of Baul songs, the luscious fruit of a multitude of trees of knowledge.

We looked at each other without speaking. Deep in his heart of hearts, he knew that if he had not been blessed with wings of song, he would have been reduced to becoming a common thief. My heart filled with love and sympathy for him. Duniya, sensitive to every change in my moods, stretched towards him and leapt into his arms.

I was shocked and disoriented by the sudden violence and extreme poverty of this way of life. The dismay must have showed on my face, for now, all attention turned towards me. Paban's father, Dibakar, came forward to greet us. An ageing lathiyal, skilled in a form of martial arts using batons, he was lithe and compact, with long, white, flowing locks and a beard, a pair of battered round glasses glinting on the edge of his nose. Paban's mother, Ulangini, returned to the hut, melting into the shadows. Neighbours who looked like factory workers, dressed in pants and shirts, kept coming and going, attracted by Paban's arrival; greeting Paban, unashamedly curious about my presence here with Duniya.

I felt stifled, hot and restless, unused to so much attention. Duniya was exhausted by the journey. Paban's vivacious sister, Anima, ushered me onto the veranda and we settled down on a wooden cot, the only piece of furniture visible. She gave us a drink of water and offered us a tiny aluminium plate of sugar wafers. The women of the house gathered around me, forming a circle, as though to protect us from the stares of intruding neighbours. Ulangini pulled her sari over her head and shouted at the assembly to leave.

'It's time to prepare the midday meal, so out of my way now. Paban, go and do the shopping and then take this ma to bathe,' she told her son.

But the crowd that had gathered in the courtyard seemed reluctant to leave. Ulangini lit a charcoal stove on the other end of the veranda, blowing through a funnel to raise a flame. A thick cloud of black smoke dispersed stragglers.

Dibakar stroked his long, flowing beard, coughing and spluttering, watching the playing out of events with a twinkle in his eye. Leaning his weight on his stick, he casually emptied a jute bag out on the floor in front of his wife. It contained some vegetables, a gourd, chillies and a cornet of teak leaves in which some catfish still tossed and turned, their great eyes distended. 'This is my contribution. My alms for today.'

Paban and Swapan exchanged looks. Although they hardly spoke to each other, the two brothers were in total accord. They stood up together in a manner which seemed almost choreographed. Their father's tone at the moment implied that he expected his sons to do better. Paban quickly took things in hand. 'Swapan, go borrow the neighbour's cycle. Let's fetch some fish from the market.'

Ulangini pulled out provisions and a traditional dao, a curved blade wedged into a piece of wood, from under the wooden cot, and, straddling it, added: 'Some oil and spices too.'

Paban frowned. 'You can get that from the grocer next door, can't you?'

Ulangini's reply was muffled as she held her sari to her nose, poking into the coal: 'We owe him three hundred rupees.'

Swapan returned with a cycle and I joined the men in the court-yard, leaving Duniya sleeping on the cot. Dibakar looked into my eyes, putting his arms around Paban and Swapan. 'My diamond and my pearl!' he declared of them. Paban's eldest brother Amulya and his middle brother Promulya looked on indignantly. 'And we're coal and cowdung, are we?' Amulya's tone was sarcastic.

The women all roared with laughter. Paban disappeared with Swapan, pushing his cycle. Three separate households lived in this compound. Paban's parents lived in the main house with his youngest brother, Gopon, who was still at school. The two elder brothers, Borda and Mezda, lived in two separate huts with their wives and children, at a higher level on the hillock. The courtyard was communal. Meals were too.

Mezda came to sit by me. Unlike his wild-haired brothers, he had cropped hair, wore trousers and a frayed shirt, and was neat and elegant. Although unemployed, he told me he was an active member of the local Communist Party of India-Marxist or CPI(M) unit, which had promised to secure jobs for him and other men of the colony. As I write almost three decades later, he's still waiting.

Borda had a shock of curly white hair, a young face, and sharp eyes. He was dressed in a long saffron robe. His hair had turned white when he had gone loco one day, stopped going on his rounds of madhukuri and begun to write songs. Premature greying was a gene which ran in his family. Paban's hair turned white early too when he began to write his own songs in the nineties, and discovered a new world of hackers, stalkers and pirates when trying to protect his intellectual property rights.

The women cleaned the rice whilst sitting in the courtyard, their saris drawn over their heads in the presence of Dibakar, their father-in-law. They giggled merrily when they saw me share a hookah with the men in the darkness of the veranda. Promulya's wife, Kalpana, strong, dark and beautiful, came forward and asked me to hand her the pipe as well. Everyone laughed even more.

The sun was blazing in the sky now. A huge pot of water began to simmer on the chula stove. Borda's wife went and stood by her mother-in-law. She drew the mortar and pestle from under the wooden bed, and ground ginger and cumin and chillies into a paste. Borda returned from the canal, and put a basket of kolmi saag, edible bindweed, next to his mother.

'I plucked these from the edge of the canal. I think there's enough for all of us.'

Duniya, who had nodded off on the cot, clambered back into my lap, clutching on to her battered brown bear with its glinting, beady eyes. The children of the house crowded around us, curious, as they were prepared for their bath in the sunny courtyard.

Duniya was equally intrigued as we watched Dibakar strip them, lay them on his knees, and rub their stringy bodies down vigorously with mustard oil. The children then ran down the hillock to jump and swim and sport in the canal. After their bath, the children ran in dizzying circles in the courtyard around us. Duniya looked around, amazed, from within her safe place on my lap. This was a sea change from her crèche on Rue du Moulin des Prés, in Paris.

I counted seventeen people, including the children who clambered on to my lap the minute Duniya vacated it. Duniya turned back to observe them, but then ran off to play with a litter of brown puppies which were suckling on their worn-out mother as she basked in the courtyard.

Paban reappeared then with some water chestnuts, which he cracked open and fed to Duniya. The other children crowded around to take their share. The entire family held him in high esteem, it was clear. He was their provider, their protector, the genius of the family. Paban showered his love on them, teasing his brothers, joking with his brothers' wives, ordering everybody around; he was quite different from the subjugated person I'd seen until now among the other Bauls, and even with me.

We shared the simplest meal of rice, dal, saag and a diabolically hot fish curry, eating with relish. After the meal, I offered to help the women, but they declined, smiling at me sceptically. Duniya and I retired to the wooden cot on the veranda, watching the women sweep and mop the floor and draw up drinking water from the well that served the area.

Around us were the sounds of workers hammering, of men and women and children; the lowing of a cow and the sharp trill of a bird, and, far away, the rumbling of the trains carrying coal and steel to Kolkata. I was overpowered by sleep as I watched the discreet movements of the women in the courtyard, and drifted off, listening to Paban as he spoke softly to his parents.

I awoke to the sound of instruments being tuned. Night had fallen, and we walked outside to the darkened courtyard so Duniya could take a pee. When I asked her to squat under a tree she protested, affronted by this final rupture with French toilet training. I insisted. She obeyed. When she finished, she sobbed in my arms. But when she saw Paban waiting for us on the veranda with a torch, she jumped into his arms, her outrage at these new ways forgotten.

Inside the hut, Swapan was seated on a narrow wooden bed, waiting for us to join him. He was ready to accompany Paban with his khamak plucking drum, which he played with an eye-shaped mediator. Swapan was very quiet, and seemed in absolute awe of his elder brother. He had a Baul chignon on his head and a wild fierceness about him, and when he sang, his eyes turned upwards, only the white of his eyes appearing like quarter moons under his half-shut lids. Mezda played a pair of small bronze cymbals.

The tiny room was so crowded that there was hardly any place to sit or stand. All the members of the family had gathered around, and some neighbours had dropped in as well. Myriad faces glowed in the soft light of a single oil lamp which lit the room. Paban and Swapan began to sing together, two brothers in harmony.

On the earth's breast,
Large currents of water
Streams full of anguished cries.
In the year 1385
The dam burst on the River Damodar,
People ran to the school building
With infants in their arms,
I saw in the waters of Satighata
A great bridge,
Its iron posts and pillars,
Lying in the water.
Many ox carts, many old men and women,
Many canals and rivers got carried away,
Floods rose in every house
People were killed as walls fell down.
Bardhaman, Bankura, Medinipur, Manbhum,
Dumka, Patna, Murshidabad, Birbhum,
Over sixteen territories, tearing iron pillars,
Water has spread all over ...

Borda had written this song after the severe floods in the Damodar river valley area in 1978, which corresponded to the year 1385 in the Bengali calendar. The Damodar River, which emerged in the Chhota Nagpur plateau in what is now Jharkhand, to our west, had changed its course several times over a century, wreaking havoc on every occasion. To add to this cataclysm, some thoughtless officials had, in a panic, let down the floodgates at the Durgapur barrage, causing severe flooding in Bankura. Paban had been in Kolkata for a concert, following which he had gone shopping for saris for his mother and the women in his family for the festival of Durga. The great city was submerged as a bore tide rose up from the Bay of Bengal to the Hooghly River, which overflowed into the streets. Paban was stranded for a week but made the most of it by singing every day and cooking and distributing khichuri, earning a small fortune from a middle-class Kolkata public, who were delighted with the new way of life the floods had brought with them. When he returned home to Durgapur, his purse full and bursting with spirits, he found the family sitting around the relics of their mud house, which had been washed away as the Damodar River changed its course and found a fresh path to join the Hooghly. His dream, after this, was to build a concrete house for the family.

Detaching an ektara from its hook on the wall, Paban plucked the string with his index finger and tuned it to his own voice. A soft, persistent drone filled the room. Paban handed me the instrument casually and I accepted it. It was a gesture that would change my life. The ektara had been given to Paban's father by a very old Baul sadhu, long deceased. I turned it upside down irreverently to look at it, peeking inside its dark interior, and noticed that Paban was watching me.

The ektara had a large round rice-eater's belly, made of a dried gourd, cut open on top and at the bottom. A bamboo pole about a foot long, split down the middle, was attached to the open top of the gourd in the form of a mini Eiffel Tower. The bottom of the gourd was covered with goatskin, held tautly to the base of the drum by a ring woven from strips of bamboo. Another such ring was placed on the top end, from which a frame of gut string zigzagged over the entire circumference, holding the instrument together. Paban said it was the very emblem of the Bauls. The gourd with its telegraphic pole represented the human body and the metal wire along its axis, the spinal cord through which energy could be transmitted.

My instrument was volatile, even more so than most acoustic instruments, and as fragile as a hothouse flower. When I had finished looking inside it, I turned it back to its normal position and tried to play it; but it was out of tune again. Paban asked me to hold it straight and steady. He squeezed its bamboo neck once more, tightening its key with one hand, asking me to pluck the string while he did this. He varied the pitch till he was satisfied, and then let go. Pulling his small wooden tambourine, his dubki, out of his bag, he began to sing. I accompanied him gingerly at first, but when I found that the instrument was responding of its own accord to the music, I let myself go.

From the moment I began to play the ektara I felt released, armed with the means to offer myself to the pilgrimage I was about to undertake. It gave me a centre, permitting me to anchor myself in a magnetic field, a sphere of sounds and songs, of music and of human love: Baulsphere. I was a transmitter, emitting sonic waves to create the shruti, the diapason, for Paban's incandescent voice – the transmission tower of his radio station so to speak!

I learnt more about Paban's family over the next few days. Like Paban himself, Dibakar had been born in the village Mohammedpur in the district of Murshidabad, and belonged to the caste of malakars, who traditionally made garlands of flowers for village deities. He performed the ritual dance during the fertility rites that accompanied the festival of the Dharmaraj, the aspect of Lord Shiva that is Lord of the Animals and of Dharma. Dibakar, wearing a massive and heavy wooden mask of the primeval father, would lead the sacred dancing around the deity to the roll of the dhol, the nahabat and the nagara, three traditional drumming instruments used in this part of Bengal. Dibakar had also become a lathiyal, practising the martial art at night, secretly, as it had been banned by the British. During the day, he worked as a bodyguard for the local landlord.

To his two elder sons, Dibakar transmitted a keen knowledge of plants and flowers, of magic and alchemy, of martial arts and combat. Today, Borda still practises ojhagiri sorcery in the colony. He is frequently called upon to exorcise evil spirits. Mezda learnt the martial arts and, when he was made redundant from the local graphite factory, his skills made him a useful recruit for the militia maintained by the local CPM party bosses.

Dibakar's two younger sons, Paban and Swapan, had been born after Dibakar lost all his ancestral rights and took to the calling of his Vaishnava origins, begging for alms: they became mendicant singers. Cut off from their earlier family traditions, neither Paban nor Swapan learnt martial arts from their warrior father. Instead, from early childhood, they hung off trains and sang their way through life; eking out an existence for their impoverished family. To them, Dibakar transmitted his knowledge and love of song and dance and music, as well as philosophy. They embody the mood of renunciation and asceticism that overtook him in the second half of his life.

Anima, Paban's only sister, was vivacious and active in the running of her father's household. In between Paban and Swapan in age, she was married to Badal, a destitute weaver. Endowed with a harsh, melodious voice, Anima sang powerfully, although only inside her father's home. She listened to no one, her husband least of all. Wild, free and spirited, she was adored by her brothers.

Gopon, the youngest brother, was the only literate member of the family. He went to the local high school, didn't do too well in his studies, but was an excellent sportsman. Born in a shack by the railway line in Sainthia after the family finally left the village of Mohammedpur, he would later face serious difficulties in negotiating the world. Literacy among the scheduled castes, tribes and other 'backward classes' (as they are known) carries its own curse; the despair and rage which comes from the knowledge of exclusion. Gopon became angrier and angrier over the years. And he would never learn to sing or play an instrument.

The story of how the family migrated to Durgapur slowly unfolded. I learnt of how the village of Mohammedpur became an impossible place in which to live following the death of the landlord for whom Dikabar worked. This was a decade after the land reforms of the 1950s, which came with India's independence. Subsequently, the landlord's land was divided into smaller plots among his inheritors, who found that they had no use for Dibakar and others like him. Dibakar had too many enemies in the area from earlier feuds.

His means of subsistence endangered, for a while he tried to survive in the village, but he lost his rights to cultivate the land he'd once considered his own. Without land, Dibakar and his family were quickly impoverished. Defenceless, severely afflicted with eczema, he desperately looked for remedies. Finally he was obliged, like many others, to leave the village and look for other work.

Shahid, a young neighbour, came with news of employment. He was acting as a middleman for the owner of a brickfield in

Barrackpore, in the hinterland of Kolkata. He was to take thirty able-bodied men from Mohammedpur to work at the brickfield for a few months. Dibakar was left with no choice but to accept his proposal. He took fourteen-year-old Amulya, the eldest, with him, as a cook for the team of labourers. Shahid advanced him some money, which he left with Ulangini so she could take care of Promulya, Paban and Swapan, still a babe in arms.

The events that followed became so painful that even now Dibakar and Ulangini spoke of them with great distress. Shahid was a crook. Soon after the men had begun work in the brickfield, he returned to the village to make payments to the families, or so he claimed. It was a ruse. He promised to return in a few days' time with news from the village. A week passed by. Then two weeks. Meanwhile, Dibakar used up the money which had been given to him by Shahid to buy provisions for meals for the team of workers. When he asked the owner of the brickfield for some more to shop for provisions, the man insisted that he had already given the sum covering their salaries to Shahid. He'd also given him money to buy provisions, he claimed. He produced a piece of paper that had been signed by Shahid.

Dibakar addressed the brickfield owner with the dignity of a chieftain. Under no circumstances could the men from Mohammedpur be expected to work without food. But the man insisted that since he had already paid their salaries, they were obliged to stay and work for him.

Dibakar returned to the tent to relate the story to those waiting in the camp. They realised that they had been trapped. That night, a small group attempted to leave the labour camp. The brickfield owner retaliated by calling in policemen, who beat them brutally with their batons. Dibakar and Amulya were unharmed as they were working in the kitchen at the time.

After this, a police picket was installed inside the brickfield. Provisions were procured under the policemen's watch, but no one was allowed to leave the compound. For the next couple of months they lived as if inside a prison camp, with no news of Shahid or of their families.

The situation was getting desperate. Dibakar knew that he would have to find a solution. One day, he spotted a relative of his deceased landlord master over the boundary wall of the brickfield. The relative was a lawyer and had probably come to the Barrackpore courthouse, which was not far from where they stood. As the man got off a cycle rickshaw on the main road, Dibakar called out to him. The wall guards posted towards the gate took no notice, luckily.

The lawyer came over and greeted Dibakar. The two spoke to each other across the wall, and Dibakar recounted the trials of the duped villagers during these past few weeks. The lawyer was shocked, and reassured Dibakar that he would help him. He had some work to finish in court that morning but promised to return early that afternoon and do what he could to get them out of this hell-hole.

He arrived in the early afternoon as he had promised. He walked straight into the brickfield owner's tent. Very soon, tempers flared and voices were raised. 'How dare you imprison the people of my village? Release them at once!' the lawyer demanded. Tensions ran high inside the camp.

They heard the brickfield owner insisting that he had paid three months' salary to Shahid, and that the workers had to stay till the end of their term. This meant another four weeks at least.

The brickfield owner was, however, no match for the lawyer. 'If you don't let them go at once, I shall move the law and we shall see what you can do. You cannot keep them here by force and you shall pay for this in the court of law.' The lawyer spoke in a commanding tone that left no doubt that he would act upon his words.

Then, walking out of the tent, he stood by the gate and directed the men to leave. Meanwhile, the men of Mohammedpur, led by Dibakar, advanced towards the gate with their bundles and their possessions. The policemen, who were crowding the gate, backed away and lowered their sticks at the behest of the authoritative lawyer.

The lawyer turned to Dibakar and handed him some money. 'Move out quickly. There's no need to wait for your salaries. They will never come. Go home at once!'

The group, led by Dibakar, made their way to the district where they lived by train. In the evening, they finally walked back to their village, as they had longed to do for weeks.

They were met with tears of joy and lamentation. In the absence of the two men in her family, life in the village over the last few months had been very painful for Ulangini. A couple of weeks after Dibakar's departure to the labour camp, she had run out of funds. At first, her neighbours collected rice, procured oil and vegetables for her. Dibakar, as the head of the old landlord's army, had been a very important figure in the village, and, as the wife of Dibakar, Ulangini had enjoyed power and prestige. A proud woman, she had felt humiliated by her neighbours' magnanimity, and had been aware of the sly smirks and the nudging of elbows behind her back.

Left to fend for herself and her four younger children, she had sent Promulya, her second son, then only twelve years old, to work as a shepherd. His meals were taken care of by the owner of the flock, a neighbour. She put Promulya in charge of five-year-old Paban. Swapan and Anima, still babes in arms, stayed at home with her.

The two brothers left every morning to graze cattle in pastures outside the village, and returned at twilight once they'd sent the cattle back to the fold. Promulya tells me how, as a child, Paban already had a special spark of light in him, how untamed and free he was. He would sing along with the birds and the insects, miming their sounds. Crickets chirped, and partridges whistled ti tarrrr ti tarrrrr in the shrubbery, surprised by the intrusion of humans, whilst bright green parrots cried and whirled over the groves of fruit trees in full bloom. Paban would be humming a tune, hopping and dancing and playing drums on whatever he could lay his hands on.

At midday, the two brothers would share a meal of chhatu, uncooked chickpea flour, which Promulya had carried to the fields, tied in a bundle inside a thin cotton towel, and slung over his shoulder. They were constantly hungry, foraging for maize and sugar cane in the fields.

'Hey Allah kurbat! Lathir bhitor sharbat!' (Allah's works are great! A stick containing sherbet!) Paban remembers a visiting neighbour shouting, when they brought their plunder from the fields back to their mother.

One day, some Santhal boys from a settlement in the forest appeared and passed by the spot where Paban and Promulya sat, watching over the grazing cows. Descended from Afro–Aurstral forest dwellers, the Santhals were the first people to inhabit the western parts of Bengal and their domain stretches through the forest belts to the contiguous states of Bihar and Orissa. They enjoy a rich musical tradition, especially singing and dancing.

These boys were armed with catapults, bow and arrows. They greeted Promulya in their own language and passed by. Paban ran after them, curious to see what they were up to. The Santhal boys chattered amongst themselves, preoccupied with their search: they were hunting field rats.

One of them sang a sweet, sad melody with a catchy refrain that Paban picked up right away and sang back to them to attract their attention. They turned to look at him gravely, pausing for a while. Suddenly, one of the boys, who had run a little ahead, flung himself down and blocked a hole under a tamarind tree, signalling frantically to his companions. The others all ran up to him and began to dig furiously around the hole with their arrows. To the amazement of the two brothers, huge quantities of unhusked rice gushed out of the earth.

Promulya and Paban watched as the Santhal boys followed the sound of screeching, till they uncovered the nest of a family of field rats. Carefully blocking the exit, the leader of the group inserted his hand and drew out the creatures, one by one, throwing them on the earth. The others grabbed them and hit their heads with rocks to kill them.

The rats, plump from their diet of grain, were thrown onto a fire of straw and twigs which the boys built in a jiffy. They skinned and cleaned the entrails of the roasted animals, rubbed them down with salt and chilli from little newspaper packets they carried with them, and began to eat them hungrily. Seeing the two brothers looking on, they invited them to share their meal. Paban was the first to taste the meat. It was stringy but delicious, and tasted like rabbit, he found. Promulya followed suit.

Next, the Santhal boys took out a sack and began filling it with the rice that overflowed from the rat warren. Promulya was carrying an empty gunny sack which a farmer had given him, and he followed suit. By late afternoon, several warrens had been dug up and sacks of grain collected from the underground tunnels of the prodigious field rats.

Exhausted by their hours of labour, the boys finally gathered in a circle. The Santhal boys sang a song, playing the flute and the dotara, while Paban thumped on a broken pot which lay in the fields. The sun set behind the sated group. Promulya and Paban returned home that evening jubilant, with their heavy load of grain. Ulangini said nothing. When Promulya suggested to his mother that the discovery of the underground granaries might mean they could store up for the monsoon season and stay on in the village, she burst into loud sobbing. Were they now to live on charity from the Santhals and pillaging field rats? When Dibakar returned from his trial at the labour camp, she pleaded with him for them to leave the village for good.

During this time, Paban began to display the same spirited thrust of energy which had made his father a survivor. Barely six years old, he began to accompany Dibakar, who had now chosen his new vocation as a Vaishnava, a mendicant, on his rounds. In the household of one of the babus of Erol, a village near Mohammedpur famous for its worship of Kali, he heard the songs of the fakirs and sages for the first time.

> O my spirit, you body clock, you golden cowrie,
> Who is the carpenter who has built you?
> He winds the key, and lets it be, and now, my spirit,
>   you body clock, you tick tock.
> He makes an earthen box and puts a machine inside,
>   where the all-merciful comes in to hide.
> He made a clay doll and put a machine inside,
>   where the all-merciful comes in to hide.
> Praise be to this carpenter, who hides inside every house,
> None but the all-merciful knows how. [1]

Recognising his joyous spark, the fakirs embraced Paban fondly and encouraged him to play the tambourine. Enraptured by their frenetic rhythms and enlightened souls, he begged his father to buy him a dubki. The instrument became his second skin. He played it night and day, and organised little ceremonies with his brothers and sisters, during which they would dance and make offerings to imaginary deities in time to his tireless percussion, to his rapping of the popular tunes, rhymes and couplets that he picked up from all around him.

> Dhin taker beta tin tak!
> Aami dite thaki, tui khete thak!
> O tor ma redhe che pui shak!
> Aami dite thaki tui khete thak!
>
> (Dhin tak, son of tin tak!
> I keep giving, you keep eating!
> Your mother cooks pui greens
> I keep giving, you keep eating!) [2]

Leaving their mother in the village, Paban and Swapan would accompany their father on trips which sometimes lasted for days. They visited many villages in the district. The three of them would leave home at dawn and walk to the main road to board a bus. Sometimes, the bus conductor would stop and make them get off halfway, because they could not pay their fares.

They would then approach the nearest village and sing the name of Hari, begging from door to door; often visiting as many as ninety to a hundred households. Occasionally, they would be offered water or tea. In this way, they would also collect rice, dal and vegetables, and then find the shade of a tree in which to rest at about three in the afternoon. They would wake, prepare a meal and then continue to walk to the next village in the evening. If they collected a lot of rice, they would sell some of it to the local village grocer. With money, they could board a bus and travel into the town of Khandi, where they would visit the shops and markets. They would collect provisions and then return home to Ulangini.

It was on one of these rounds that they met Dadang, a holy man venerated by the shopkeepers of Kandhi. Stocky and muscular, he would strut down the main street naked, his penis swinging like a pendulum in front of him, beating a rhythm on his pot belly with a stick. Legend had it among the local shopkeepers that Dadang brought luck; if he entered a shop, all the merchandise sold out that very day. So shopkeepers solicited him enthusiastically, making offerings of food and clothes which he took no notice of. Shamed by his nudity, they would try to cover him, but he would rip the clothes off and return to his natural state at once.

At night, Dibakar and his two younger sons, Paban and Swapan, often slept next to Dadang, in the same shelter, by the Kali temple. He was kind to the children and brought them food to eat. They, in turn, played pranks on him; poking his genitals with a stick while he was asleep, and giggling and shouting as he leapt up and chased them. When Dadang died some years later, the Santhals venerated him as a manifestation of the deity Marang Buru.

Despite the success of these trips, Ulangini urged Dibakar again and again to leave Mohammedpur, wanting to leave the past behind. Finally, leaving the two elder sons at home, the family set off one day for the fair at Vairagitala: the first stage of a new life. The road to Vairagitala went in a straight line past the village of Panchthupi, about twenty-eight kilometres from their own village, which it took them two days to reach. They stopped overnight at Panchthupi, named after the five ancient Buddhist stupas scattered around the village. It was the end of winter: the villagers were observing the festivities of Saraswati Puja. Paban remembers watching children celebrate the festival in the village courtyards, dipping their fingers in milk to write the Bengali vowels on banana leaves: Aw Aa, E Ee, Ou Ouo, A Oiy, O Ou in order to appease Saraswati, the goddess of knowledge, the arts and music, who is often depicted floating on a white swan, playing her bina or lyre. Looking at the children writing, Paban knew he couldn't join them because he had to move on with his family. They went on to the town of Kirnahar, and there Dibakar decided that they would take the train to Ahmedpur.

It was the first time the family had boarded a train. They managed to scramble on with all their bundles but the carriage was so crowded that somehow Dibakar got left behind. Ulangini remained on the train, confused and frightened, clinging to her children. She got off at Ahmedpur, deciding to wait there for her husband. An old sage with a beautiful face came up to her and spoke to her very kindly. She talked to him for a long time and told her children that the old man resembled her father. Cooking their meal next to the station under a tree, she invited him to share their food. When Dibakar finally arrived by the evening train, it was already dark.

The family spent the night at the station, and the next morning they continued to Sainthia, a township on the railway line in the district of Birbhum. Now about forty kilometres away from Mohammedpur, they squatted on the railway platform. Promulya and Amulya joined them there a few days later.

As the year advanced and the heavy rains and violent winds came, Dibakar realised that it would be impossible for them to stay on under the open sky. Ulangini could not cook under the meagre shelter of the tree they had camped beneath, because the rainwater put the fire out. So Dibakar rented a room in the colony next to the station for thirty rupees. He decided to settle in Birbhum; their old life in Murshidabad was behind them now. Promulya and Amulya made friends with the neighbours and got jobs at an oil mill. When the mill closed down three months later, they started plying rickshaws.

In the meantime, Paban and Swapan, with their musical talent and their training from Dibakar in asking for alms, became regular buskers on the Darjeeling Mail. It was on this train that Paban met the handsome young Kolkata poet Amit Gupta, who soon became his mentor.

Amit took his protégé to Kolkata and introduced him to Shakti Chattopadhyay, Sunil Gangopadhyay and Deepak Majumdar, the triumvirate of modern Bengali poetry. Amit rented rooms in nearby

Durgapur, from where he ran his affairs, and inducted Paban into his business of spraying pesticides in the factories of the Durgapur–Asansol coal and iron belt. When Ulangini railed about his continuous absence from home – Paban was only fifteen – Amit encouraged Paban to move the family to Durgapur. He showed him a strip of vested land on the banks of the Durgapur canal where the landless were being encouraged to settle. Paban persuaded his family to make the move without much difficulty; it would be easier for them to survive in a city than in a small town. They bound and strapped all their possessions to a bullock cart, and trundled all the way to Deshbondhunagar Colony on the outskirts of Durgapur, where Paban and I had found them.

After spending a couple of days in Durgapur, I was ready to head to Kenduli. Paban's family seemed reluctant to see us go. Stay for longer, they asked us; Makar Sankranti, the day of the new moon, is still two days away. I saw their smiles disappear when Paban announced my plans to them. They surrounded me, eyes forlorn. They always benefitted from the patronage of Paban's friends and admirers from the city; it was only natural that they wanted to make sure they didn't lose mine. I held my ground and continued to get Duniya dressed for travel in her tracksuit, socks and sneakers, ignoring their silent pleas.

To my relief, Paban stood by me, firmly turned his back on our audience, and helped me pack my bag and fill our water bottles. We said goodbye to the family and, taking Duniya by her trusting little hand, left for the bus station after an unusually late lunch. But by the time we reached the station, the last bus had already left. It was not even five in the evening. Paban told me it would not be safe to take a private taxi as it was risky to travel after sundown; the Kaksha jungle was full of danger. Remnants of the armed Naxalite organisations of the seventies had taken refuge in the forest area, and turned to banditry. They'd been known to hold up solitary cars at night.

Paban hung his head, avoiding my eyes, and looked very guilty. I realised that the go-slow technique, perfected by strikers and unionists in West Bengal over the past decade, had been used by Paban and his brothers to sabotage my plans to leave them. I was furious with myself for not having realised this earlier. This was my first indication that I'd have to keep a sharp watch to prevent myself and my children from becoming entangled in the net often laid down by this wily, impetuous, charming family of survivors.

When we returned to the colony we found the entire family congregated once again, squatting in the courtyard in the semi-darkness. The sky was lit up with the ruddy glare of the coke oven, the unnatural light transforming their silhouettes into ghostly figures. A man shrouded up to his nose in white cloth, with a skele-tal face, rasping and coughing, crouched in the centre of the circle. Paban embraced him heartily and introduced him to me as his uncle, Dibakar's youngest brother, Shuhankar Das.

Paban whispered in my ear that Shuhankar was a destitute music teacher and that he was in the terminal stages of tuberculosis. Poverty had gutted him like a tree ground to dust by termites. Dibakar had invited him to spend a few days with the family, and now implored us not to leave, to take care of him. Searching Paban's face I could see he was deeply affected. Shuhankar had once been a brilliant jhumuria and played all kinds of instruments. Jhumurias are bards who live in the forest regions bordering Bengal, Bihar and Orissa; unlike the Bauls, who are mystics and ascetic philosophers, jhumuria are folk poets. Jhumur songs are sung in the forest regions among nomadic peoples such as the Santhals who practise jhuming, slash and burn cultivation. Shuhankar's vast oral reper-toire of folk songs would disappear with him.

Our entrance had created reverberations in the silent circle, which broke up as Paban shouted orders for lamps to be lit and made plans for dinner. The women slipped away like phantoms. Duniya was fast asleep in my arms, so I laid her down on the wooden cot in the veranda. Ulangini and Anima helped me take off her shoes and put up the mosquito net. We lit a lamp, an aluminium bottle with a small wick. The flame fluttered at first and then became strong, throwing up giant black shadows that bobbed up and down with its movement.

We spent an evening of song inside the family's hut, sitting on their single wooden cot. Paban and Swapan forced Shuhankar to sing and recorded him on a crackling, beaten-up tape recorder. He coughed fitfully at the end of every phrase. They all drank potent Bangla country liquor, and their words began to slur. I turned my face away to hide my tears. To my disappointment about being thwarted from leaving for Kenduli that day, was added an over-powering sympathy and sorrow for Paban and his family.

Shuhankar's song was melancholy, coquettish and innocent.

> Where are you going to, pretty maid?
> The bells in your feet jingle jangle,
> Ranaka jhanaka jhanaka
> I am sorrow and sadness.
> Don't peep at me
> Your eyes lined with kajal,
> Don't cheat me
> My life cannot bear this pain.
> The bells in your feet jingle jangle,
> Ranaka jhanaka jhanaka ... 3

Shuhankar's song reminded me that I resembled those village girls and farmers' wives who leave home with the rasik poets, as the jhumurias are also called, in a state of trance. In these past few days, something had changed between Paban and me. Our playful friendship had deepened. I was frightened. How could I resist the sweetness of Paban's song or deny the pathos of his situation?

A rap on the door interrupted my thoughts just then. Some of the local elders had gathered and wished to meet Paban, whose visits were few and far between. A small log fire was crackling and hissing in the centre of the courtyard. The old men sat down around it, the flames flickering on their faces, greeting us solemnly as we joined their circle.

'Jai ma!'

'Jai Tara!'

'Jai Kali! Kalkatta Wali!' – Victory to Kali! To Kali of Calcutta! (They were paying me a tribute!)

Paban spread a blanket for us to lie on by the fire, and wrapped another blanket around me and Duniya. We watched the flames. The sky above was starry and the sickle of the moon curved directly above us.

Next to us, Dibakar squatted on the ground in the centre of the semicircle of elders, swinging on his haunches, chewing the end of a neem stick. He coughed and spat and rasped for a while. As he turned towards us, he had a twinkle in his eye.

'I was never afraid of anything except she-devils and man-eaters!' he declared to his audience.

I wondered if he was referring to me. I said nothing, and in the hushed atmosphere he began his story.

'I was returning to Mohammedpur late on a moonless night. I had had a few drinks with the Kandhi precinct officer to overcome my fear of the dark. Stick in hand, I set off alone on a track which would take at least three hours to lead me back to the village. The road led through a teak forest on the opposite edge of which was a small Santhal settlement. There was not a soul around. The only sounds I could hear were the howling of foxes and the chattering of owls. The landscape looked dangerous. Giant shadows loomed around me like the ghosts and sprites of Mother Kali!

'Suddenly, in a clearing in the wood, I saw a naked black woman, upside down, walking on her hands, holding a pot with live embers around her feet. She dropped the pot as soon as she saw me. Red sparks flew around as the embers dispersed; in my drunken state, I thought they flew out of her bloodshot eyes. The pot splintered into pieces as it fell to the ground. Her matted locks and necklace of seeds meant that she was a dakini – a wild female spirit – and that she might hold me prisoner as a captive mate. I was terrified but held my stick in my hand. Then, I rushed up to her menacingly, lifting my stick high in the air to deliver a deathly blow:

'"Wait till I finish with you, you witch!" I cried.

'The woman threw herself at my feet. "O Baba Bhairava, forgive me!" she whined, in a nasal voice.

'She begged me not to reveal what I had seen. I rushed away and hurried home.

'I realised that she was practising pisatch sadhana, the most dangerous and macabre of all tantric disciplines, involving scatological practices and necrophilia. In the daytime, she lived like an ordinary person and, in the night, she secretly practised her sadhana in the forest. I spoke to none, fearing the consequences of breaking the promise I had made to the woman. A few weeks after this incident, I heard that a woman pisatch had been stoned to death by the villagers who lived by the forest.'

What could this woman have been doing? These regions of Bengal were full of the remnants of all kinds of occult tantric practices from ancient times. What was *I* doing here? I was in the heart of a patriarchal village society where the status of women was practically non-existent. Dibakar's story pointed to the conundrum of my entering this world with Paban. I could be a dakini and not a yogini. My presence here was tolerated only because, being the daughter of a Kolkata babu, I had the honorary status of a male. Were I a village woman, I would surely be in big trouble. Village women who discovered the potential of their energy, who learnt a skill or an art, who tried to free themselves from the shackles of orthodox patriarchal village society, were lynched without hesitation unless they entered a religious sect or were patronised by a guru. The choice for them was between being farmers' wives, or becoming prostitutes and slaves in the cities.

Seeing the doubt and anxiety written on my face, Dibakar picked up his ektara and sang with a smile in his voice:

> The cry of the tigress
> Makes my heart tremble
> When I go to the forest of Madhupur
> O who will come hunting with me
> The name of the tigress:
> Flower divine
> On her face, she sports a thick beard,
> She's got no eyes,
> She sniffs out her victim! [4]

A silence filled the courtyard as the drone of the ektara stilled. Above us, the night sky was clear and filled with stars. Someone pointed out the Saptarishi mandala: the Ursa Major constellation, the crossbow and the plough. A pipe of ganja was shared among the elders. At Paban's request, it was passed to me, a great honour and recognition of my equal status among them. As I lit up the chillum, smiles lit up the faces of the grave old men. Night fires were starting up all around us, and the smoke hung low over the fields beyond the colony. Every so often, a train whistled by and the ground thundered under us.

'Off with you now,' Dibakar finally said, dispersing the assembly. 'Paban and our ma have to travel early tomorrow morning.'

Dibakar's words were calculated to reassure me. With just a few words, he had let me know that he accepted the unusual friendship that had developed between me and his beloved Paban. And we were free to leave now.

III

KENDULI: FESTIVALS, STARS AND A SINGING HEART

Illustration overleaf: Krishna touching Radha's feet, symbolising female ascendancy in the act of love.

How does this unknown bird
Flit back and forth,
In and out of his cage?
If I could catch him,
I would bind him
With the chains of my spirit.
But I can't get a hold of him,
He still flits in and out.
His cage has eight rooms and nine doors,
Surmounted by a room of mirrors,
O my heart, the cage you dream of,
Made of weak bamboo
Can break any moment.
So, says Lallan, the bird can break free from the cage,
Escape, who knows where. [1]

THE LAND that is home to Paban and the Bauls is a vast stretch of hills, plains and forests watered by enormous rivers from east and west, and bordered by a loop of steep snowy mountains in the north and east. In the south, it flows into a massive delta and scatters into tiny islands to meet the Bay of Bengal.

However, if territory could be marked by songs the way birds mark it in flight, then this is what the Baul landscape looks like. In the cool blue hills, which form the lower ranges of the Himalayas, lie its eastern limits, marked by the strumming of the silk strings of the dotara in the mountain chalets of Shoshtofel or Chesterfield, in the Shillong basin.

Southeast, the staccato rhythms played on the khamak by Giribala Dasi, the last of the ancient Baulinis, cleave the air in the outskirts of Agartala, capital of Tripura, next to the Burma and Bangladesh border. Here, a process of orogenesis, during which the tectonic plate broke away from Africa in the night of time, has knocked the Indian subcontinent against China to form the highest mountains in the world. Further east, this process has pleated the earth into steep, bare hills. Lower down, it has folded itself into rain forests and lush valleys latticed by innumerable streams and waterfalls, which cascade in raging muddy torrents to join the great rivers of Bangladesh: the Surma, the Meghna and the Padma.

The northern limit of the Baul landscape is defined by the high notes played on the dotara of Kalachand Darbesh, a Baul singer from Dhupguri in north Bengal, just south of Bhutan and Sikkim, the Himalayan kingdoms beyond which lie Tibet and China. Bengali pilgrims and scholars travelled to Tibet over a thousand years ago and left behind them traces of songs sung in mysterious sandhya bhasha, twilight language, the texts of which were enigmatic and told the secrets of the body.

The southern limit of the Baul landscape is in the Muslim dargah of Ghutiarisharif in the district of the South Twenty-Four Parganas, south of Kolkata, Baruipur, across the mangroves of the Sundarbans right up to the Bay of Bengal. Here, the rattle and thumping of tambourines of the fakirs and Bauls vociferously dialoguing with each other have almost faded away in recent years as Sharia law takes over from that of the marfati, the Islam of the Sufis.

The western limit of the Baul landscape lies with the slow bass roll of the duggi drum and the drone of the ektara of Hrishikesh Mahato, a Baul singer from Purulia on the hilly forested Bengal–Bihar border. This western limit is known as Rarh Bangla and coincides with one of the more arid areas of Bengal, containing its most ancient memories. Its red soil and golden hills were inhabited by the first nation in this part of the world, consisting of tribes of Afro-Austral and Tibeto-Burman origin. This is where we were now.

Numerous festivals occur within the radius of the Baul landscape, often as part of agricultural fairs, and held in accordance with a lunar calendar. The first chain of festivals is that of the great melas of Kenduli, followed by Ghoshpara, Agrodwip and Sonamukhi. The second chain consists of those Baul festivals held in guru ashrams. The third chain, crucial to the survival of Baul science and art, are held in the homes of disciples. Bauls and fakirs, astrologers and soothsayers, itinerant scroll painters and practitioners of all manner of acrobatics anchored in yoga across the land, from Bankura, Birbhum, Murshidabad, Nadia and even remote corners of Bangladesh, flock to these festivals to meet members of their fraternities, linked together through common and ancestral gurus. There they perform with each other in marathon singing duels and receive teachings from the great Baul gurus.

Kenduli is the first and most important mela in the Baul festival season and Bauls from all over West Bengal rush there, a huge, floating population of pilgrims.

Swapan, Paban and I left Durgapur early in the morning to take a bus to the Kenduli Baul festival. Pilgrims, itinerants and vendors jostled against each other and crowded the buses in a fevered frenzy of excitement. Conductors slapped the sides of the buses, soliciting clients. 'Kenduli! Joydeb! Kenduli! Joydeb!' they cried, hailing the great medieval poet and patron saint of the fair. Joydeb is the author of the *Geet Govind*, an epic poem which celebrates the passion of Krishna and Radha. Born in Kenduli, he became the court poet of the king Lakshmana Sen, ruler of Bengal in the late twelfth century, and was one of the 'five jewels' of his court, the others being the poets Umapatidhara, Sarana, Govardhana and Dhoyi. Chased from Kenduli by a hardening Brahmin orthodoxy as waves of Islam spread to Bengal from the north and the west, Joydeb wrote his magnum opus in Puri, in neighbouring Utkala, now Orissa. The Brahmin priest of the Jagannath temple, perceiving his aura, married him to his daughter Padmavati, the temple dancer. At her feet, he wrote the great song of the love play between Radha and Krishna which ends with the phrase:

> Dehi padme ballava mudaram!
> (Radha's foot on the head of Krishna!)

An image of feminine ascendancy in the act of love.

The *Geet Govind*, a literary chef d'oeuvre, continues to inspire Indian artists and musicians to this day. The Kenduli festival began, almost eight hundred years ago, in honour of this great poet, and was also called the Joydeb Mela. Over time, it developed into an agricultural fair as well.

After a ride of about forty-five minutes through barren fields and young teak forests, we got off at the banks of the River Ajoy. We set off on foot for the Joydeb Mela on the other side of the river – which separated the district of Bardhaman from that of Birbhum – crossing the dried-up river on a temporary dirt road, behind a convoy of groaning, creaking bullock carts loaded with pilgrims visiting the fair. Red dust from the laterite soil of Birbhum had risen to the sky, flushing it saffron. The dark silhouette of a giant Ferris wheel signalled the location of the fair, and Paban pointed out the domes of temples and prayer flags where thousands of Baul singers and Dasanami sadhus congregated.

Dasanami sadhus are of ten denominations: Auls, who are ascetics of Sufi origin given to repetitive chanting in the style of qawwalis; Bauls; Sains, who believe that the guru is the spiritual preceptor; Darbesh (the word derives from dervish), a mendicant Hindu order who carry begging bowls; Bairagis, Vaishnava ascetics who wear tilak, the mark on the forehead symbolising the third eye, and beads and who often shave their heads and practise seva or service to humanity; Vaishnavas; fakirs; Nagas, male worshippers of Shiva who practise extreme physical self-chastisement to the point of sacrificing their sexual organs to become one with Shakti or the feminine principle; Nathas, the original yogis who are masters of sexo-yogic techniques; and tantrics.

We passed through alleys of shops selling eclectic mountains of wares: farming implements, baskets, fishing nets and tackles; lithographs of Kali, Shiva, Radha and Krishna; clay pots and clay gods; bangles, saris and scarves, winter wear, earrings and beads; shola, a light, white balsamic wood, intricately carved into effigies; marriage hats and wall hangings and decor; bowls and dishes, crudely cut out of grey stone and granite, glinting copper and bronze vessels.

We stopped to watch the histrionics of a famous kirtan singer from Nabadwip. Paban said her name was Radharani. She was a fair and rotund belle, dressed in a flashy orange sari, with white flowers and marigold garlands twisted in her hair, her arms jingling with gold bangles, her chest gleaming with chains of gold, her high-pitched melodramatic voice lifted incantatively, as she chanted verses from the *Geet Govind*.

> Radha, obsessed with unfaithful Krishna, confides in
>   her girlfriend, Lalitha, who tries to distract her.
> Lalitha says: the kokil is black,
> Radha answers, black are the eyes of Krishna.
> Radha sees her lord Krishna everywhere!

Radharani's public shouted appreciation with loud cries, and the drumming rose to fever pitch, cymbals clashing as ululations filled the air. I would have tarried for a while, but Paban seemed determined to carry on.

We passed a tousled pelican, a pair of scruffy monkeys and a snorting, muzzled black bear performing on a stage. They advertised a village circus. We paid a few paise, and entered a garishly coloured tent decorated with synthetic drapes bearing purple and yellow scallops; inside, a pair of Siamese twins, two village girls, were being displayed in a room of mirrors, reproduced to infinity. We followed a queue of people up to the two sisters, who rapped with the public.

'I'm Ganga!' announced the right head, tossing a right plait.

'I'm Jamuna!' exclaimed the left head, tossing the left plait.

'I vote CPM!' declared one head.

'I vote Congress!' said the other.

'Jai Bangla!' chortled one head. 'Victory to Bengal!'

'Jai Bharat!' giggled the other. 'Victory to India!'

The crowd cheered and laughed and threw coins at them. Paban did the same. I felt claustrophobic. Duniya squalled, up on my shoulders, and we staggered out of the tent and back into the crowds. Outside, we caught a glimpse of Subal, singing a song inside a tent. Paban explained to me that the song celebrated the menstrual cycle when I asked him its meaning.

> A girl is Ganga, Jamuna and Saraswati:
> Every month, tides rise within her,
> Form the confluence of three rivers of three colours,
> The first day it's black, the next, white and the third a pearly red.
> Who can plumb the depths of a woman?
> Maheshwara knows only a little bit about her. [2]

In the meantime, the volume on the mikes on each side of the alley was raised many hertzes above what the human ear could bear, drowning out Subal's song. They blared out the latest Bollywood hits and Paban and Swapan merrily joined in the refrain of a popular Hindi song. They had a double repertoire, singing film songs as well as mystic ones with equal gusto!

Next, we took Duniya for a ride on the Ferris wheel, to get away from the crowds which thronged the fairgrounds. Duniya and I sat on one side of the swinging metal seats, holding on to the rails, and Paban and Swapan sat on the other, facing us. The Ferris wheel, a massive steel and chrome affair, ran on the power of a noisy generator and the spokes were designed to resemble the tentacles of an octopus. We swung higher and higher in the air at regular intervals, as the attendants ushered the public in. Paban pointed out the sights of Kenduli. To our left was a massive parking lot with buses, taxis, private cars and police vans crowding the entrance of the fairgrounds, which stretched for about two kilometres in every direction. In front of us was the bed of the River Ajoy, with just a few narrow rivulets of water in the middle of a large stretch of white sand, milling with pilgrims. The red soil of Birbhum and teak forests trembled in the horizon, and way beyond were faint grey-blue traces of the Shushunia Hills.

Beyond that were Bihar and Nepal. Further west, I pointed, were Bhutan, Tibet, Afghanistan. The brothers looked amazed when I told them I'd been there. To our right, below us, was a patch of green, a thick grove of banyans. In the heart of this grove, Paban told me, was Tamalatala, the principal Baul monastery where the Baul singers and their gurus congregated every year. We could glimpse the dome of a terracotta temple, caught in the aerial roots of a banyan. This was the temple of Shiva, where the poet Joydeb was said to have attained enlightenment.

Joydeb must have had the restless soul of a wandering Baul. He never stopped under the same tree for more than three nights. We would spend three nights here too. Three life-changing nights. Paban! Paban! Paban!

We headed now towards the Tamalatala, returning to the main alley and meeting, on our way, many Baul singers dressed in orange robes, the attire of asceticism. For the Bauls, wearing a particular costume in order to sing symbolises offering up the breath as a sacrifice to their gurus and to the Baul wind. Casting aside daily apparel and donning the robes of an ascetic is therefore a noble gesture. It also made them look extraordinary.

Other Bauls, including Paban, wore patchwork robes. These patchwork garments have a ritual significance and are usually gifted by gurus to mark those disciples who are *vanaprastha* – 'struck by an arrow', so to speak, and who are capable of firing such arrows as well. The arrow is a metaphor of the deepest core of human energy, which lies coiled deep within the solar plexus and which the Bauls personify through their pantheon of saints and embody in their performances. In representing this sacred cosmic energy, they become one with it and transmit it through their songs, music, dance and storytelling, transcending the confines of time and space. I was to see how their audiences, equally if not even more devotional, often worship the Bauls as living gods and give them alms in the form of tea and puffed rice, offer them shawls to wrap around themselves, or pin notes on to their costumes to mark their appreciation and gratitude.

Today, many Baul singers greeted and embraced Paban, who slipped speedily through the dense crowds like water over rocks, making a passage for us. We stopped at the Radhavinode temple, where I leant against the wall with Duniya in my arms. This was all very new and confusing for her, and I held her close. We were dizzy from the Ferris wheel, both beginning to tire. Paban and Swapan stood on either side of us, protecting us from the constant stream of people thronging the alley.

Then they led us to an inner courtyard in a cottage by the temple. We sat to rest for a while, under a tree with yellow trumpet flowers which were strewn all over the courtyard.

The cottage was made of clay and thatch. An old Vaishnavi, draped in white cotton, was in charge of the ashram. She brought us water. Paban disappeared and returned with refreshments: puffed rice and onion bhajis and bananas. He requested the old Vaishnavi to bring him a bowl, and she brought out a bronze thali – a large, high-rimmed plate. Paban poured the puffed rice into the thali and threw the fritters in, mixed them with his fingers. Then he handed us a ball each, and Duniya and I squatted in front of him and ate. The old lady ate too, after reaching out and blessing Paban.

He teased her lovingly. 'Ma, come to me! Let's make love.'

She smiled back at him. 'What can I do, my boy? I have no partner. We Vaishnavas serve others.' She sprinkled some water on a tulsi mancha, an altar which adorns every Vaishnava household, on which an Indian basil tree had been planted.

Behind us was a frieze on the temple wall. Paban folded his hands out of respect for Mahishasur Mardini, Durga, as the saviour of the world, the slayer of demons with her crew of consorts. I teased Paban, tugging at the curl which fell over his forehead like a corkscrew.

'So, you call yourself a Baul, do you, yet you worship gods made of stone!'

He stopped short, electrified by my touch. I withdrew my hand quickly, suddenly self-conscious.

'No, it's you I adore! Why look at a stone goddess when I have a live one beside me?'

He was flirting with me now.

We went around the temple, on which were displayed the ten incarnations of Vishnu and the battle between Rama and Ravana, as well as couples locked in passionate lovemaking. The crowds of pilgrims were so dense in the alleys that we moved step by step; a slow, sludgy river of bodies. I felt little fingers behind me feeling the clasp of the chain and locket around my neck. Turning back, I saw a young village girl behind me. She looked innocent enough, but broke into a naughty grin when our eyes met.

After a final struggle through the crowds, we arrived at an embankment on the riverside where the path was high and free. I put Duniya down on the ground, and we stretched our legs, breathing in great gusts of air. The embankment marked a water-shed between the River Ajoy and the village of Kenduli. Before us, thousands of pilgrims were bathing in the sparkling blue river, having first set up their tiny tents on each side of a path to the river bank. Each tent contained a divinity; inside, red-robed tantric men and women displayed figures of Kali surrounded by her ogres and spirits, foxes and crows; white-robed Vaishnavis displayed Radha and Krishna.

Suddenly, the crowds evaporated. We were in an immense vault created by a grove of banyans, almost a secret foyer. We had arrived at the monastery of Tamalatala: in the space of a few minutes, we had moved into another age. The thick canopy of trees cut off the cacophony of the fair. In the dappled light Baul couples, old and young, dressed in saffron or patchwork robes, sat facing each other, nested in the enclaves formed by the overhanging roots of the banyan trees; eyes locked on each other, blazing with love, their dark, saintly faces serene and statuesque. They came to life when Paban greeted them. They seemed to know him well and greeted us vociferously, embracing us and looking deep into our eyes. Paban touched their feet in devotion.

These ascetic couples graced the fair with their presence every year to re-enact the spiritual scenario of the *Geet Govind*. The very trees of this grove, the central tamala tree with its dark glossy leaves, which gave the name to the Tamalatala ashram, were a part of the imagery of this great poem. The tamala is black, said Lalitha, to Radha. And Radha answered, besotted with Krishna: my lord is black!

We entered the central akhra, or place of learning, of Tamalatala, where Sudhir Baba, an old Baul sadhu with a tranquil face and quiet manners, received us graciously. We were seated under a canopy of tamala and banyan, and treated like royalty. This particular ashram was adjacent to the crematorium, and traditionally opened its doors to all. Belongings of the dead were usually distributed in the ashram, to the poor, and every single person who passed through was fed a simple meal by Sudhir Baba and his wife. In tandem, they received donations and alms of rice. Paban made them an offering of a hundred rupees.

Looking around me, I saw that the women present largely outnumbered the men. The importance that the Baul singers and sages held for women in Bengali village society was clear here. Here was where they got some respite from the extreme tensions of being farmers' wives and daughters and mothers, deriving consolation from Baul songs to contend with the tribulations of daily life. It was here that widows and old women, rejected wives and runaway daughters, could seek shelter and solace.

We joined the pilgrims for a meal of rice, dal and vegetables, served from pails and slopped clumsily onto our plates of woven leaves. The liquid dal trickled through our leaky plates, onto the ground. Duniya began to cry. She'd learnt to keep clean by Western standards from the age of a year and a half, and it was hard for her to accept this sudden entry into another world. How could I reassure her? She was barely two and a half. I explained to her that the earthen floor was our table, and that once the meal was over, they'd pave a new floor; that our leaf plates, prettily woven into a spiral with sticks, were disposable as there were no dishwashing machines here.

Sudhir Baba, noticing her discomfort, sent for a bronze thali which came by special delivery on the head of a young Baul. He distracted her with a little brown pup; Duniya was all smiles again. He also told me to look for a decent place to live in, as soon as the festival was over, as though he'd read my thoughts.

'You need quiet and peace to become a Baul,' he told me.

'You mean, I need to be quiet to become noisy, is that it?'

Sudhir Baba laughed and turned to Paban. 'You've found a good fairy, don't ever let her go!'

After lunch, Paban prepared a space for us to rest in the veranda of a small thatch cottage, the ashram of Sudhir Baba. Bundles of hay appeared from nowhere and were spread on the floor, covered with a blanket. We were screened off from the rest of the visitors by a mosquito net, over which Paban draped a cover. Exhausted by our journey, we fell asleep instantly. I woke up to see I'd been sleeping in Paban's arms, unwittingly caught in an enchanted, invisible circle.

That night I followed Paban from akhra to akhra, wading across a dense sea of humanity, through the warm charcoal darkness, under a constellation of twinkling lights from earthen lamps, carefully carrying Duniya. Thousands of Baul singers and sages thronged this secret foyer of saints and singers, dressed in orange, wearing necklaces made out of tulsi beads and round, red, knobbly rudraksha seeds, and sporting beards, wild haired and soft mannered, loud voiced and vigorous in their singing and dancing, bells jingling at their feet, their drums rumbling. Those who were here from the river valleys of the Ganges performed bhatiali melodies, traditionally sung by boatmen. They sang of life as a river, the human body as a boat and the boatman or the helmsman as the spiritual preceptor. Those who came from the hilly regions of north Bengal, from Siliguri and Dhupguri, drew inspiration from bhawaiya songs from the forests of Bengal and Assam. They sang of the forest as life itself, the human body as the elephant which crossed through this forest fraught with danger and the mahout as the supreme guru.

Soon Paban pitched himself into the arena of song; I accompanied him, closing my eyes, and listened to his cries and groans, trying to keep the ektara in tune. His fingers bled as his little drum thundered, punctuating each cry.

> For you, my beloved, I'll become a yogini,
> I will throw off my conventions, my dignity
> O what is this country, O moon of Nadia,
> Which has imprisoned you?[3]

It was difficult for me not to identify with the words of the song. The audience consisted largely of women, young and old. Many wept with emotion; I was not the only one to be moved by Paban's singing. The women came up and pinned rupee notes onto his patchwork robe, embraced him passionately and kissed me. In spite of the extremely orthodox quality of the village society that surrounded Kenduli, the presence of the Bauls had created a magnetic field of complete liberty in which people were briefly free to become themselves.

And now, wild Paban flung himself into moods and postures with complete abandon. Thundering on his dubki, he sang one song after another, songs of Radheysham Goshain, Nilkantho Goshain, Bhaba Pagla and Lallan Fakir and of many unknown authors, in his deep, velvety voice, pouring like liquid into the ears of his auditors. He had a massive repertoire and could build up a variety of moods and tempos; the village public who were gathered here simply adored him.

Old sages also responded to Paban's mystic heart. Shombhu Das from Ilambazar and Deben Khepa from Bolpur leapt up and began to dance to a continuous, repetitive jingle he was playing on his dubki. Paban was the road, the Kabaa was in his eyes and many Medinas in his heart. I could hover there for ever.

I was beginning to fall in love with him. It was visible to all those around me; an old bare-bodied sage with a faded cloth around his loins came and stood next to me, and he smiled kindly as though he had divined my feelings.

'Ma, these Baul singers are saints as long as their songs fly like kites in the wind. When they stop singing, they are just ordinary mortals. Like glow-worms, they glow in the night. If you see them in the day, they are ordinary, dull and wooden.'

He was clearly asking me what lay behind my infatuation. Before I could even take stock of my own feelings, Paban strode up to where I was sitting, Duniya sleeping beside me. Ripping off his jubba, the multicoloured patchwork coat that displayed his special status as a Baul and dervish, he collapsed on the ground with his head on my lap. He was drenched with sweat from his efforts and exuberant, sure of himself now. I handed him a towel, a fresh kurta and a black quilted Nepalese coat from my bag, a gift to me from Terai.

The old man who'd spoken to me was a village yogi and he lingered near us while Paban dressed. The old man invited us to visit his ashram, which was by the riverside beyond the grove of banyans. I had by now lost all sense of time and space. Stars winked at us from beyond the foliage of the great banyan trees, and each step Paban made was a jingle and a dance. We were both in the thrall of love. The night was soft and dark. There was a strong perfume of sandalwood incense in the air, a kokil warbled in the thick dark foliage of the tamala tree above us. A meander of the River Ajoy shone before us like a curved half moon, and the sandbanks shone and glimmered with wavering yellow petals of light, lamps of thousands on a pilgrimage to sensual love. Beyond lay the forest, where, in a little hut, on a bed of ferns, Radha had triumphed over Krishna in the *Geet Govind*. All the elements of the settings of the great love poem still survived, as though caught in a web of immortality. We seemed to be caught in the same web.

Paban lay at my feet, on his stomach, watching me closely and making me conscious of our irresistible attraction. I was ready to abandon myself to him completely.

The old sage vanished, as he had appeared. Leaving Duniya, still asleep, in the care of Sudhir Baba and his wife, Paban now led me away from the fair to the banks of the river. We raced each other over the riverbed for a mile or two till the lights and noises of the fairgrounds receded in the distance. Then we stopped suddenly in unison, bound by an invisible force and came together, yoked by our passions, a churning, cataclysmic union of two disparate galaxies swirling into each other, tongue to tongue, lip to lip, cheek to cheek.

We returned, both chastened, to the akhra at the Tamalatala, where Bauls' songs continued all night, punctuated with coughing, spluttering, quarrelling, curses and incantations. Paban now embarked on a marathon of duels in song with the other Baul singers. Some songs were questions to the guru, others answers.

How can I find pure and innate love?
While seeking true love, a storm churns up the river of passions.
In the hope of finding the jewel of love
I have walled in the confluence of the three rivers
But a single push of a wave, destroys the dykes I've built.
How can I speak to you of that Love?
Passions turn into loving vines,
Love cannot prevail unstained by desire.
Love and devotion are the supreme masters
And even the master of passions has his own master.
How can I know love without passion?
Lallan tells himself. 4

At three in the morning, we wound up inside a long, dark barn reeking of liquor. Paban brought sheaves of straw, which he spread on the floor. I stretched a blanket over them and covered Duniya with a sleeping bag. Then Paban lay down and fell asleep immediately. Duniya whimpered in her sleep, and I remained wide awake though tired to the bone. I was thinking about what had happened, unable to decipher fact from fiction.

A man's voice, deep and resonant, interrupted my thoughts: 'Who are you, pagli? Why have you brought your child to Kenduli? I have children too. I've left mine at home in Kolkata!'

Surprised at this intrusion and irate at being called pagli – a madwoman, I snapped back at this unknown male critic, who seemed the epitome of a moralising Bengali babu. 'Kolkatar babu master, I don't have a wife in Kolkata with whom I can leave my daughter!'

In the darkness, I discerned a bald-headed, bespectacled Bengali babu sitting in the doorway. I must have struck a chord because he fired up. 'How dare you talk to me like this! Do you realise who you're talking to?'

'I don't know and I don't care.' I was irritated now beyond measure.

'I am the greatest poet of Bengal!'

I didn't react. Paban lay asleep like the dead next to me, exhausted after all his exertions. There was no hope he'd wake up to protect me.

The man edged closer to me. Poking me in the ribs unceremoni-ously, he began to babble. 'Pagli! You will never survive! I know the local Deputy Inspector General. I'll have him evict you from here!'

Another voice interrupted him with a string of obscenities. 'Shut up, banchot – you sister-fucker! You tool of the Congress Party! Leave her alone!'

I recognised the voice of Dilip, a neighbour of Paban's from Durgapur, who had accompanied us to the festival. Dilip, quite tipsy, had taken up the cudgels on my behalf.

'You CPM ruffian, I'll tear your balls off,' the bald-headed man shouted back at him. Realising that they were both very drunk, I turned my back on them and fell asleep, while political and personal insults hurled over my finally resting head.

It was late morning when we awoke. The two men lay stretched out near us, sleeping like the dead, their arms enfolding each other like long lost brothers. Paban, after procuring tea, bananas and biscuits, prodded the bald-headed man awake, forced him to drink some tea and introduced him as Shakti Chattopadhyay, poet laureate of Bengal!

Shakti would one day become an adorable friend. He would rattle at the gates of my father's house in Jhautalla late at night, shouting in his stentorian voice, 'Paban, tumi bari aachho?', echoing the lines of his very famous poem: 'Abani, Tumi Bari Aachho?':

> Bolted doors, the neighbourhood sleeps still
> All I hear is the knocking of the night.
> Abani, are you home?
> Here it rains all the year round
> Like grazing herds the clouds here drift,
> The green blades of grass
> Look askance as they choke my door.
> My heart near suffused with ache,
> Is bound for far away.
> I fall asleep
> To hear the knocking of the night.
> Abani, are you home?

Taking Shakti by the hand, Paban led us to the river. We breathed in the morning air. Bells were clanging in the temples and the shops were still shut. The winter sun was weak and a thin layer of smoke and mist covered everything. We drank chai out of clay pots in a small shop.

We had three days and three nights at the Joydeb Mela. Three nights in which I accompanied Paban as he sang and fell deeper in love with him. But I wanted to let the relationship develop in its own time; for now, I was ready to head on to Shantiniketan. I needed to settle down for a while and build a nest in which I could raise my children. I needed peace and quiet to reflect on the new direction my life was taking. Paban decided to move with me there.

We left Kenduli, taking the long straight strip of the dirt road over the sand bed of the Ajoy River, joining a procession of pilgrims departing from the fair; villagers loaded with goods, beggars and mendicants, itinerants and strange folks. We passed a small man with scruffy hair and ragged red robes carrying a stick on one shoulder, on which was a steel ring with a hornbill chained to it and a small tin trunk slung over his shoulder containing bones of hornbills which had been threaded and made into amulets. A tantric sexologist, he sold aphrodisiacs. He didn't look as though business had been good. The hornbill didn't seem horny and squawked in displeasure, a steely light in his beady eyes.

Sexual prowess and performance was a major obsession in this three-penny world. It was not only the Baul singers and the tantrics and Vaishnavas who were besotted with sex; it was this entire old floating population who believed in the rejuvenating powers of sexual intercourse.

IV

SHANTINIKETAN: SECRET ARTS OF LOVE AND INITIATION

Illustration overleaf: Radha with Krishna playing the flute. The union of the amorous divine couple is revered by the Baul singers of Bengal. Krishna's flute represents the sublimation of sexual energy into musical expression.

PABAN AND I were wedged in between my sleeping bag and a wickerwork basket in which catfish tossed about. We were on top of a bus bound for Bolpur, the largest town near to Shantiniketan. The lower branches of the trees on the roadside slapped our faces. Duniya gurgled with laughter as we lost our balance and fell on top of each other each time the bus careened to a halt. Paban's spirits were high as well. His wild, curly locks were tied back in a pale yellow bandana with motifs of Radha and Krishna inscribed on it in washed-out red. He wore his old patchwork jacket with its myriad colours, embroidered with a multitude of motifs: a flying bird, a jumping fish, a blue starry sky, a heart. The word 'BAUL' was stitched on it in Bengali and English.

I dipped into a little guidebook to Birbhum District, in which the university town of Shantiniketan lies. The guide was written in Bengali by the poet Amit Gupta, companion of Paban's teens. In Birbhum, I learnt, you will find worshippers of Shiva and worshippers of Shakti. Here you will find an amazing mixture of cultures and languages: fakirs, dervishes and Bauls, Hindus and Muslims, Vaishnavas and tantrics, and among the forest people, the Santhals and the Mundas; both Christians and animists. Birbhum belongs to everyone.

There was a faded picture of Nabani Khepa, companion and inspiration of Rabindranath Tagore. In the photograph, he wore the robes and turban of an ascetic and held aloft an ektara: the classic posture of the Baul; his noble, bearded face turned up, stretched and held out to a saffron sky, his mouth wide open in a cavernous roar of joy.

Paban sang a song written by Nabani Khepa as I looked at the old photograph, encouraging me to sing along with him.

O bird in the cage of my heart,
Sing the name of Radha and Krishna.
You sing the name, I hear it,
I sing the name, you hear it.
O bird in the cage of my heart,
Sixteen names and thirty-two characters
Subtract twenty-eight,
That unsaid name has four characters.
Sadhus know that name,
The profane don't.
O bird in the cage of my heart
Sing the name of Radha and Krishna.
When you were in the womb of a woman,
She called for Krishna.
You've left that country
And come to this one,
Yet you don't even once take the name of Krishna.
O my spirit, take the name of Krishna
And your bestial life will come to an end.
Then your human soul will find its seat
If you change your habits, you'll be rich. [1]

There was a promise of fulfilment in the song, within easy reach of all. The melody was based on raga Bhairavi, a morning raga; the mood was plaintive, that of a fettered bird trapped in a cage, the rhythm slow and majestic.

We moved on, down the straight long road, listening to this wonderful song as it played out. Then, at a bus stop, Paban cried out to familiar faces: two Bauls clad in saffron robes. They joined us on the roof of the bus and Paban introduced them to me. Dinabandhu I knew from Georges Luneau's documentary film. Cascades of long wavy hair hung down to his shoulders, covering an even-featured face, full, sensual lips and twinkling eyes. He was girlish, flirtatious, and slipped his arm around Paban's shoulder. Chinmoy was reserved, almost wooden, and had the fine features of a prince from an old Mughal miniature. Paban called them Dinu and Chinu.

Dinabandhu lived in a village called Ichhapur in the suburbs of Durgapur, and his father ran a paan shop. He was a talented singer but told us he had recently stopped singing to run his father's business. Chinmoy had come to West Bengal with his mother and crowds of other refugees from Bangladesh in 1971. His father had been a fighter for the Mukti Bahini and was killed in the war against the Pakistani army. Chinmoy had spent a short stint with his uncles in Kharagpur who were railway mechanics. His nostalgia for his mother and the songs they had sung together made him run away from his uncles and return to her, to where she lived in the refugee camps near the Bangladesh border in Bongaon. There, in the evenings, he would raise his beautiful, reedy voice in song around the fire with the other refugees, bound by a common past, survivors of the same shipwreck. Chinmoy soon met Subal, who introduced him to the Baul network in Nadia, and before long Chinmoy met the beautiful Durga Das, a Baulini with whom he now lived in Tribeni.

The Bauls now embraced each other heartily, looking deep into each other's eyes as they did so. No gesture was casual with them. Duniya left my lap and wrapped herself around Paban, jealous that his attention had turned from her. She kissed him on his cheek, pulling him away from his friends and towards me. The other two pinched her cheek, enraging her, and proceeded to focus on me as I pacified Duniya, holding her to my chest.

'So this is your new khepi? Is it? And now we old khepas are all forgotten!'

They touched my feet, murmuring 'Jai ma! Jai ma!' and turned back to Paban, waiting for a cue.

Paban answered with a song, handing me the ektara and asking me to defy the laws of gravity as the bus lurched and bumped over potholes made by the monsoon rains.

> Heart of a fakir,
> Words of the heart.
> Chillies grow on bamboo trees,
> Aubergines grow on ridge gourd vines.

In the morning, an engagement,
At midday, a wedding,
In the afternoon, the wife comes home
With a child on her lap! [2]

Many-layered meanings were suggested by the enigmatic verses of this song, which I'd first heard Paban sing in the documentary film *Le Chant des Fous*. Now, hearing the song in real life, it seemed to take on a new dimension. The song itself was like a crystal, reflecting subtle nuances of colour, endowing our lives with fresh facets, both brilliant and ephemeral. Paban had explained to me that the song was, in fact, about Baul initiation. In the morning, the Baul gurus initiate their disciples with a few magic words; at midday, the Baul couple become wedded to their gurus, often the guru father and mother in tandem; in the afternoon, the initiated woman returns home with a newborn child: her male partner in the guise of his Baul avatar.

The two Bauls gleefully supported Paban with their instruments and vocals. Duniya bounced up and down with the music, joining in spontaneously. I was enthralled. The earth sped past us. It was on top of that bus, caught like the catfish splashing next to us, that I finally began to realise I was trapped like a hapless bird in a mist net of songs.

'Whatever you do, never get initiated,' my aunt had told me. Her words of warning returned to me like a clarion call. I was playing with fire. Was I being naive to believe that I could enter into this charmed world without abiding by its laws? In addition to their long apprenticeship of invocations and songs, incantations and music, fables and stories, Bauls like Paban believed that divine knowledge was to be found within the body, to be attained through rigorous physical discipline in an emotional and sexual relationship with a life partner, guided by a true guru, in jugal sadhana. It was only now beginning to dawn on me that this was perhaps how Paban saw me: as a patra, a receptacle for divine knowledge. Yet I didn't see myself as a receptacle for anyone but my children.

I turned away from Paban to look at the countryside. The world was my tight-lipped oyster.

Chhap chhap chhap chhap chhap! The catfish splashed inside the wickerwork crate. Paban, sensing my withdrawal, tried to draw me out again.

'Some catfish, like koi,' he told me, 'can climb trees. On hot nights before the rains come down, clay pots are tied to the laddered trunks of palm trees to collect sap, which ferments into liquor as the day advances. If a tree grows next to a pond, the sap sometimes overflows into the waters and the koi, maddened by the savoury juice, climb the laddered palms using their gills, in a frenzy of thirst. When the pots are lowered in the morning, fish are found swimming in the juice, and provide an excellent accompaniment to palm toddy.

'The catfish families live in shoals and dig deep tunnels into the earth. Sometimes, when the drought hits and dries out the ponds, a great thrashing can be heard late into the night, flushing out these subterranean shelters. Men and women descend upon the tunnels with night lights and shovels and quintals of fish are caught and the liquor flows and there is great celebration.'

And so, Paban calmed my fears. There was the promise of an entire universe behind this flat countryside, deep and rich, waiting to be explored.

Life first began on earth when marine creatures learnt to live away from the great waters. So the grunion fish, which leaves the water to mate on land, must be a distant ancestor of the koi, whose tenacity is proverbial. We women, who live in the arid zones of patriarchy, whose tenacity is also proverbial, can be compared to that of the climbing perch; we are surely direct descendants of the grunion too.

After a short trip to France to pick up my son Krishna and to tie up a few loose ends with Terai and Katoun, the four of us settled into rented rooms at the back of a sprawling bungalow within the precincts of the Visva-bharati University in Shantiniketan.

The area that we were now living in was an arid zone; in spite of Tagore's dreams of plenitude, water was still scarce in Shantiniketan. It flowed in dribbles once in the morning, once at noon and once again in the early evening. I left the tap on every night so as not to miss a single drop of water. It was the rumble and gurgle, the mouse-like squeaking and squirting of water in the pipeline, which awakened me every morning. I then filled pails, drums, containers for the morning wash and bath, filled the kettle for tea, lit the chula stove, washed the dishes and prepared the morning meal.

Lighting the chula was a slow, complex and poisonous procedure. The traditional chula has a small aperture paved over with clay and an iron grille sitting on top of it, under which are three humps acting as the stand. Cowdung cakes and then bits of coal and charcoal are heaped on top of the chula for fuel. Kerosene is splashed on to light it, and soon a smoke jet of carbon emissions clouds the environment within a circumference of about two metres. I had to light it and jump back, or run to a corner of the compound, waiting for five minutes for it to smoke itself out; till the embers glowed and flickered.

I wasn't used to cooking at floor level so I finally opted for a gas stove, much to the amusement of the visiting Bauls, who found my standing at the stove in the kitchen masculine and droll as they were used to seeing women crouch to cook. So that I didn't alienate them even more, I spread mats on the floor of the living room in place of the traditional colonial sofa and carpets. The only concession I made to modern living, apart from the stove, was a wooden bed and a rosewood cupboard with a full-length mirror, slightly warped, with a turnkey lock.

News of our musical love affair had spread far and wide thanks to the Baul grapevine. The Baul singers who lived in the region collected around us like honeybees buzzing around a hive. There was nothing that the singers and sages loved better than an amorous couple who would possibly follow the path of Baul jugal sadhana.

Two Debens were regular visitors. Each morning Deben Das of Surul would come tiptoeing into the garden, playing his dotara softly, singing a song of melancholy beauty through his splayed teeth. He was emaciated, fragile; a refugee from East Pakistan who had lost all his property after the partition of India in 1947. Torn from his roots, he had busked on the trains till he gradually found his way to West Bengal two years later, when he had settled in the village of Surul a few miles outside Shantiniketan.

Deben Khepa, the second Deben, was a joyous, sprightly old man in his eighties, tall and strapping, with a shining bald pate and a crown of white hair slung low on his perfectly oval skull. We bumped into him first in the bazaar in Bolpur, the town nearest to Shantiniketan, when Paban invited him home. He usually arrived with the first light, in the mists of dawn, solemn and radiant. I served him tea and thin arrowroot biscuits.

Soon other Bauls got news of my open kitchen, and every morning by the time Paban awoke, they would be sitting in a circle on our veranda: the famous Nabani Khepa's daughter Radharani and her husband Dhananjoy, a brilliant percussionist who was familiar with Paban's most ancient rhythms; Bipadtaran, a Baul from the village of Gargaria whose habit it was to visit and sing to the grand dames of Shantiniketan, busking from bungalow to bungalow within the university compound; all joined in.

The Bauls were a garrulous lot, a little like the witches of *Macbeth*, especially after their first cup of tea. I'd already had a major dose of the stories of Radha and Krishna, and so was relieved when they regaled us with songs and tales of other legendary couples: Billu Mangal and Chintamoni, Chandidas and Rajakini, Lakhindar and Behula, Roop Bhan and Rahim. Billu Mangal and Chintamoni were sixteenth-century lovers from Birbhum in West Bengal, who chose to die together rather than renounce their love; Chandidas was a famous Vaishnava poet of the fifteenth century whose muse was Rajakini, a washerwoman; Lakhindar was bitten by the snake goddess Manasha, but saved by Behula, his wife, who revived him from death by singing and dancing for Bramha, Vishnu and Shiva. Because of a curse, the twelve-year-old stable girl Roop Bhan was married to the infant prince Rahim when he was only twelve days old and they spent a life together as mother and son before they became lovers. Rich and intriguing, the stories captured my imagination.

I learnt how Deben Khepa was eighteen years old when he first heard that a great soul, Rabindranath Tagore, had called out to the whole world to come and open the gates of knowledge in Shantiniketan. Knowledge, stated the poet, must be acquired in natural surroundings. He opened a school in 1901 and the Visva-bharati University in the town in 1918. Responses came from all over the globe, from France, Japan, USA, Germany, Argentina and Africa; Gandhi and Einstein both came and reiterated Tagore's ideals. Attracted by this message of glorious peace, Deben Khepa left his village for Shantiniketan, finally settling in nearby Bolpur. Tagore gave him food and shelter, heard his songs and became his friend.

It's possible Tagore was drawn to Shantiniketan because of the presence of many Baul singers: Radheyshyam Goshain, Rauterar Khepa Baba, Monohor Khepa, Shankar Baba, Nitai Khepa of Betal Bon and more. Deeply inspired by Baul philosophy and by their magnetic personalities, he wrote a great many songs using popular Baul melodies and infusing his texts with their spirit; almost a third of his songs are called Baul Anga, or the Baul part of his poetry.

In Shantiniketan, Tagore established close links with the great Baul singers Nabani Khepa and Panchanan Das and, from the accounts of Deben and Radharani, possibly shared a pipe or two with them. To my ears, Tagore's melodies and rhythms were like Western chamber music, to be sung sitting down, demurely pumping at a harmonium. There was none of the dancing, the earthy violence and intensity, the trance-inducing swing and cacophonic rhythms of a Baul performance, which was grounded in constantly being on the move on the hard and lonely road, on being steeped in their art. And yet Tagore did more than anyone to promote the Bauls.

Tagore was particularly inspired by the Baul master Lallan Fakir (1774–1890). For many years he shuttled between the towns of Shantiniketan and Shilaidaha, where Lallan had lived, in what is now Bangladesh. He went on to publish some of Lallan's songs. Today's Bauls still sing with passion the songs of Lallan Fakir, and recount his unusual tale.

Lallan was born in Jessore, in present-day Bangladesh, into a high caste Hindu family. He set out on a pilgrimage to Puri, Orissa as a very young man but was abandoned in Kushtiar in East Bengal by his companions when they found him afflicted with smallpox. Fortunately, he was nursed back to life by the great dervish Shiraj Shah. Childless, Shiraj and his wife then adopted Lallan as their son and spiritual successor. He spent a few years with them, rowing in the waters of a great lake archipelago spread over several districts called Chalan Bil, dotted with tiny islands, on each of which were small monasteries of Bauls and fakirs.

When Lallan returned home to his village, his wife, pressured by orthodox Hindu village rules, refused to let him into her home as his stay in a Muslim household had made him impure. He returned to his Baul fraternity in Kushtiar in 1823, travelling once again from island to island, to complete his sadhana with his preceptor Shiraj Shah, till he finally settled in the small village of Muslim weavers among whom he found his second wife and spiritual companion, and established his own order.

Duniya took to our new life here, romping around with the local children. She was used to the Bauls by now; they spoilt her and took her off for cycle rides and she enjoyed being the centre of attention. But I was anxious about Krishna, who was more reserved, and how he would take to life here after his regulated life in Paris with Terai and Katoun. I need not have worried. Paban took on his new role of father with complete dedication, thereby winning my heart completely. When we had first moved in he had taken Krishna to look at a litter of newborn pups, crowding under a stairway at the back of an old colonial bungalow. Krishna was thrilled; real puppies were much more interesting than stuffed or virtual ones. He was almost five now, little things drew his attention, filling him with wonder and amusement.

'Maman, look! The clouds are changing colour.' 'Maman, look! The tree is going crazy in the wind.' 'Maman, look! The rain's making the ants panic.'

He spent hours playing indoor games with Paban and his younger brother Swapan, who often came from Durgapur and spent time with us, always with an urgent message for us to return there.

After breakfast, the Baul singers would disappear on their rounds and I would take the children outdoors to play in the garden. We would settle down on stone benches around a stone table, with crayons and pastels and paper, in the shade of a Japanese cherry tree. Paban was nocturnal and tended to wake up late by local standards, but when he did, he joined us in our improvised outdoor school. Our main textbook was in fact a picture book, a gift from Deepak Majumdar. It told the story of Huien Tsang and his pilgrimage to India through the country of the White Bone Ogress with Monkey, Piggy and Sandy. We often acted it out, much to the amusement of our visitors.

These mornings marked Paban's initiation into the world of reading, writing and drawing. When he saw that the children had picked up the alphabet in no time, he tried to read along with them and in a few weeks began to decipher the texts of songs in the innumerable cheap editions of Baul songs left behind for him by Baul poets and singers. Our visitors watched and commented on these developments.

The Bauls believe in the power of speech; books for them are stale knowledge, cut off from the sources of language. Deepak Majumdar, a frequent visitor, warned me that Paban's memory, entirely oral, would suffer if he learnt to read.

'We have our world and they have theirs,' he told me.

I could not agree with him. 'Can we not be elastic?' I asked. 'Swing between multiple visions of the world, like the monkeys above our heads who swing from branch to branch?'

Deepak smiled at me derisively.

The monkeys paused on the parapet to watch the children play. It seemed as though it was they who were the natural inhabitants of Shantiniketan.

Life was pleasant in the winter, and I had all the time in the world to digest all that we'd been going through. Paban and I were absorbed in each other and in the children. Mornings glowed with dew, and by midday, we were warm and sunbaked.

We walked about aimlessly with Krishna and Duniya, who were enjoying living outdoors. We walked to the shore of the Kopai River, whose currents were swift, the water waist deep. Krishna and Duniya were natural water babies – swimming was deep in their oceanic genes – and we floated in the river, letting the currents take us down it, holding hands. Like pelicans on a fishing cycle, we repeated this over and over again. I spread thin cotton gamchas on the sandbanks, and rubbed the children with mustard oil while they tried to wriggle away to freedom.

Paban had become a child among my children and the three of them often ganged up against me. Krishna and Duniya watched my face as Paban defied me, when I insisted on his not washing our clothes with polluting detergent in the river. Then, he flung the clothes to dry in the sun and wind, over bushes and trees, much to the glee of the children. They laughed uproariously when Paban exuberantly ordered me to hold one end of my red and blue sari to dry while he held the other; collapsing with laughter when it flapped and fluttered like a happy flag in the wind, and resisting me when I tried to wrap it back on.

One morning, we went for a walk in Bhubandanga, the university campus grounds. After we'd sat down, Nabani Khepa's second son, Lakhon Das Baul, strode towards us, handsome as a Sioux chief, his long straight hair flying about him. Paban invited him to join us on the grass. We were tranquil, basking in the new spring sun; my few moments of respite before I prepared for the midday meal and for the second stream of visitors. Lakhon smoked, lazily.

Suddenly there was uproar behind us: a herd of cows were creating a commotion. On the other side of the field towards the Science Faculty, on the main road into the Visva-bharati University compound, was a huge monkey who looked like an incarnation of the god Hanuman himself, chasing the cows. The cows, which had been grazing till now, stampeded, mooing and bellowing in fright.

The ape, an elderly male, was in his turn being chased by a pack of wildly barking stray dogs. He paused, changed direction, bounded over to join our circle and sat down cross-legged, pressing his face into his knees.

Lakhon was quick to respond to the animal. He spoke tenderly to reassure him. 'Father, are they bothering you?'

The ape, swiftly recognising his sympathetic tone, laid his head on Lakhon's lap in a posture of surrender. Lakhon massaged him and smiled triumphantly at us, as though he had just managed to convince the world of his magical powers. The children were wide-eyed with delight, though a little scared of the enormous creature. After a few moments, they plucked up courage and crouched on Lakhon's knees, stroking the animal. The ape sat up again, crossing his legs once more like the rest of us, twitched his ears and gravely accepted an aubergine which was being proffered to him by a man from the crowd that had collected around us. After a couple of bites, he tossed it aside, leapt onto a passing rickshaw, and disappeared from sight.

We all laughed, relaxing again. Lakhon took his bag off his shoulder. Made of patchwork, the bag was an exquisite piece of craftsmanship. The corners were drawn in and sewn together, with shoulder bands which crisscrossed over each other. Motifs of tiny birds and fish, embroidered in coloured threads, darted into its corners. As he untied the bag, he demonstrated its five openings, representing the five elements, Khiti, Ob, Tej, Morud and Boom: Earth, Water, Fire, Air and Cosmos.

Paban, jealous of the attention I was giving Lakhon, snatched his bag from him and rummaged inside, then laid its contents out on display. Lakhon, imperturbable, smiling faintly, continued to roll tobacco and hemp together, watching Paban as he laid out his ornaments: necklaces and bangles, precious stones and a small piece of sandalwood. The two could gossip and quarrel till the sun reached its zenith. They had known each other for years, and Paban told me there had once been talk of his marrying Lakhon's daughter Bhabani, only negotiations were dropped when Dibakar refused Lakhon's offer of a dowry, which he judged to be too low for his talented son. This did not seem to have come between them.

'Ma, there was a time when the atmosphere of Shantiniketan inspired me to reach great heights. Perhaps it was the huge trees or the presence of a great soul. But I don't feel the same here any more. Something has left us. It's like that Hanuman, which became ours only for a few moments and then went away. I don't like to stay here longer but would prefer to lead a monastic life in Sheori, next to my father's grave. I'd be delighted, Ma, if you'd come and visit me in Sheori or in Mehednagar.'

He embraced us heartily, and strode off majestically, disappearing into the crowds. Shantiniketan had clearly lost its allure for Lakhon.

My first impression of this town was that it had an atmosphere of sterility. Emaciated old people lived here, shuttered in their dilapidated bungalows and wrapped in memories of the transient glory Tagore had once given it. Their withdrawal from reality was indicative of a shrinking of the arteries of the town's spiritual essence. Tagore had lauded a lifestyle close to nature and espoused the philosophy of Baul poets and philosophers, but how could he teach sensual life and the concepts of democracy to the caste-conscious, puritanical society that had taken over the administration of the university?

Tagore had created the Paus Mela, a multicultural and multidimensional fair, with the idea of creating a bridge between the indigenous popular living arts of the local region and the cultures of the West. He cleverly timed the Paus Mela during Christmas, aware that people from all over the world would visit Shantiniketan during this period, especially as it corresponded with the winter holiday season in Europe and America. But now the Baul singers were reduced to abject creatures who wandered the mela, forced to line up for meal tickets and a few rupees for singing a song. Tagore had hoped that these projects would spiral upwards into a fecund and rich communion between city and village. In half a century, that spiral had been straightened out and reduced to a conformist straight line, separating the world of the babu from the world of the Baul. If only Tagore could have foreseen that the destiny of a place like Shantiniketan after his death would finally be determined not by the individuals he had drawn there through his personal magnetism, but by the continued impoverishment of the village and forest world that surrounded it, a hardening of caste attitudes and a total obliteration of the sensual and imaginary life of its women. The poet's dreams faded out with his life.

By the thirties, Lakhon's father Nabani Khepa had already wearied of Shantiniketan, sensing perhaps which way it would go. Tired of the sycophants, promoters and property dealers who had gathered around Tagore when he won the Nobel Prize and became an international celebrity, he quit the small town with his family. He bundled his children Purna, Radharani, Chakradhar and Lakhon onto a bullock cart. With his wife Brajabala by his side, he trundled, disgruntled, towards Bakreswar, where he felt he could plumb greater depths within himself. Bakreswar was famous for its seven hot springs, said to contain chemical and curative powers, and the sage Asthabakramuni was said to have attained illumination here.

Nabani was by then famous throughout the land. As his cart passed by them, people from the villages bordering the road solicited him with offerings of food and shelter, asking him to stop and visit. Finally, he stopped under a giant banyan not far from Bakreswar. The local people rejoiced and within a few days, they had provided him with a shelter, given him land to cultivate and cattle to nurture. There Nabani and his family lived peacefully for a few years – until one ill-fated day.

The new rice had just been harvested. Lakhon, still a little boy, hopped from one sheaf of paddy to another. The women prepared pithas and fritters of aubergines, lotus stems, green bananas and bitter cucumbers for the festival of Nabanya. At midday, when the water was warm and the fish rose to the surface to feed, a net was cast. A large fish was caught in the main reservoir. Nabani sat in his asana, the place where he performed his practices, and began his daily ritual: he packed his panchamukhi chillum with a fine mixture of tobacco and hashish. When it was ready he dabbed it with snake venom, which he kept in a tiny mother-of-pearl casket. Silence reigned supreme. Nabani's ashram was separated from the village by a grove, and it was easy to ignore what happened in the village.

Suddenly a morol, an elder with a voice in the village's affairs, burst in on Nabani: 'Father, get ready to leave for Bakreswar immediately!'

Nabani lifted his head very slowly and looked at him without uttering a word. The man was obliged to bend down quickly, touch his feet and change his manner. 'Khepa Baba, there has been a death in the village. It is our custom that when someone dies on the day of Nabanya, all of us must accompany the body to the cremation in Bakreswar, and then bathe in the Jivanakund to be purified. The others are already on their way. You are the only ones still here.'

So saying, the man left. Nabani turned to his wife, Brajabala: 'We are leaving this village this instant.'

His tone made the children realise the gravity of his statement. Purna hitched the cart to the ox at once. The family mounted the cart and took the road away from Bakreswar, returning in the direction of Shantiniketan. As they left, Nabani lit his five-headed pipe and sucked on it, crying, 'Jai guru!'

After a long time, Brajabala turned to Nabani: 'Why did we leave the village?'

His response was simple. 'How can a Baul live among people who expect him to run after a corpse?'

Several days after our encounter with Lakhon, we took the early morning bus to visit him in Sheori. On the way we decided to halt at Gopalpur, where Nabani's wife, Brajabala, now a widow, lived. The early morning sun gleamed on the dewy earth. Serpentine tracks traced on the red soil of Birbhum wound into the horizon, disappearing into clumps of date palms and banyans, teak and tamala trees and tall grass flowers. The tracks of ascetics, they led to sacred places of pilgrimage: to Tarapith, Bakreswar and Dubrajpur.

A Baul clad in patchwork robes beckoned to us from a tea shop next to a bus stop. He was long and willowy and seemed to sway in the breeze. It was Chakradhar, Purna and Lakhon's youngest brother. We got off the bus and followed him to the home which had been built for the family by Nabani, in Gopalpur. It had been his final home with Brajabala, about ten kilometres away from Shantiniketan, but in little danger of intrusion from the middle-class urban population, who still remain incarcerated within the precincts of the university. Nabani must have known they were unlikely to venture out this far. Travelling can still be dangerous outside zones clearly demarcated by electric poles.

Brajabala continued to lead the life of a Baul, the ascetic life of a mendicant. Every morning, she set off on madhukuri, on a round of the neighbouring villages, beating time with her metal cymbals and singing the name of Hari. The customary seven fistfuls of rice sufficed for the day and villagers willingly offered this to her, often adding some lentils, vegetables, fruit, milk and oil to their offerings of rice. They would also offer her cotton saris, and every year a piece of thick, rough-grained silk which they wove themselves.

When we arrived in Gopalpur that morning, Brajabala was seated on a little wooden stool, anointing herself with a tilak of sandal-wood, resting after her madhukuri and morning ablutions. She wore a choli blouse and a sari of fine white cotton, as well as a thick creamy scarf of rough, handmade silk and four strings of tulsi beads. Her silver hair was drawn into a knot at the nape of her neck, framing a dark, kindly face burnished in the sun. She welcomed us into the circle of her serenity. A mat was spread out for us by Chakradhar's wife, Pratibha, who invited us to settle down on the veranda.

'Tell me, who are you, where did you come from, and where are you going?' Brajabala quizzed me, her voice teasing but friendly.

'I am a wanderer on a pilgrimage and you are my divinity, I will go where you send me!' I answered her carefully, aware that here every single word would carry weight.

She looked surprised at my answer, though not at all put out by my effusiveness. A little thoughtful, she went into her hut to search for provisions, then questioned me from a pool of darkness. 'What sells first in the bazaar?'

We were served bowls of puffed rice and steaming new potatoes, and tea. It took me a while before I found an answer.

'What sells first in the bazaar? Rice? Salt?'

'No, no! Even before any transaction takes place in the market-place, what sells first, what is the first thing exchanged?'

'Words?' I ventured hesitantly.

'Hari bol! Hari bol!' exclaimed Brajabala. 'A true Baul's answer! Your store will always be full.'

I received bhiksha – alms – for the first time in my life: some rice and dal and potatoes. And it's true to say that I've never run out of them since. The blessings of a Baulini go a long way ...

In the evening Paban disappeared, leaving me with Brajabala and Pratibha. When he did not return after a few hours I was in anguish. Why had he said nothing to me? We had quarrelled that afternoon. Swapan had come with a message for him to go to Durgapur, where there was a fresh crisis: his uncle Shuhankar was back again and this time was obviously dying. Paban had given all our savings to Swapan, as he felt guilty about not having given his family any money for a while. This meant that I'd have to go to Kolkata and ask my father for money, something which we'd managed to avoid doing till now. I had been financing my stay in Shantiniketan by giving private lessons in French and English, and by doing the occasional translation into French. This had given us enough to cover our costs. But I could not afford to finance Paban's family and had told him he needed to make a choice; he had walked off in response.

I felt tired and angry. The winter sky was full of stars, but the lack of electricity made the children gloomy. I was discovering a stubborn, wilful side to Paban's nature. Was he just using me? And was he now with some village belle? After all, he came from the lower depths of society, a place where survival was a vicious game; the niceties of middle-class conduct were beyond him.

The intensity of my feelings for Paban overpowered me at that moment. He was ambiguous and fragile. He had invaded my world and changed my daily life irrevocably; the world I saw around me had become meaningless without his presence; he was the back-drop, the diapason, the drone behind all action.

We were breaking all the rules of our respective worlds. Our love was subversive and endangered us and all those around us. Fears came buzzing into my mind like the mosquitoes which stung our feet. But they cleared out like night pests in the light of day, whenever Paban began to sing. He had a trick of cheating time, and in his presence all my fears about the future evaporated.

At about ten in the evening he appeared in the doorway. I could tell by his guilty face that he'd been drinking. I kept my silence. Nothing I could say would make sense now. Outside, the sky was brilliant with stars, the pond was twinkling with the phosphorescent lights of a thousand glow-worms. We sat quietly on the earthen floor and ate our meal. I wondered if his home and mine could ever be the same.

Was I not, as friends still point out, the contingency that was pushing him away from his profound nature? Whenever he left me it was to return to a world which had a natural claim on him. Realising this, I felt I must tell him immediately that I would like to leave. But, before I could say anything, he began to tell me a story.

'An old man and an old woman lived on the bank of a lake in a little hut. Every morning, at sunrise, they would bathe in the lake and then the old man would remain to fish tranquilly, while the old lady would carry back a pitcher of water from the lake and finish her work at home. She would water the basil plant, swab the floor with a mixture of cowdung and mud, light the oven and place a pot of water on the fire.

'Now one day the old man came back with five koi fish still alive and jumping inside a pot. The old lady settled down on her stool and took her dao. She spread some ash on the floor and then rubbed the fish, still squirming, into the ash to get a good grip on them, for koi fish live in slime and are slippery. She scaled them on the back of the chopper, cleaned and cut them. She then fried them with great care and put them aside. She heated a little oil, threw a pinch of onion seed and a few green chillies into the oil and once the seeds spat and hissed, poured in some water with a little turmeric and salt and plunged the fish into the soup.

'The old man sat on his mat while the old lady strained the hot steaming rice. He was so hungry that he could hardly wait. The old lady served him a heap of rice on a banana leaf which she had washed with great care and served herself another heap.

'"I shall eat three fish and you shall eat two," said the old man, "because it is I who have caught them!"

'The old lady, stung by his selfishness retorted: "I have prepared them and I have cooked them so it is I who shall have three and you shall have two."

'"But had I not fished for them, we would have had no fish at all."

'"And had I not cooked them, you wouldn't be able to eat them at all."

'Neither of them could change the other's mind, so they decided that whoever was the first to speak would have two fish, and whoever could keep silence would have three. An hour passed by, and then two, and then three. And then a whole day passed, and then another and then yet another. But neither of them spoke.

'In the meantime, their neighbours, who had noticed their absence from the lake, peeped into the hut and saw them stretched out stiff on the floor. Assuming them to be dead, they sent for the undertakers to carry the bodies to the cremation grounds. Five undertakers arrived, placed the two bodies on a bamboo cot, which they balanced on their shoulders, and set off for the cremation grounds, chanting, "Bolo Hari, Haribol!"

'It was almost evening after a very hot day.

'"They will burn quickly today as the wood will be nice and dry," remarked the chief undertaker, who led the way.

'At the entrance of the funeral ground, the old man suddenly sat up.

'"All right, I agree: you will eat three and I will eat two!"

'The five undertakers were terrified, thinking that the dead had come to life and were planning to devour them, as they were five in number, just as the fish were. They dropped the bamboo cot and ran for their lives. The old man and the old lady, weakened by their fast, got up and slowly trudged back to their cottage.'

Paban was telling me the life of a couple was a struggle unto death. There was no getting away from each other now.

*

We had frequent visitors in our time in Shantiniketan, attracted by the fame of the Baul singers, which had spread through the West in the seventies thanks to the modern European theatre movement. Jerzy Grotowski, a legendary Polish theatre director, declared that the sources of theatre in Europe were dead, and incited Western actors to steep themselves in oriental traditions, pointing to the Bauls of Bengal as one such 'living source'.

Ramananda Das Baul, Grotowski claimed, was a personification of 'the human divine'. Ramananda had been a great Baul singer, the adopted son of the old Baulini Chintamoni, and had once lived in Nichu Bandhgora on the outskirts of Bolpur. He smoked a lot of ganja and began mixing up the texts of his songs, and one day disappeared for ever. As he suffered from epilepsy, some said he was dead while others believed he was still somewhere in the Himalayan region, possibly in Gangotri.

Key theatre figures, including Peter Brook in Paris and Andre Gregory in New York, were among the disciples of Grotowski. Grotowski encouraged his students to face their darker sides and to explore their emotional and physical limits. Personally, I've always felt that this was a dangerous initiative for those not firmly anchored in life. But inspired by Grotowski's example, visitors to the Bauls have since included actors, musicians, poets, ethnographers, photographers and writers, music producers, agents and impresarios from around the world.

Jonny, an alto sax player from Sweden, was a regular guest of ours and accompanied Paban everywhere. He quickly picked up a smattering of Bengali, learnt to eat rice with his fingers, pick the bones of fish with his teeth and to stand on his head and practise pranayama. Jonny, whose name is pronounced Yonny in Swedish, and whom the Bauls soon cheekily began to call 'Yoni' (the source and origin of life, i.e. the vagina), stayed for six months on his first visit. He was soon well known in the villages by the banks of the rivers Damodar and Ajoy, where Paban was often invited to perform. His dazzling blond hair, which reached his shoulders, and his 'golden horn', his alto saxophone, made him stand out in the flat Bengali countryside. Children in the villages soon became familiar with his name. They came running to him from all directions, shouting his name as soon as he appeared on the horizon like a lost Percival: 'Yonny, Yonny, Yonny!'

Jonny's skin would turn scarlet, and his blue Nordic eyes would water, when he heard this cry. He would crawl into the nearest shelter and hide his face in embarrassment. He was not used to so much attention, nor to the communality of life among the Bauls. Most Bauls lived in small huts where the only piece of furniture was a wooden cot and, at night, they slept packed like sardines on a communal mattress.

'That's how most of the poor live in India,' I explained to him as gently as I could, when he complained and asked for a room of his own.

In spite of his naivete, Jonny genuinely tried to imbibe the culture and the lifestyle of the musicians he emulated. He was not a hacker, a stalker or a pirate. He seemed entirely unaware, though, that the very act of transporting himself from a remote suburb of Gothenburg to the edge of Bolpur town made him a vehicle of the globalisation he was trying so hard to resist.

On his second trip Jonny brought with him Katrin, his partner, an actress who was an intelligent and independent Swedish beauty, with a strong character and sharp wit. She promptly got herself a bicycle and shuttled between Bolpur and Shantiniketan. She told Paban frankly that she wanted to learn the sexual techniques described in some Baul songs. This left Paban flustered and troubled for days; Grotowski's techniques were devices to train and develop sophisti-cated, urban European actors. Trying to lift techniques from this utterly different world that was agrarian, deeply religious and poor was tantamount to drawing water with a sieve. There was much to be learnt, I felt, from the words of Baul songs.

> O my heart fakir, words of the heart,
> Hawks come to the tree
> The cat comes to the tree
> And the fish spawn are all devoured
> By the triangular fish.
> O my heart fakir, words of the heart ...
> And Paddo, the scoundrel, is so clever
> He draws water with a sieve ... 3

The extreme pressures of modern life had forced the Baul singers to make a profession of their ancient celestial craft. Traditionally, Baul gurus gave the Baul singers a baina; an honorarium to book them to sing in their monasteries during festivals dedicated to the gurus and to Krishna, the supreme preceptor. These akhras, or places of learning, were in turn patronised by village folk. But this entire support system had collapsed over the twentieth century. In this situation, and in the absence of patronage from common village folk, Baul singers had become reduced to mercenaries, eking out their existence by singing for their supper.

Many of the Baul singers therefore regarded this new interest in them from young, beautiful, talented and affluent white people as a miraculous promise of survival. This made for a particularly deadly equation: these disenchanted travellers, seeking spiritual solace, opened their hearts and their pockets to the Bauls. The Bauls in return, famished and avid, wound themselves around them. Both groups were caught in a serpentine coil of mutual dependency.

Most of them no longer practised madhukuri. Instead, they climbed onto the trains to Kolkata and busked on them, living at the mercy of the commuters' goodwill. The luckier ones, endowed with talent and good looks, managed to make a career of their singing. They were avaricious, abject and downtrodden, forced to live double lives. Younger Bauls were frequently forced into prostitution by their patrons, often unscrupulous contractors and dealers, rough men who lived in the coal area. Only a handful of older Baul singers and sages, who lived in their remote ashrams, were still in contact with their songs' deep meaning. They shook their heads at the ways of the Baul youth, who only sang for money and gain, having lost their true spiritual and artistic vocation. Even Paban, with his natural musical genius, sometimes sang like a parrot, without a remote inkling of what he was singing about.

'Nakal korey pabi ashal,' Gour Khepa told me one day, laughing. 'It's by faking that you get to the real.'

*

Being multilingual, I had to be careful not to fall into the trap of being an intermediary between Paban and our Western visitors in this complex interaction. In any case, I had a busy mother's life running the house and an open kitchen for visitors, who were frequent. I scowled dreadfully to keep these young visitors away, banged my pots and pans, swung my brooms and brushes and took on the posture of an angry mother goddess.

Cooking meals at midday always made me hot-tempered and intolerant, and I would quarrel with Paban who encouraged the visitors crowding our house to stay for lunch. I only calmed down after the traditional midday chillum on the veranda, followed by massaging soothing coconut oil on my scalp and ablutions with buckets of cold water.

The Baul singers and sages who clustered around Paban commented on the daily dramas played out in our home, pointing out that the only way for him to avoid such scenes was to leave home entirely. Fortunately Paban was immune to their advice.

During the Paus Mela at Christmas, when a certain section of Kolkata society descended on Shantiniketan, the intrusion into our privacy became unbearable. But I had no one to blame but myself. I had built a halfway house, to bridge the gaps between Paban's world and mine. My open door was an open invitation to being trampled upon in the ensuing stampede of Western pilgrims towards the Baul singers.

'Khaachhilo tati tat bune, kal holo tar gan shune!' goes the adage: the weaver ate happily, weaving on his frame. It was hearing a song that destroyed him.

One night Paban and I returned home at about two in the morning from the Baul akhra at the Paus Mela, the children asleep in our arms. When Paban unlocked the door, we found Jonny and Katrin with a group of musicians and actors squatting in our living room. They had somehow let themselves into our home even though we had made sure to double lock the door before we left.

These young people, still adolescents, were determined to get into our lives even if they had to break in. They'd borrowed the services of a child acrobat at the fair, helped him slide in through the bars of our windows and open the back door for them.

I was furious and feverish with exhaustion. 'Would you ever behave like this in Europe?' I yelled at the foreigners.

Jonny, Katrin and their friends stared back at me defiantly. I stomped past them to a little room opening into the garden at the back of the house and put the children to bed. Paban followed me in anxiously and shut the door behind us without bolting it. We went through our nightly rituals, lighting a mosquito coil, putting up the mosquito nets as a double precaution and making sure the children were covered. My temperature was rising: I popped in some aspirin and drank water. We chatted softly before going to sleep; the lizard clicked on the wall as usual.

Suddenly Jonny burst in through the door with his blue eyes blazing. He knelt at the foot of our bed folding his hands in prayer. He had evidently been chosen by his group as an emissary.

'Joy guru! I have six weeks in this country. Please teach me prem sadhana ... '

Prem sadhana is the yogic discipline of breath control and retention of seminal fluids practised by the Bauls. The aim of such a discipline is health and longevity. It's this technique which is popularly referred to as tantric sex and which has titillated the interest of many a visitor to this world. Jonny had conceived the idea of a sexo-yogic initiation into this ancient char chandra (or 'four moons' practice) of the Bauls as a kind of six-week workshop.

In prem sadhana, the four moons in the body represent the four corporal fluids: menstrual blood, semen, urine and faeces. It's through the subtle control of the flow of these seminal fluids that Baul gurus help their disciples reach the sources of inner energy. The mysterious words of Baul songs only hint at these practices, which are practised in secret within the Baul fraternities to this day.

But Jonny was asking the wrong people. Neither Paban nor I had been initiated into this esoteric core of Baul practice. Although Paban sang their texts like an angel, our love life was completely spontaneous and unplanned.

I realised that Jonny was not acting alone. Katrin, who wanted to see how far she could go with Paban, was encouraging him; behind every uncertain fellow, there is a strong woman. Seeing that Paban wasn't likely to be helpful, Jonny decided to play on his insecurities, aware of how strong the rivalries were among the Baul singers when it came to winning over allies and disciples.

'If you don't teach me, Katrin and I will attach ourselves to Viswanath in Suripara. He says he will be able to help us,' he declared.

Despite my derisive laughter, Paban was unsure how to respond and finally sat in the lotus position, showing Jonny some basics of yogic breathing which I'd never seen him practise before. Ultimately, however, Paban had to reveal to Jonny that he had not yet learnt the sexo-yogic techniques leading to the retention of sperm. It was a discipline that could only be communicated by a reliable guru.

'I am a Baul singer, not a Baul sadhu,' Paban confessed to Jonny, looking at me sheepishly. 'You will be better off with Viswanath Das of Suripara. He's a sage, and more experienced than I am.'

Paban showed Jonny out of our bedroom, his face a little sad.

'We are not gurus to be initiating disciples,' I told him, slightly delirious now. 'We're not going to start a cult, are we? Dress up as guru and guruma?'

'Maybe some day,' he whispered to me, stroking my feverish head to sleep.

'Over my dead body!'

Within a few days Jonny and Katrin settled into Viswanath's ashram in Suripara, on the other side of the Bolpur railway station. Then, after a month or so, they went off to Puri on a Baul honeymoon with Viswanath and his wife, Padma. Puri, where Joydeb wrote the *Geet Govind*, is a place of pilgrimage for the Bauls and fakirs.

The foursome checked into a beach hotel where crêpes Suzette were served for breakfast and you could sit by the Bay of Bengal playing chess on cement tabletops designed as chessboards. Some of the hippy beaches of Goa had shifted there.

In the meanwhile, Georgio, a violinist from Italy and a friend of Katrin's through the Grotowski network, had checked into a dorm in another hotel not far from his friends. One night, Georgio noticed that his neighbour in the dorm had a black instrument box under his bed; the man turned out to be a sitar player. They shared some chai, and Georgio felt the man was quite stressed out, drinking heavily and yelling oppressively at the hotel staff. Late that night, Georgio returned to his hotel after spending the day with his friends to find the lobby infested by policemen: the corpse of the sitar player had been found on the beach. He had drowned in the sea that night. Foul play was suspected.

He had possibly been involved in a drug racket, a hotel boy told Georgio.

Georgio went up to his dorm to retire for the night, a little shaken. The cot next to him was empty. But the black case still lay under the bed; no one seemed to have noticed it.

Georgio opened it, to see a brand new sitar gleaming inside. He struck a note or two and was transported by the quality of its resonance.

Early the next morning, Georgio went to have breakfast with Jonny at his hotel, and told him about the sitar player and the sitar. Then the idea struck them both, simultaneously, as they began to tuck into a pile of crêpes with honey. The sitar player was dead; they could take his sitar, which seemed to have been forgotten by everyone. There was no harm in this. After all, it was all for a good cause. Jonny had been planning to buy one for a friend in Sweden – here was a golden opportunity to get one free.

The two young men hatched a plan. Jonny would come to Georgio's hotel in the night. Georgio would tie a rope around the sitar and let it down from the roof. Jonny would then take the sitar to his hotel and hide it there. He would transport it to Kolkata the next day.

They went to the market to buy rope and a couple of cotton saris to fabricate a winding sheet. Then they returned to Georgio's hotel and wound the sheet around the sitar, tying it securely with rope.

That night, Katrin intercepted Jonny as he was about to set off for Georgio's hotel. The manager of the hotel where the two of them were staying had invited Katrin to have a drink in his room, and she wanted Jonny to accompany her as she was afraid of the intentions of the hotel manager, who had obviously been lusting after her. Swedish women were reputed to jump into bed with all and sundry, and the fact that they had come here in the company of a Baul couple renowned for their knowledge of sringara rasa and the rites of maithoon, sexual intercourse, must have titillated his fantasies even more.

Jonny, forever flexible, accompanied Katrin to the manager's room. After a smoke of Bhubaneswar gold and a drink of coconut arrack, the couple left the manager to his own devices. Katrin returned upstairs to Viswanath and Padma, and Jonny hit the beach, stoned and drunk, hyperventilating and hallucinating.

By this time, night had fallen. Security guards and armed policemen were posted all along the beach. Jonny staggered past them to Georgio's hotel, but under the influence of psychotropic substances each minute seemed to stretch to an hour. There was no sign of Georgio, and it was too dangerous to hang around on the beach. Jonny knew by then that his blond hair and his fair face would be spotted all too easily against the black night and the black sea, so he returned to his hotel. It was only nine thirty. So, after waiting for another half an hour, he returned to Georgio's hotel, covering his blond hair with a dark bedcover, walking slowly and steadily.

Georgio was now on the terrace and waved at him. He lowered the shrouded instrument slowly to Jonny but as he did so, the sitar strings, which were not yet properly set, knocked against the parapet, resonating loosely and loudly, setting off the barking of dogs. Finally, Jonny managed to catch it. He untied it and returned into the night, clasping the sitar to his bosom.

At dawn he was still on the beach. The ocean was grey-blue, triangular shadows of the sails of fishing boats floated in a cluster on the distant horizon. The beach was crowded with fishermen heaving their boats into the sea. The waves were violent, slapping against the shore, signalling undercurrents. There was not a surfer in sight, only

Bengali and Marwari families clustering together in front of a safe place to bathe. But the beach no longer seemed to Jonny what it had been the day before; what had seemed fun before was now spiked with fear. A watery death and a night's furtive thieving had given the new day an uneasy pall.

As soon as it was time, Jonny left by rickshaw for Chandanpur, about ten kilometres out of Puri, to catch the train to Kolkata. He wasn't eager to be spotted with the stolen sitar at Puri station; the effects of cannabis had waned but he was still paranoid, certain he was being followed. Viswanath, Padma, Katrin and Georgio boarded the train at Puri, and they were all reunited in Howrah station, checking into a hotel on 'Shudder' Street.

We happened to be nearby in Kolkata at that point, where Jonny asked me if I'd keep the sitar for him. I scolded him. 'We are in India, not Europe. What if you had been caught? You could easily have been accused of having murdered the sitar player to get his sitar. You can never tell what will happen in India. And how do you know the sitar is not stuffed with drugs?'

Jonny left, hanging his head and hugging the sitar to his chest.

Years later, we found the sitar hanging in a smörgåsbord restaurant in front of the quiet lake of Karlstadt in Sweden, a memento of an unknown musician pulled in by the great waters. Jonny and Katrin are separated now. Today, over two decades later, Katrin is the mother of Viswanath's gorgeous daughter, Sunna, who has the looks of an Inuit beauty and the spirit of her grandmother, Khandi Ma, one of the great women Bauls of the early twentieth century. So much for the retention of sperm!

'When I first saw you, I thought you were a maiden from a house of devotion!' Subal Das had said when he first met me in Paris. He visited us in Shantiniketan when the monsoon finally came and we were homebound by the rains. The light is particularly beautiful in this season. That year, the red earth glowed under the cloud-covered sky and gusts of wind made the ripened mangoes fall to the ground.

By this time, the stories of Jonny's request to Paban for an initiation into sexo-yogic practices had circulated around the Baul network in Bolpur. Jonny had confided in Viswanath and Padma who in their turn told Gour Khepa, who, in a moment of great hilarity, immediately broadcast the information loud and clear in a chai shop at Bolpur station. The Bauls, gossips and raconteurs, were hugely tickled by this interest generated among young white people in the four moons practice of Baul sadhana.

'Today's plastic Bauls have chemical gurus,' cried out Gour Khepa, expressing his disgust with modern contraception and its consequences. Baul couples practised natural contraception, restricting lovemaking to the few days of the menstrual period. This, then, was the secret core of their practice of ulta sadhana.

Brahminical law considers a woman's body to be impure during menstruation. The Bauls, who oppose this law, declare that the menstrual period is the most obvious indication of the presence of cyclical lunar currents in the human body. They consider roj, the menstrual flow, and beeja, sperm, to be the sacred elements which ensure the continuity of mankind. Purusha, man, in order to discover the inner secrets of his body must be led by Prakriti, woman. We are all women, except for a few moments, state the Baul gurus, recognising the uniquely male capacity for erection and the shortness of its duration!

At the time of Subal's visit, I had been helping Paban paint tar on the bamboo rafters of our veranda. The night before, when Paban and I had turned towards each other, my bottle-green angora cardigan must have dropped off the wooden bed to the floor. In the morning, to my surprise, it was nowhere to be found. Paban, still sleepy, opened one eye at the pile of dark green dust on the floor and whispered: 'Ghun legechhey. Woodworms. We must get some tar.'

After a cup of tea, he cycled off and returned with an aluminium pail full of tar from a grocer's store in Bhuvandanga. We got to work right away, fabricating a brush out of a length of bamboo and some rags. Paban stood on a ladder and I held the pail for him. The tar was heavy and sticky, and it spread from my fingers to my hair, making the children laugh. When we were done, Paban asked me to fetch the jerry can of kerosene, soaked a rag in it and began to rub the tar off my hair. I suddenly got the feeling I was being watched. Paban stopped painting and cried out: 'Jai guru!'

Subal stood in the garden like a ghostly apparition. His small, shrunken body was curved into three distinct angles, a tribhanga dance posture, his chignon tilting to the left and his eyes closed in slits over his high cheekbones. When I asked him to come in and sit down, he did not move but remained, standing inscrutably in the garden by the Japanese cherry tree, tuning his ektara. His hair, which was dyed jet black, added to the impression of a geisha ceremonially awaiting instructions.

Paban whispered to me that I should spread a mat for him on the veranda. For some reason, he didn't want Subal, his musical guru, to enter the house. He cried out to him: 'Come here, pethni buri, old witch, let me colour your hair with some tar! Your ektara is out of tune as usual!'

Subal sat on the veranda while we retired to bathe and change. Paban whispered into my ear that Subal, the old rascal, had pretended to the world that he had given him a diksha mantram and was probably thinking of exercising his right as his guru to initiate us into the Baul four moons practice now that the cat was out of the bag that Paban was still a novice in this area.

The first single cycle of Baul sadhana lasts twelve years. It's a process of impregnation, like many oral traditions of India. It requires becoming steeped in the vast repertory of Baul songs in order to apprehend and then become agents of the Baul philosophy and way of life through a practice of songs and stories, music and dance, body practices, rites and rituals, under the watchful eyes of Baul gurus. The next cycle of sadhana – jugal sadhana, life as a couple – lasts yet another twelve years. Paban had completed his first cycle; it was time to enter the second. This is what Subal had come to initiate Paban and me into.

Paban had first met the Baul singers when his father, Dibakar, had taken him and his brother Swapan to Kenduli at the age of ten to beg for alms. The Baul sadhus and singers took to little Paban instantly and taught him a few songs, which he learnt with lightning speed. Many Baul gurus and singers like Jaya Khepa and Shombhu Das, Sanatan Das and Purna Das Baul told Dibakar that he must let go of his son, who was a child prodigy.

Dibakar took them seriously. Returning to Sainthia he shared his thoughts with Paban's mother, Ulangini: Paban must be allowed to go out and find the right gurus, and himself. So Paban started busking on the local trains. Swapan followed him everywhere, accompanying his ecstatic singing with his steady, funky rhythms on the khamak. Paban now had the power to make money whenever he wished. As soon as he began to sing, coins would pour on him. And on the trains, he met many Bauls who also busked on the trains: Gour Khepa and Phoolmala, Dhona Khepa and Viswanath Baul, Norrotom Das and Madhab Das Baul. They invited him to their ashrams. After handing over the cash they had made on the trains to Swapan to give to Ulangini and Dibakar, Paban would go off alone on the Baul itinerary through Birbhum, Murshidabad and Nadia district. He would travel with Gour Khepa to Baul festivals in the tiniest and most humble Baul ashrams.

Over the next few years, Paban picked up a repertory of Baul songs and he returned again to Kenduli, this time to sing in the Baul akhras. It was here, at the age of fifteen, that Paban met Subal and was enchanted by his singing. Subal invited him to visit him in his ashram in Aranghata and to visit Bhaba Pagla. An adept on Kali and a guru for many of today's Bauls who continue to sing his marvellous songs, Bhaba's powers of enchantment were such that wealth was showered upon him by his disciples, who were middle-class people: merchants, shopkeepers, rich farmers, contractors and dealers, as well as artisans and folk artists. He had a musical and poetic genius and wrote a vast repertoire of Baul songs and songs to the goddess Kali, which he set to music himself. In the lavish gatherings which he held in his ashram in Kalna, he would play percussion with spoons, devise his own vibraphone with glasses and play his ragas and melodies, play the flute, play the fool. He spent his wealth on nourishing his disciples, buying the best fish, which he carved and cooked himself to feed all and sundry. With all the cement that dealers presented to him, he built houses for his disciples and an elaborate network of grand houses and gardens in his ashram. All those around Bhaba became rich; Paban too, as he sang Bhaba's songs.

> The river's full of waves,
> Why don't you see?
> Why do you try to row your boat by yourself?
> I have faith in the saviour of life;
> Give him the hull.
> Bhaba, the madman, was rowing his boat,
> But it broke midstream.
> Now he's drowning and crying out to the passer-by,
> 'Help me, O saviour, help me!' 4

Subal fed Paban's hungry soul with songs. Sundari, Subal's young and beautiful wife, who was tall, slim and enchantingly sweet-tempered, took charge of his body. Subal, forever mysterious, would disappear with his many disciples for days and even weeks, leaving Sundari without any money. And Paban was outraged at his neglect of Sundari, forever and always brimming over with sympathy for women, and would go off to busk on the train and bring her back money.

The relationship between the Baul and his guruma, like Krishna and Radha, has a sexual charge, although it is not usually consummated. According to popular belief in village Bengal, Radha was Krishna's aunt, older than him, and Radha's husband, Ayan, was Krishna's maternal uncle. Radha, as Krishna's preceptor in the rites of sexual love, was also his incestuous aunt. Baul gurumas, like Radha, initiate their husband's students and teach them of sexual desire. Many, like Ma Goshain, Hari Goshain's partner, revel in telling dirty jokes. This is a potentially explosive relationship – a spiritual ménage à trois. There are Baul gurumas who have crossed the line and fallen in love with their disciples, but these transgressions remain a closely guarded secret in the Baul world.

Paban spent months away from Durgapur now, much to the rage and frustration of his family, who tried to bring him back to them, but it seemed as though he had already grown out of their mould. Money came to him quickly and he spent it exuberantly, inspired to holiness and generosity by the example of Bhaba Pagla, who exerted a profound influence on him and to whom Paban returned again and again.

Swapan, who continued to accompany Paban everywhere, would sometimes have to snatch rupee notes from his over-generous elder brother to take them back home to the family, before they went elsewhere. Paban's friendship with the poet Amit had led him to Calcutta, where he met the great musician and composer Gautam Chatterjee and began to work with him and with a new band called Mohiner Ghoraguli. Amit helped Paban produce his first album. With it, his fame as a Baul singer spread and he was invited to play all over the land. Paban's travels took him to the remotest corners of Bengal and his songs became legendary by the time he was eighteen.

Subal stayed with us for a month, sleeping on a mat on the veranda. Every morning he was up before me, sweeping the dead leaves off the courtyard, lighting the chula and preparing the tea. He befriended the cleaning lady who was attached to our bungalow and organised a second kitchen on the veranda. He took over Paban's attention, whispering and cackling like an old hag into his ear. But I didn't mind.

At last, after these enthralling, exhausting months, I had some time to myself.

Evenings were sublime. Paban recorded Subal and learnt his songs quickly. He had a prodigious memory and knew entire texts after having heard a song only once or twice over. Subal sang, of course, from his magnificent repertory of Baul and bhatiali songs.

O my fickle friend,
I weep for you,
Raise me a home by the riverside,
Raise a home by the riverside.
Four paisas float in the water,
Frangipani blossoms cost two or four paisas.
It is hard to get the dirt off the blossoms,
It is hard to get the dirt off the blossoms.
Come, friend, and sit by me,
Don't put your hand on the pomegranate tree.
The blossoms are only just budding ...
The blossoms are only just budding ... [5]

We were both overwhelmed by the beauty of Subal's rendition, which was patterned with quarter tones and quavering blue notes. The song was nostalgic, slow, with a floating cadence reflecting the pull and push of river currents. It was a traditional bhatiali song from the riverine lands of Dhaka district in East Bengal, the country of Subal's origin and that of my father and mother too.

Paban and I looked at each other silently. His message to us, though subtle, was clear: love between man and woman demands infinite patience. Subal hadn't initiated us into prem sadhana but his song had brought us together as no teachings could. Subal's wisdom lay in his art.

Those few days with Subal brought back the initial zest with which I had begun my journey into the Baul world. Coping with life in Shantiniketan, with my new family equation with Paban and the children and the frequent visits from foreigners and Bauls, had pushed my original questions to the back of my mind. Now, in Subal's compassionate presence and relieved of my hours of house-work, I was reunited with my search.

V

GHOSHPARA TO AGRODWIP: MUSIC, WOMEN AND SORROW

Illustration overleaf: Radha and a basil plant. A pot of Indian basil adorns almost all Vaishnav homes in Bengal and symbolises devotion and service to humanity.

S UBAL'S VISIT galvanised us, sending us back into action. Paban and I decided to follow the Baul trail through Bengal with his band, who accompanied him on the khamak, dotara, flute and tabla. It would give us a chance to connect together with the deepest part, the heart, of Baul culture. It had now been over a year since we had met and begun that first journey into the Baul world; over a year since we'd begun to live together as a family, the four of us.

All through this time, we hung on trains, walked for miles, travelled incessantly from festival to festival: from akhra to ashram, all over the Baul map. Swapan played the khamak and sang along with Paban, Jagannath played the dotara, Naba played the flute, Madhu played the tabla. As for me, I played the ektara, joining in the singing and playing, much to Paban's delight. And Duniya and Krishna would play in the garden with the neighbourhood kids, joining in the music and the dancing from time to time.

After a while, Madhu dropped out of our band; there was a lot of pressure from his Brahmin landowning family, who wanted him to get married and feared the consequences of his attachment to Paban and the Bauls. Then, Swapan also dropped out. He was generally moody in any case, but his reason, he told us, was that he didn't want to leave his mother's side.

On Dol Purnima, the night of the March full moon dedicated to the love play of Radha and Krishna, we visited the Satima Mela in Ghoshpara, which commemorated a local saint, Satima.

Many of her devotees, particularly those from the Sufi-influenced Kartabhaja fraternity, gathered in Ghospara every year at this time. Women in the nineteenth century were practitioners of sexo-yogic acts, initiators of ancient sexo-yogic cults. Satima, a simple village woman of the mid-nineteenth century, became famous for her sharp wit and lacerating tongue: a vac siddha woman. For she raised the delicate and explosive issue of the balance of power between sexes, accusing the Bengali upper classes of surrendering to their colonial masters; she said that Bengali men, feminised by the presence of their British colonists, had as a result become oppressive masters in their households. They incarcerated their daughters and their wives, all the while indulging in debauchery and alcohol. To me, having returned to Bengal more than a year ago and having observed the life of the women of rural Bengal for many months now, it seemed that nothing had changed even now. The events of the days that followed proved this to me without a shadow of a doubt.

I was curious to discover how the Bauls celebrated Holi, the spring festival of colours which coincides with Dol Purnima. To my surprise, the atmosphere of this fair was surprisingly muted and orderly; it looked more like a massive refugee camp than a festival. Tents were spread across a grove full of large shade trees, and large cooking pots bubbled peacefully all around us. Only the women in white who had played with abir – powdered dye – bore witness to Holi, their saris stained pink and green. We headed for Subal's akhra, which he'd started almost twenty-five years ago. In it, he had created a network of relations consisting of many disparate religious communities: in addition to Padabali kirtans which expressed the emotions of Radha and Krishna, marfati and murshidi songs were also sung here, the former emphasising the importance of gurus as the preceptors of spiritual knowledge and the latter celebrating the spiritual life as opposed to the constraints of Sharia law.

Subal knew how to manage a Baul festival, run a community kitchen, organise a stage and services for all visitors. As a young man, he had worked for a coppersmith and as an actor with a small folk theatre group. He had a great sense of theatre and his performances were subtle and explosive, comparable to the greatest of kabuki masters. Today, he received us unostentatiously and silently, shrouded as it were, lying wrapped from head to foot in a cocoon of cloth. By him, a crowd of rowdy young Bauls, his disciples, horsed around.

Paban, quick to interpret Subal's posture as a signal that the singing in his akhra was not to begin till later in the night, led me to a neighbouring akhra.

There, Noni Pagla, a genial, smiling tantric sadhu, sat in the midst of things like an emperor, surrounded by four splendid young women and his mataji, his female consort. He greeted us warmly and we were served karan, country liquor mixed with the water of fresh green coconuts. I told Noni Pagla that I was disappointed not to find any powerful women in this Baul world. He smiled at me sadly, then whispered into Paban's ear. And the next day, we went to visit a female tantric sadhu.

Gourima's ashram was a little thatched hut. Only those who knew Ghoshpara well could reach it; the only access to it was through a small lane behind the crematorium. The dead burnt beside Gourima night and day. An ethereal beauty, she sat in the yard outside her ashram on a small, intricately embroidered mat, lost in contemplation. My eyes were riveted on her.

It was impossible to divine her age. Her matted white locks were covered with an orange veil, which framed the soft contours of her fine-boned face. She wore the flowing red tunic of a tantric sage; necklaces of white cowrie shells and rudraksha seeds were coquettishly strung in pretty, decorative loops around her throat; red, coral and white conch shell bangles adorned her hands from wrist to elbow, jingling against each other – even when lost in contemplation, she moved constantly as she fed the fire, fondling a pair of iron tongs which she used from time to time to add logs, poke them into a flame and then push the dying embers and ashes to the side. She refreshed herself from time to time, pouring liquid into her throat from a tall, narrow brass pitcher.

Behind Gourima was a small, dilapidated red-brick temple nested in the aerial roots of a banyan. Gourima rose and turned towards her little hut. When she stood and began to walk, I saw that she was tall, slim and graceful, moved like a vine in a light breeze.

Inside her hut, through the open door, could be seen an image of Shiva's consort Bhairavi, clothed only in clouds, cascades of hair hanging loose, trident in her right hand in a mudra of protection and a fresh citron in the left one.

I whispered in Paban's ear that she was perhaps the last of the Bhairavis, a vestige of an ancient world of tantra and yoga in which women were preceptors, and that we should drop all other projects and dwell here for a while.

'Ma, I have some questions to ask you!' he began, addressing her all of a sudden.

Mistake. Gourima quivered with rage, and her soft voice was suddenly raised high in scorn: Paban was given a verbal drubbing for his lack of courtesy.

'I! Me! My! That's all you men think of! Do you think you are the centre of the world? You are nothing! You will become nothing!'

The men who had gathered around shouted, 'Jai ma! Jai ma!'

But her mood changed like quicksilver just then. I sat on my haunches next to her, my knees touching hers. As though she'd heard what I'd said to Paban, she addressed me.

'Vamachara is a ritual to be conducted by women, but now, as you can see, tantra is dominated by men. We sadhus know that tantra originally belonged to women. Brahma, Vishnu and Shiva transformed themselves into women before they could see the Goddess in her sublime form.'

As if on cue, a group of exuberant young women in coloured saris arrived on the scene. They approached Gourima and knelt before her, touching their heads to her feet, and gave her offerings in little newspaper packets: sweets, fruits and paan leaves. She blessed them munificently. The women, laughing and shouting at each other, brought out mops and brooms from inside the little hut, swept and swabbed the courtyard. They seemed almost to be infusing energy into the ground, so vigorous were their movements, so robust their vitality.

Gourima rose again to cover the stones in the altar under the banyan tree with sindoor, vermilion powder used to denote marriage, settling on her haunches. Then, in a single gesture, she took a fistful of fine white powder from a paper packet and poured it in a fine spiral drizzle on the earth, drawing a simple diagram: a triangle in the interior of a circle.

'A yoni and a lingam?' I wondered.

'A male trinity englobed in a female sphere,' was the answer.

Her reply was clever. She knew how to turn things around to her advantage.

I watched as the first woman placed a clay pot on the mandala. The second filled the pot with water. The third woman returned from the river with a fresh pitcher of water, and kept it aside. The fourth and fifth women plucked leaves from the trees in the grove and handed them ceremoniously to Gourima, who covered the opening of the pot with five kinds of leaves and a green coconut. She bent over the pot, pasting all the leaves red with vermilion and sandalwood paste, and then, turning towards me, put a red spot on my forehead with her index finger; turning to Paban, she put a red spot on his forehead too.

Now, I don't ever use sindoor myself; sindoor symbolises acquiescence to the laws of marriage in Bengal. I had sworn as a child never to wear it after seeing the suffering which marriage had brought upon my mother, an accomplished artist, forced to choose between life and art. Paban, being a Baul, respected my choice – the Bauls themselves never use sindoor, rather they use sandalwood paste and tilak mati, made from chalky clay from the river banks, to anoint themselves – although the women in his family in Durgapur and Mohammedpur badgered us about my wild, unparted hair from time to time. But we were in the presence of a sage, and content to be her playthings.

The women began to sing. Paban tuned his dotara and joined them. Slowly the tempo built up. He sang a hymn to the mother goddess.

> Pacify the body, O mother Tara,
> You who chases pain, O source of life
> If you don't, dear mother, who will calm it?
> On your left Lakshmi and on your right Saraswati,
> You ride the lion, O saviour of this world.

Gourima, finally appeased, prepared a pipe of cannabis which she offered Paban. Mysteriously, the Doms, who burn the dead, appeared around us and shared the pipe with her. The smoke clung to her, making her look as though she would disappear by some sleight of hand.

The pipe made a round and came to me.

Gourima now raised her voice again: 'Saraswati is a favourite of the veshyas, the prostitutes. She is the goddess of knowledge. Like them, she is celibate. Her morality is obscure to ordinary beings. She goes to the depths of her soul and her body to search for knowledge. Saraswati is mahavidya – she who is endowed with great knowledge, and you women are vidyas – the personifications of knowledge, made flesh and blood. Without you, no man could ever become a saint!'

By the time we returned to Subal's akhra, it was very late at night and the full moon shone bright over the mela grounds.

Halim Fakir from Rampurhat and his wife Man Kumari sat with Subal and greeted us warmly. We had met them in Kenduli. Man Kumari was the daughter of a Brahmin but had left home to become Halim's spiritual partner. She sang a song of Lallan Fakir's in a rough deep voice.

> People tell me:
> O I've lost my caste, I've lost my caste,
> O what is this strange factory?
> No one wants the truth,
> They only prevaricate ... ta na na na ... [1]

Many Muslim fakirs were present here. They included Shahjahan Miah, a blind Baul singer from Dhaka, Humayun Fakir from Kushtiar and Gholam Ali from Joshor. They came every year to attend Baul festivals in West Bengal. Subal told me that in the old days, he had crossed the border every year to visit the fakirs and Bauls of Kushtiar in East Pakistan, now Bangladesh.

This transmigration of the Baul soul was vital to the preservation of a massive repertory of songs and a centuries-old network of itinerant minstrels. None of these men knew how to read or write, but had a vast oral memory. They were many currents in diverse streams, flowing into a veritable ocean of songs. Hailing from the lowest strata of Hindu and Muslim society, they were poor peasants and itinerant artisans of all kinds, tinkers and tailors, carpenters and potters, firecracker men and birdcatchers, coppersmiths and black-smiths, painters and leather craftsmen, lute makers and carvers, small merchants and traders, policemen and railway workers, vendors and petty thieves and, of course, local dealers of cannabis and country liquor.

The Baul singers shared the same simple language, the same social milieu and the same spiritual and aesthetic values as their audience. As they twisted and turned, stamped and stormed, they blew the breath of life into those who listened, pinching high notes on their lute strings, beating iron tongs, practising zikr – a form of continuous chanting that involves circular breathing: 'Hey Allah! Hey Allah!' Hari bol! Hari bol!

Subal turned to me and said, softly:

> Ma, a mad wind blows hearing the sound of a Baul's lute.
> There are those who go mad with rage and others,
>   like me, mad with joy.

Subal and Paban started to sing now. I began to see them now in their real context. They did not pretend to foresee the future or console past sufferings. Anchoring themselves in their songs, in ordinary everyday life, they teased and provoked their audience, inspiring them with reflections that were sometimes pleasant, sometimes disagreeable. While they echoed the joyous spirit of religious experience, they condemned the narrow bigotry and hypocrisy of organised religion. Their songs, expansive, rapturous, anarchic, had the power to evoke and amplify emotion in a way which exceeded the power of prescribed words.

*

Spring was here with its warm winds and air laden with the perfume of honeysuckle and jasmine. We made a small detour from Bardhaman to go to Garifa to pick up band member Jagannath, who was to accompany us to the Baul mela of Agrodwip which would take place ten days after the full moon of Holi.

We got off the train and walked backwards in the direction we had come from, along the railway lines and into the suburbs on the edge of the small town – which was itself on the edge of the huge industrial hinterland of Kolkata – winding our way through narrow lanes till we came to a large pond. Jagannath's cottage, with a red tiled roof and walls, was perched over the pond. The courtyard, walled in with cement and recently whitewashed, was pungent with the odour of camphor and mint; he ran a flourishing toothpowder business. Three women, Jagannath's mother and two wives, one of them with a child on her lap, sat around the veranda silently like cats, turned away from each other. Jagannath's mother told us he was not at home, but that we would find him in the market.

We made our way to the marketplace through a labyrinth of lanes. Jagannath was holding a demonstration sale in the main square of an open market. There was a large crowd gathered around. Two young apprentices, dressed in Baul costume – Baidyanath, a boy of fourteen, and Khepachand, not more than eleven, we would soon discover – accompanied him. An old percussionist with the tilak of a Vaishnava whom Jagannath treated with a mixture of contempt and deference acted as the diapason, the rhythmic throbbing of his hand drum providing a track to this little street play. A wreck of a man, his cheeks were drawn and he seemed to hunch under the weight of his drum. Sridam, who played melancholy notes on his dotara, had drooping shoulders, equally drawn cheeks and mournful eyes. On the whole, the performance in the marketplace was saturnine.

Jagannath tested the crackling, whistling microphone, shouting in a hoarse voice, 'Hallooo halloo, testing testing,' and snapped open a medium-sized black tin trunk revealing bottles of an assortment of shapes and sizes which contained balm and toothpowder. Sridam and the percussionist fumbled around in the meantime with their instruments, which they tuned lackadaisically, while Jagannath concentrated on his performance.

'Play, you son of a pig!' Jagannath growled to Sridam under his breath but loud enough for all of us to hear. This was another Jagannath, different from the merry, warm-hearted person I'd seen so far. His movements were stiff and jerky, unlike his usual fluid manner when he joined in the singing at a Baul akhra.

Now, he introduced the two young Baul singers to the audience, who closed in on them. Rapping in high speed, he lifted his voice in chant.

'Brothers, sisters and friends! Here is Khepachand from Nadia! A genuine Baul! With a direct link to the cosmos! If you want to travel in time, just hang on to his song line. It's a free ticket to Vrindavan.'

At this point he picked up Khepachand's little pigtail, traditionally sported by Vaishnavas, and stuck it vertically in the sky like an antenna, as if authenticating his divine status; to loud applause from the crowd. Khepachand, right on cue, danced, sinuous and serpentine, striking some sharp, staccato notes on his khamak. His trousers, torn to shreds, showed through his short Baul tunic. Squinting at the public, a smile on his small face, he belted out a song in a powerful voice, at once child-like, melodious and exquisite.

> O my heart, take the name of Hari just once,
> Be not arrogant about this human body.
> This human body is just a jar of clay,
> If it breaks, it will splinter in pieces.
> O my heart, those broken pieces,
> Will never come together again.
> O my heart, take the name of Hari just once,
> When the day is over, night will come,
> You will go alone to the final darkness
> Youth, so fulfilling now,
> Will vanish for ever.

Within half an hour, Jagannath had sold his bottles of tooth-powder and cans of balm, and had extracted the teeth of people who came forward from the crowd to more loud applause and cheering.

Jagannath was articulate in a way Paban could never be. I thanked my lucky stars for this.

Subal had warned me when we'd told him that we were going to visit Jagannath: Bauls who channel their musical energy for commerce are a dangerous lot. Jagannath had hired the services of these young boys, from families of poor Bauls, for their sparkling musical talent. He was also exploiting them cruelly, and the boys were fearful of him. Paban accepted the situation as normal; I found Jagannath's behaviour unpalatable.

The Agrodwip Mela took place on a little island on the Bhagirathi River in the district of Bardhaman, close to the borders of the districts of Nadia and Hooghly. We arrived in the town of Kalna, the nearest connecting point, after changing trains in Bardhaman, where we met Swapan eating jalebis and snacks on the platform. He was weary, but ready to join us. The rail connections were not easy and travelling was very tiring and long drawn out, here. We were deep in the Vaishnava world now.

In this small town was the Sri Gourango Mandir, famous for storing the personal belongings and manuscripts of Sri Chaitanya Mahaprabhu, whom Bauls claim as their original preceptor. All Bauls belong to one of the six 'families' of gurus and their descendants. These gurus are, in their turn, the descendants of the six great Baul century, all of whom were disciples of Chaitanya: Sri Advaitya, Nityananda Mahaprabhu, Ramananda Goswami, Gadadhar, Srinivas, Jabban Haridas. (With the exception of Jabban Haridas, who was born an untouchable but raised to the status of goswami because of his wisdom, the goswamis were all gurus of Brahmin origin.) Kalna is also known for the Devi Bhabani temple, where Bhaba Pagla meditated and wrote many songs to the mother goddess, which are now part of the repertoire of many contemporary Bauls.

It was a fairly long walk from the railway station to the fair. We were in the rich alluvial plains watered by three rivers: the Bhagirathi, the Damodar and the Ajoy. We crossed through groves of giant palms and bamboos by the river. The earth was fertile, densely cultivated, divided into fields and groves full of mango, jackfruit and papaya, laden with fruit; great flowering trees, blazing with new blossoms. At the river bank Paban vigorously greeted Tinkori Chakraborty, whom I had met on the train out of Kolkata at the beginning of my journey into rural Bengal; he was delighted to see his friend.

Hare Krishna Radha!
Allah Rasool Khoda!

Tinkori returned the greeting instantly. Turning to me he added, 'You know, now it's all piyaj-roshoon-aada!' Onions! Garlic and ginger! He was referring to our first meeting on the train when he'd told us a story about a poor wandering Baul.

He began to babble furiously, complaining to Paban about his lost life, cursing his wife, swearing at the world. Paban listened silently as we crossed over to the island on a wooden dinghy, carved in one piece from the trunk of a jackfruit tree, which ferried pilgrims back and forth. There were many new Bauls' faces here, ones I hadn't seen before.

Even the colour of the soil in this tropical part of Bengal was different here from the rusty red laterite soil of Birbhum. Here the clay by the river was a soft sandalwood colour, and the furrowed earth in the fields a rich dark brown. The colours of the costumes too were different here; white robes and saris rather than the flamboyant oranges and crimsons of Kenduli.

Ascetics, men and women with marks of sandalwood on their foreheads and thick ropes of beads around their necks, greeted us, bowing low in greeting and looking deep into our eyes as they embraced us in their traditional manner, touching cheek to cheek and holding us to their chests.

The Agrodwip Mela, third in the chain of major Baul festivals and held after the Joydeb Mela in Kenduli, had grown around the mansion of a local family, the Ghoshes.

The Ghosh family had been holding this carnival or mahotsava for over a century. A recurring pattern in each of the Baul melas is a commemoration – of a saint as in the case of poet Joydeb in Kenduli and Satima in Ghoshpara, or of an event, as in the case of Agrodwip – which is often at their origin.

Legend had it that Lord Krishna had appeared in a dream to one of the ancestors of the Ghosh clan in the mid-nineteenth century. The next morning, he found a black statue of Krishna floating up to him from an eddy in the stream near his house. He installed the statue in a temple and made ceremonial offerings every year to commemorate the auspicious event of its discovery. Thereafter, a Baul mahotsava grew around the Krishna temple.

I began to imagine how it had all started.

First, some great Baul gurus of the nineteenth century, perhaps even Shiraj Shah with his disciples Lallan, Duddu Shah and Panju Shah, had graced the Ghosh family's fair with their presence a hundred years ago. Perhaps when such great sages had come to the fair, the scenario had been very similar to the one I was experiencing now with Paban and Gour. Villagers had surely gathered around them as they listened to all the local gossip and scandals, poked their noses into the conjugal relations of their disciples, and improvised songs, skits and plays to interpret Baul philosophy and impart it to them. And such moments of grace had turned the fair into a mahotsava, which was how Agrodwip grew in stature and came into its own.

When we arrived this day, the thundering of a multitude of drums – khols, dhols, nagaras and nahabats – and the clashing of gongs and cymbals greeted our ears. A dholot or procession of ecstatic dancing men and women draped in white cotton, their faces rapt like ancient statues, circulated around the sanctum sanctorium, the seat of the gurus, chanting, 'Hare Krishna, Hare Krishna, Krishna Krishna, Hare Hare!' The continuous throbbing of the khol drums and the clash of cymbals induced their trance-like dancing, a fusion of many into one single moving body.

A rich patron of the Gouriya Vaishnava akhra, a fraternity of orthodox Vaishnavas, had offered three rupees a day and all meals for three days to anyone who would sing nama kirtans, chanting

Hare Krishna repeatedly, at the festival of Agrodwip, and many poverty-stricken Vaishnavas were only too happy to comply.

> Hare Rama Hare Rama Rama Rama Hare Hare
> Hare Krishna Hare Krishna Krishna Krishna
> Hare Hare!

Incessant chanting filled the air. Tinkori told us that recently the number of kirtaniyas, or kirtan chanters, in the festival had increased a hundredfold. What's more, the kirtaniyas had encircled the akhras and the sheer volume of their noise stifled the voices of the Baul singers.

There was a fundamental difference between the approach of the kirtaniyas and that of the Bauls. The kirtaniyas chanted divine names in a state of bicched or rapture, a little like the quawwaliyan devotional singers did, mourning their separation from God and seeking Him. But the Bauls did not seek. They were finders. They decried organised religion and sought the divine within; they were joyful and celebratory.

Piercing through the collective chanting, Gour Khepa's voice rose like a charge of electricity, soaring into the highest notes way above the range of the kirtaniyas, and then descending far below; he was a vocal acrobat who used his voice to leap to the heights and then plumb the depths.

He was singing in the main akhra: 'In my body torch light, O Guru, light up the battery of knowledge ...'

We settled down in the Samudragarh akhra, where Tinkori ran the show. We were well taken care of. Paban and I were treated with ayurvedic massages for our aches and pains. It was hard for me to differentiate between Sufi and Vaishnava here because most of the men and women wore white. We were truly in a world which lived in synergy, Hindu and Muslim, and had done so long before the very term was invented.

In the meanwhile, Duniya went off romping with Bodi Pagla, a madman, but one who seemed essentially harmless. Bodi was a sanyasi who had gone over the top when he practised his sadhana, and he had never returned to his normal state. At times, he could be violent, Tinkori warned me, worried that I had let Duniya go off with him. I trusted Bodi, though, as he was very gentle and funny with me. He begged for alms from Paban and then bought me some muri and begunis, puffed rice and aubergine fries. While Duniya accompanied him, Krishna sat resolutely by my side, tucking into the basket of fruit which was offered to us.

The kitchen in the Agrodwip Mela was a medieval affair. Rice and dal and vegetables were poured into basins which had been dug into the ground and paved over. Everywhere, there were signs of a deeply lived aesthetic life. Alpanas, temporary drawings made with rice flour with a proliferation of ferns and lotus blossoms, birds and fish, had been painted all around the akhra and in front of the beautiful thatch akhras in the heart of the Agrodwip Mela.

We were fed a copious and delicious lunch, organised by Bappa, a tall, handsome and exuberant young Baul from Krishnanagar in the Nadia district, obviously very popular here. Bappa had been an active Naxalite in the sixties and early seventies. Then he turned against the violent politics advocated by the Naxalites of his area, and became a Baul. We talked and talked and waited for night to fall, for this was when the kirtaniyas would pack up and go to sleep; the Bauls, those nocturnal creatures, would take over and sing all night, Bappa forewarned.

And they did. Gour Khepa, who took pride of place here, installed an echo microphone through which he played his khamak like a whiplash, filled with the obvious intention of provoking the orthodoxy. All night, the cacophony of his barking khamak kept us from sleeping too deeply.

Ecstatic, possessed, Gour wept with joy, cried out the news of his felicity, shouted the fact of his gaiety, singing raging songs of the heart, telling lusty stories of the body, the repository of the soul. It was not difficult to understand why the puritanical village society around him, founded on hierarchy and rigid dogmas, despised and feared this energetic, nomadic, most iconoclastic minstrel.

Wherever he went, Gour seemed to evoke strong emotions, as he had at that concert in Paris when I had first seen him perform – from open hostility and condemnation to undiluted joy and fervour.

The next morning, we joined the reigning Baul guruma, Meera Mahanty, at her akhra. Meera was a flamboyant figure. A large, round woman with a fair and fleshy face and great tigerish eyes, she was dressed in garish orange and had garlands of marigolds and white blossoms wound around her thick cascades of hair. Her spiritual partner was a big man too, a bearded, long-haired sadhu who sat beside her on a large, raised platform, never once raising his eyes. Many sadhus, fakirs and Bairagis sat all around her. They all turned to us, greeting us with invocations and showering us with petals. Paban was ready to sing now and began to tune his new dotara. But Meera asked him to wait his turn, smiling sweetly. I was surprised to see Paban defer to her. I was accustomed to seeing him enter a Baul akhra and take over the space entirely. I soon realised why.

The Agrodwip Mela was Gour Khepa's territory. He was the son-in-law here and had the privilege of exercising his authority. Meera Mahanty was his wife, Haridasi's mother and Gour's mother-in-law. Gour and Meera Mahanty were affiliated to the same guru, Haripada Goswami of Nabasana in Bankura, considered to be the greatest and most authentic Baul guru of our times. Hari Goshain, she explained to me, was from the Modhom Goshain parivar, and in his turn Modhom Goshain was affiliated to Sri Advaitya.[2] Baul fraternities have a network of gurus, which they trace back to Shri Chaitanya Mahaprabhu and his six Goshains or Masters.

We were irksomely stalked in Agrodwip. Both Noren, a Mr Punch of a man who had been a railway guard till he was suspended, and Lal Baba, a potbellied tantric sadhu, latched on to us and popped up wherever we went. Noren was a harbola, a mimer of birds and beasts. He took up the post of the procurer of tea and hemp, whistling like a teal all the while, lighting the chillum for the pot-bellied tantric who shouted:

Ganjar jogar kor!
Boro loker chhelley ke fakir kor!
(Procure some hemp!
Make a fakir of the son of a rich man!)

Their constant presence soon began to chafe. We were roused from sleep in the morning to find dozens of kokils cooing amorously at each other on the canopy of trees over our heads, in answer to Noren's summons. In the evening, when Paban and I argued, Noren mimed the bark of a stray and roused the dogs around us to such a point that we could no longer hear each other. Finally we decided to shake off our stalkers.

On the third day, after lunch at the Baul akhra, we took the children to the shade of a veranda in the village for a nap. After ten minutes, sure enough, Noren arrived with the potbellied sadhu in tow, walking fast. They lay down for their afternoon nap on the other end of the veranda. The heat was sweltering.

I waited for half an hour till I was certain that they were asleep. Then I shook Paban and the children awake. We packed our things quickly and ran all the way to the Kalna railway station. There was no train due for a while, and I was worried that our two stalkers would wake up from their nap and follow us to the station. We waited, tensely; the children, still sleepy, were transfixed by the mortal hiccup of a mangy dog which walked across the railway lines and disappeared into the bushes. After almost an hour, a train arrived in the direction of Howrah. We were free!

After Ghoshpara, we went to the annual commemoration festival at Bhaba Pagla's, who had died in 1982 at his ashram in Kalna.

Through this year of travelling, I had come to realise that the world of the Bauls portrayed in Luneau's film *Le Chant des Fous*, which was at the root of my journey, was idealised, exotic and imaginary; belonging to the realm of cinema, having nothing to do with the nitty-gritty and social stigmas of the world in which the Bauls lived.

I, and many others, felt that the Bauls were losing hold of the real meaning of their craft. Faced with dire poverty, many Baul gurus lived by exploiting their most faithful followers; some encouraged the use of alcohol and drugs, indulged in the most promiscuous sex and punished those who tried to escape their rule. Gour Khepa's tyrannical treatment of his first wife, Hari Dasi, which had resulted in her untimely death, and his subsequent avidity and cruelty to his urban followers – all of which everyone knew, and I soon heard about – outraged me.

Hardly a year after Hari Desai's death, Gour had married a tough tantric sadhuma whom he met on a pilgrimage. He then took on a disciple from an upper-class urban family, a theatre actor from Delhi, whose personal fortune he fleeced, subsequently establishing himself in a flat in south Kolkata and copying Deepak's bohemian though middle-class Kolkata lifestyle. Over a few months, he drank and smoked himself into a violent and schizophrenic state. When his disciple saw the light and abandoned him at last, Gour Khepa finally decided to cut himself off from the world in a small shack on the outskirts of Bolpur, where he now lives with a brood of stray dogs and cats.

Many Baul singers, realising the high esteem in which their philosophy and their songs were held in France, were keen to travel on the international shuttle, unaware of the struggle and tragic loneliness of such a journey. The real, authentic gurus like Hari Goshain today found themselves isolated; unable to find the right adharas, or vessels, to receive their knowledge.

What we witnessed at Bhaba Pagla's ashram only further confirmed my belief. We arrived in Kalna, entering the inner sanctuary of the akhra, to take a look at the mystical paintings of Bhaba Pagla, who had died three years earlier. A relatively unknown aspect of his life, these surrealistic self-portraits showed flowers emerging from his feet and clocks tick-tocking under his fingernails. The deluded devotees who had collected here to celebrate the festival of the ashram imagined that Bhaba's spirit was still hovering around them.

We settled in one of the ashram's havelis, or grand houses, for the night. The next morning, the atmosphere in the ashram was tense.

Slime rotted in choked drains in the inner courtyards. We sensed the hostility of the villagers when we went for a walk to explore the countryside around the ashram. Moreover, we found that we had stumbled into the middle of a bitter legal battle between Bhaba's elder and younger sons, over his estate. There was also an ongoing battle of wits between Paban and the resident Baul over how to correctly interpret Bhaba's songs.

We returned to join a session of singing at the temple. The mellifluous notes of the harmonium were broken by the whiplash of Paban's furious khamak. The heat was unbearable. Two vagrants joined us, one a vendor of bangles, the other a beggar without limbs. We crossed over to an inner courtyard where a couple of Hanumans were locked in cages. Visitors to the ashram threw their leftovers at them. The monkeys had curry all over their bodies, and there was food rotting on plates of teak leaves next to them. Dogs fought over the plates, snarling at each other and at us as we left the ashram.

Paban, unconcerned by the conflicts around him, set one of Bhaba's songs to music. Some years later, he would record it in Peter Gabriel's studio in Wiltshire.

Row the boat gently, don't tie it to the banks,
There's no one in this land to call your own.
All is unknown,
Light floats in the infinite skies, mixes with the
    soft breezes,
Know that you must cross to the other side,
And it will not do to keep sitting.
To a far country you must go,
If you pitch your boat on the bank, everything will
    lose sense.
Don't you realise that everything is fleeting,
No one will remain beside you for ever.
So many temptations come to devour you,
How do you dare stay in one place?
Row your barque to the beautiful shores,
Should you begin now no one will oppose you.

With great joy, Bhaba rowed the boat,
The boat broke midstream,
I don't know how to swim, what will become of me,
I don't even know how to hold my breath.
Row the boat gently, don't tie it to the banks. 3

Our last stop was at Garifa, at Jagannath's. Embers glowed in an iron chula in front of the doorway.

Paban froze. He told me urgently that this was a sure sign of a death in the household. Sure enough, a pained heavy silence hung over the house.

As we rushed in, we heard the terrible story of what had happened from Sridam, the dotara player, who came out to greet us. The day before, at one in the afternoon, before the midday meal, Jagannath's younger wife had set herself on fire with some kerosene.

It was impossible for us to divine, at first, what exactly had happened. Jagannath had returned home a few minutes before when we entered. His fair face was red, scorched by the fire of the cremation he had just attended. His voice was hoarse and heavy when he finally spoke. He embraced Paban and broke into sobs.

'I was hard on her. I built these walls around her, waited too long to set her free, to travel and to sing along with me, heart of a singer that was hers, heart of a wanderer, more than mine.'

Was he being truthful or trying to save his skin? The woman had had frightful fits of coughing, and had complained to me and Paban about being enclosed by the elder wife and mother-in-law, being obliged to do all the housework while her son was placed in the charge of the elder wife. She was choking in the asphyxiating binds in which the Vaishnava Baul community holds its women. If she had been a singer, as Jagannath claimed, then why hadn't he taken her out to join his threepenny opera? The ease with which I travelled with Paban and my children to the Baul festivals had perhaps made her realise that she could never be free in the way I was.

How could a Baul, supposed to dedicate himself to feminine

energy, live this schizophrenic double life? The theme of our habit-
ual divide repeated itself: Paban took this society for granted, I felt
weak and feverish. The violence and enmity between the Baul
singers and the totally depressed status of the women and children
in this lower-middle-class, semi-urban world, frightened and
discouraged me, more so at this moment of blight and defeat.

But there was no time to linger; the atmosphere in the neighbourhood was thick with suspicion, and we decided to leave at once.
Our staying would only exacerbate the situation. Jagannath accompanied Paban, Swapan, the children and me. As we walked out of the
tenements towards the railway station, Jagannath spotted a house
with a sweeping view of the fields; a privileged location compared to
the other houses that huddled together in the colony and over-
looked the road. He turned to Paban and pointed to the house.

'A chemist truly understands poison,' said Jagannath, quoting a
song which Paban had been singing recently. 'That is the house of
the master mason.'

'And goldsmiths know gold,' Paban responded.

'I shall tie myself to he who knows love!' Swapan sang the refrain.

Duniya sat on Paban's shoulders and Krishna sat on the cycle
which was being pushed along by Swapan's strong arms. The two
brothers sang in unison. It would be the last time they would sing
together.

> I will fuse my mind with his,
> Our two lives will become one.
> I shall travel with him on the road,
> Suspended on his neck,
> Like a chain of jewels. 4

Tears flowed from Swapan's eyes. He was crooning, sobbing,
laughing all at once, like an infant; devastated by the scene we had
just left behind us.

'Ma, why is Swapan crying? Who has hurt him?' Duniya, ever
sensitive, began to cry too.

Krishna watched us, sitting with Jagannath on his cycle, starting to feel anxious. But Swapan laughed and stretched his arms out to little Duniya, and she leapt into them.

It was the middle of a balmy afternoon in Purbapalli on the day of Lakshmi Puja, in October 1984. I'd just finished washing the dishes and was pulling the wooden shutters together to darken the room, thus lulling the children into a siesta, when there was a frantic knock at the door. It was Gopon, Paban's youngest brother. He carried terrible news. Swapan, who had been very disturbed over the past year, had just attempted suicide.

It was difficult for him to bear the separation from Paban; Swapan had been shuttling between Deshbondhunagar Colony and our home in Bolpur but seemed uncomfortable in both. Also, the year before, he had had an affair with a young French girl who was visiting Shantiniketan during her winter holidays. He had taken her to Durgapur, where the family persuaded her to put sindoor on her head, the streak of vermilion signifying marriage, when she spent a few days with him there. She had left for France and hadn't returned nor sent for him, as she had promised she would. Swapan waited for news from her in vain, and became increasingly moody.

That morning, his mother, Ulangini, had forced Swapan to take the cows to graze in the fields. Swapan had returned home at midday, tethered the cows, entered the house and latched the door. Ulangini, sweeping the courtyard outside, heard a heavy thud, minutes after he'd retreated. Unable to open the door, she called the neighbours, who broke it open. Swapan was lying on the bed on his stomach, clutching the sides of the bed, his face distended in a grin and his eyes shining feverishly. It took four grown men to prise him away from the bed and when they did, they found that he was bleeding profusely in the stomach. They transferred him to the emergency ward of the main hospital of Durgapur immediately.

The news was so stunning that it took a few minutes to register. It was as if time had come to a standstill. I flung a few things into a bag and got the children ready. Minutes ticked by. We set off for the bus station in Bolpur, running as fast as we could. But the last bus had already left, and there was no choice but to leave the next morning; we couldn't afford to take a taxi.

At the colony a drama of tragic dimensions was being played out. The women had all gone to the hospital. Neighbours stood around, looking at us with great suspicion. Borda again related what had happened, adding that Swapan had fixed a knife against the wall and thrown himself on it; hence the stomach wound.

We rushed to Bidhannagar General Hospital in Durgapur. Swapan lay in bed, his eyes overflowing with tears. He was conscious of what he had done and was repentant. He told us calmly that he had committed hara but had been unable to commit kiri; that is, to pull the knife horizontally. One of his intestines had ruptured, but there was hope. He wanted to live.

He wept uncontrollably. The doctors had already stitched him up but he desperately needed antibiotics to prevent any infection from spreading. We needed to scrape together some funds to pay for Swapan's treatment, so the four of us, Paban and the children and I, went to Kolkata to get it. As in earlier moments of crisis in my life, my father was sympathetic and forthcoming. He immediately went to the bank and withdrew some money for us. Concerned, he asked me to leave the children with him, but I decided to take them with me; Swapan was very close to them.

We returned by train to Durgapur the next day, and rushed to the emergency ward. Swapan's bed was empty. We thought that Swapan had died. Duniya looked enquiringly at Paban. Krishna put his arms around me.

Then I noticed that most of the beds were empty. The hospital had closed down for ten days during the religious festivities of Durga, the most important religious festival for Bengali Hindus, and all the patients in the emergency ward had been transferred to nearby Bardhaman.

The emergency ward in the hospital in Bardhaman was small and looked like a scene straight out of a war zone. Patients lay around groaning in pain, swathed in bloodied bandages. Swapan lay in the midst of it, in a cot, fed by an intravenous drip. There were complications. When he had rolled about on the floor, Swapan's perforated intestines had been polluted with some grains of dust. The house surgeon in Durgapur had done only a cursory cleaning-up job and now the wound had become infected owing to the remaining dust particles. When the women of the family had tried to feed him rice, this had aggravated his condition.

We were too late: Swapan was dying of septicaemia. Even a last attempt to revive him with a steroid injection had failed, we were informed. Swapan left us later that night.

He opened his eyes and smiled at us with infinite tenderness, pulling us both close to his chest: 'Come and join me down here.'

He sat up and raised his hands above his head in the posture of the saint Sri Chaitanya, leaned back and his eyes became empty. We stayed with him for a long time.

We travelled to Kolkata and returned in a group to Bardhaman with friends and family to collect Swapan's body.

When we arrived, a member of the hospital staff told us that Swapan's body had been reclaimed and was already on the funeral pyre. We rushed to the crematorium. One of Paban's family's neighbours shouted drunkenly, 'Where is Paban? We should put him on the pyre along with Swapan!'

He swallowed his words as soon as he saw us enter the funeral grounds. Swapan was burning on the pyre. Paban's eldest brother, Amulya, and middle brother, Promulya, stood by, witnessing the drama that was in the making: the neighbours were building up a case, accusing Paban and me of somehow being the cause of Swapan's death. Amulya told us that they thought this because we had administered an injection to Swapan, causing him to die. I tried to explain that the steroid injection had been administered by the hospital as an attempt to revive him. But my words fell on deaf ears.

Paban paid us no heed. He was devastated. He wept uncontrollably. Other members of his family looked on without saying a word. His mother, Ulangini, had returned to Durgapur. I led Paban away. We returned to Durgapur ourselves, to join Ulangini and Paban's father, Dibakar, who had refused to go to the crematorium. He embraced us and wept when he saw us. Ulangini sat on the veranda, eyes glazed, in a state of shock. For six months, she wept and mourned.

For those six months, Paban wandered to all the places he had ever been with Swapan, hoping to find him somewhere. He was ridden with guilt. We traced his childhood footsteps; took the Darjeeling Mail up and down; returned to Mohammedpur in Murshidabad; strayed from village to village in Bardhaman and Birbhum and took a launch to Number Twelve Taktipur at the southern tip of the Sundarbans. Then, at last, when I saw that he was inconsolable at his separation from his beloved brother, I proposed that we visit Hari Goshain in Nabasana, in the district of Bankura. Only a guru could save Paban now.

VI

NABASANA:
HIDDEN ALTARS AND
HOLY GAMES

Illustration overleaf: Krishna on a cobra. This image represents the
legend of the divine child Krishna who dances insouciantly on the
Ananta Naga – the Serpent of Eternity. The Serpent represents the *kuna
kundalini*, the power of the breath's suction, which lies coiled inside the
orifices of the human body. According to the Baul cosmogony, a guru is
Krishna in a human form.

WE WERE on the road again, on the Patrasar trolley train, a metre-gauge train which moved slowly, twenty miles an hour. This was Rahr Bangla; here lay the drier, western lands of Bengal. The earth below was mineral red. The engine snorted a jet of black charcoal smoke, chugging like a toy train. The train passed through bright green rice fields where scruffy marabou storks fed on cockles and snails, their wings folded back, their stretched heads stuck low in the mud. Someone pointed out their nests in a grove of trees, where hundreds of chicks muttered and clamoured as the older birds fed them.

These birds had migrated here every April since ancient times, flying off again after Kali Puja in November. I was delighted to find my own path crossing that of these migratory birds: I was becoming one myself.

We were part of a crowd of Bauls on the train, old and young, all heading in the direction of the guru ashram: Chintamoni, Viswanath and his son Anando Gopal from Bolpur, Chinmoy and Benimadhav from Magra, Gour Das and his khepi Bimala from Khana Junction, and many others.

The train entered a forest. Bright green parrots swirled around in exuberant droves, brown speckled teak babblers and jet-black kokils whistled, cried, warbled and flew about, disturbed by the passage of the train. The children were with Father, who was taking care of them in Jhautalla. Paban and I were heading in the direction of the ashram of Sri Hari Goshain, whose annual mahotsava in Nabasana was part of the second tier of Baul festivals.

I was keen to meet Hari Goshain. He was one of the few remaining authentic Baul gurus in West Bengal. Living in tandem with

Nirmala, his spiritual partner, he trained his disciples in the deeper understanding of Baul philosophy, and also taught them esoteric sexo-yogic practices such as the control of breath and the retention and use of body fluids. He was the author of a vast repertory of Baul songs, each song a gem containing the essential tenets of Baul body knowledge.

Hari Goshain was not a sadhu who had retreated to the high mountains to seek wisdom through yogic discipline. He believed that illumination was to be found in this very samsara – the only cycle of birth and death, and that the sacred dwelt in the profane like honey in a beehive. He lived like most Baul gurus, among ordinary village people.

We crossed the forest into lush green rice fields and pastures. Beside the railway line, three slim young Santhal herdsmen led a troop of doe-eyed cows to graze. One of them played a lilting, piercing melody on a high-pitched flute, the two others sang and shouted, wielding sticks. Paban responded immediately, tuning his dotara to their pitch and singing to them out of the doorway of our compartment, roaring with gaiety. The Bauls encircled us and jammed with him.

> If I were a doctor
> I would sit under a tree,
> I'd sit on a chair –
> You'd see how proud I'd be!
> I would poke your skins with needles,
> I'd take twenty-five rupees for a visit
> O Santhals have made a God of me!

The herdsmen shouted back to us and waved till we were out of sight, watching the train disappear. The passengers cheered. We were getting into a festive mood again, our tiredness – after a sleepless night at the Sonamukhi festival from where we had boarded the train – sloughed off like an old snakeskin.

An anti-cyclonic electric storm, a kalbaisakhi, had risen and formed a threatening knot of clouds above us and blasted at us, then blew away as quickly as it had gathered. By mid-morning, the sun was relentless, the sky cloaked in a russet haze with not a speck of cloud to be seen. A strong, hot, nerve-wracking wind blew into our faces. Black soot disgorged by the train's charcoal engine caked our hair. There was a taste of grit, on my tongue, in my teeth.

Just then, a stentorian voice bellowed from the other end of the carriage: 'You can't become a Baul unless you're pasted with soot and dust!'

Paban swung around. Nimai Chand, an old friend and Baul musician who'd been busking on the train, came and joined us with a twisted grin. He was much older than Paban, tall, stooped and paunchy, with a high, sloping forehead, a protruding jaw and a wise, wily face.

Paban greeted him with a hug, and cockily showed off his new dotara to him. It had a peacock head, which he'd decorated with two pink beads for eyes and a tiny crystal in the place of a third eye. He'd added a cute little tuft of multicoloured thread to make a crest. A master craftsman, Paban was constantly pottering around with various paraphernalia, creating the instruments of his music. The Bauls watched him, wary and admiring, as he decorated his instruments with beads and bits of carved wood. Our lives were entangled in gut strings and metal wires, cowries and nails, burins and bamboos. In his bag, he carried a screwdriver and a saw, scissors and blades.

Nimai strummed a couple of chords, nuzzled up to Paban like a drag queen, and took on a whiny, provocative voice: 'Why must you play a dotara when I am here to play for you?'

Paban was electrified by Nimai's arrival. He'd often spoken to me in superlative terms about Nimai's virtuosity as a dotara player. But now, he turned his back to him.

Nimai moved closer till he faced me and said succinctly in English: 'Big sister, this is my heart connection. Don't push me away!' He was staging the act of taking over the show.

Paban turned obscene: 'Ei bokachoda! Chup kor!' Shut up! Asshole!

The passengers, old and young, enjoyed their scuffle; aware that, in fact, Paban and Nimai were spontaneously playing to them and pleased to be on a mobile stage, with a captive audience. Pageantry is woven deep into the very grain of Baul artistry and showmanship.

The Bauls did not look for a utopia, be it social or religious. For them, utopia was to be found in the human body, to be harnessed in the present.

Sometimes on these train rides, young boys and girls, dropouts from village life, would turn from their steely intentions of making it to the city. They would get caught in a Baul mist net. This would save them from the destiny of slavery in the city, or from joining the rigid military groups of the Maoists. Different from the Naxalites of the 1970s, these Maoist groups populated the forests all along Baul country, forming a red corridor that ran from Nepal in the north to Telengana in Andhra Pradesh. These pastoral lands that we were passing through formed a buffer between the troubled jungles and the disturbed industrial zones of Bengal. It was easy to see why the potential recruits were turned. When the Maoists spoke of a mouse and an elephant, they meant a detonator and a bomb, when they preached of red and white they meant arsenic sulphate and potassium chloride, ingredients to make bombs. The Bauls only smiled at each other secretively; for them, the mouse and the elephant are male and female genitalia and the red and white, blood and sperm.

The passengers, young and old, men and women, egged Nimai and Paban on. 'Come on, Nimaida, sing for us, please. Have pity on us ordinary mortals!' Nimai looked very pleased indeed. He stroked his side whiskers and made ape faces. Nimai's moody, skilful chords on the dotara seemed to speed up the tempo of the train and wind Paban up, till his dubki thundered at high speed in accompaniment. Nimai met him, beat for beat, and harmonised perfectly with him, binding him in an invisible musical bond. They made a magnificent couple!

The metaphor of Nimai's song, in which the train represented the human body, was the perfect song for his setting. It had been written by Nimai's grandfather, Shivananda Goswami, whose author's credits are integrated into the text in the last verse of the song in the true Baul tradition.

What you hear with your ears
Is final proof
That man is a car of pipes and taps
Driven by the wind.
A cosmos is on each side,
Fire burns within him.
Why, then, does he sleep?
Above, a water jar,
Below, a tale of fire
The pair never stop,
They move together.
On each side,
A pair of compasses
In the middle, a star eye,
Above a flag flutters in the wind!
Inside a hole,
Filled with burning coal
Five passengers stand by the door
Driven by the spirit
Look the human car goes wherever it wants!
Inside this car,
A net of chords
A single melody played on three notes,
Unite in a single chord,
Which turns round and round,
Till, like an alarm,
It produces yet another sound.
He who becomes a swan, instructs the world!
His wings spread out by the force of his wheels.
Crossing over ten thousand leagues
He goes where his spirit takes him.
To Delhi, to Manipur
He announces the state of all things!
Shivananda Driver says
It's hard for me to drive
My machine is rusty and no longer moves! [1]

Outside, the heat spread, everything a haze. Grey foxes slunk by in gullies by the rail lines, looking for shade or water. Packs of brown strays played in a waterhole. We passed more domes of dilapidated terracotta temples caught in the aerial roots of banyans and peepul. The shining green and white of an occasional mosque was a sign that oil money from far-off lands was filtering through even to these remote parts of Bengal.

At this point, the train stopped in the middle of nowhere. Around us were stretches of fields, lying fallow. Paban signalled to me to disembark, and we jumped off the train with our instruments and bags. Some passengers, attracted by the Baul magnet, also got off hurriedly. They trailed behind us. Paban groaned because his new dotara was heavy; a young Baul ran up and offered to carry the instrument for him. A couple of sturdy young men came up to us as we walked, and Paban introduced them to me as Jagannath and Lakhan, local farmers who were Hari Goshain's disciples. They relieved me of my ektara and shoulder bag.

Our companions were all devotees of Baul songs and singers. Paban always sought hands to help us carry our burden, always found shoulders to lean on, lightening the weight of our constant shuttle. There was a sweetness and reciprocity in these little gestures between him and those around him that came from deep and common feeling. Their bond had aerial roots, like the banyan trees which seemed to proliferate as we went deeper into the countryside.

We walked together Indian file, over the ridges that separated the fields, and towards a jungle. As we entered the forest the locals showed us signs that elephants had been there; a smudge of mud on a high branch. They'd had great trouble with them lately. The jungles in these areas, which lay in the passage of the River Damodar to the west of Bengal, were depleted. A century of uncontrolled mining in the Damodar valley region, from Chhota Nagpur to Asansol, had wreaked havoc on its forest resources. Elephants often trampled across fields of grain to feed on the fruit trees in the groves adjoining the areas of human habitation. Seventy-five such elephants had gone on a rampage in Bankura recently, destroying fifteen lakh or one million, five hundred thousand rupees' worth of grain.

Bel fruit, with their hard, pale green shells over a soft inner core of fibrous orange pulp, and champakala, small yellow seed-filled sweet bananas, were among the elephants' favourites. As were the mangoes, jackfruit and lychees, still raw now, but soon to ripen in this new heat, which would carry on till the June equinox, at which point the monsoon rains would bring temperatures down. Till that season and till the trees in the forests bore their fruit, the elephants would return to the farmers' fields from time to time to feed on the grains ripening in the villages.

For the moment there was absolutely no sign of any elephants, nor of the heat abating. Utterly hot and bothered, I was hoping to find one who would carry me across the jungle. Paban and his companions laughed, implying the sun had gone to my head. Paban told them I'd spent my childhood in Assam where my uncle owned five elephants, and that it was quite natural that I should expect one to be at my service. The villagers looked at me in undisguised awe, as if I were royalty.

Finally, after what seemed like hours, we arrived on the bank of a river, the Damodar. To my disappointment, the riverbed was dry and there was no way of taking the dip Paban had promised me. There was a tiny rivulet of stagnant water in the middle, not even enough to splash our faces with. Paban looked worried at my reaction. The last time he had visited Hari Goshain's festival three years ago, he told me, the river had been full. We moved on.

With the help of our guides, we now had to cross over to the jungle on the other side. The Nabasana ashram lay beyond the narrow jungle belt. I kicked off my rubber sandals and walked barefoot on the burning sand. After a few minutes, the soles of my soft-skinned urban feet began to blister. In a fury of suffering, I pummelled Paban on his chest, holding him responsible for my predicament. Our companions roared with laughter; they found my reactions hilarious. I had nobody to blame but myself for the situation I was in. If you point a finger at someone, say the Bauls, remember, three fingers point at you!

We finally got to the forest and rested in the shade of a large tree. Some children, forest sprites, appeared out of nowhere. They were Santhals. A dark, beautiful girl of about twelve, with the face of an ancient deity, gravely poured us water from a brass pitcher. She was adorned with heavy brass jewellery and beads, and wore a bit of cloth wound around her hips. Another child, a bright-eyed boy of eight with curly hair and a torn pair of shorts, had a bow and arrow. Paban picked a couple of wild bel or woodapples, cracked them open and crushed the fibrous pale orange pulp into a paste with his fingers, inside a malui – a coconut-shell bowl used by Bauls for ritual purposes. Nimai made a wisecrack about how the bel juice was a Baul colour and suggested that Paban should pee into his bowl too. Paban scowled at him darkly.

In a few minutes, we were drinking cool refreshing juice. We settled down in a circle with Lakhan and Jagannath, and smoked the traditional pipe of tobacco and home-grown cannabis. Paban sent the boy to scale a tree and pluck some orchids.

The boy stripped the forked branch of a nearby tree of its parasite flowers, disturbing the meditation of a pair of owls, who blinked and screeched indignantly. Dark, cinnamon-coloured orchids with pale, sand-coloured spots, gorgeous and remote, like the land we were in. Paban offered them to me ceremoniously. I was delighted, sufficiently recovered from the heat with the juice and now this lovely gift from the jungle. We decided to plant them in Hari Goshain's ashram.

Leaving the forest behind, we arrived on the main road which connected the town of Beliator to Sonamukhi, still in the Bankura district. Jagannath and Lakhan indicated a distant clump of trees which beckoned promisingly, but were still beyond our reach, a couple of kilometres away.

Sheltered by a panchabati, a sacred grove with five kinds of trees – banyan, peepul, bel, ashok and tamala – within the meander of a small river, the Shalini, lay the sanctuary of Baul guru father Sri Haripada Goswami.

We left the forest behind and walked the last lap of our journey over the dried-up fields. The exterior of the ashram was shrouded in the shade of trees. We walked into the courtyard. I was blinded by the April blaze. My ears were assaulted by solemn incantations and prayers offered in deep, resonant voices; by a clash of cymbals and the deep bass notes of a bhairava horn; the thunder and roll of drums and the shrill, ecstatic ululations of women.

As my vision returned, little by little, a dazzling solar system greeted my eyes. Hundreds of Bauls clad in a spectrum of colours – white, saffron, red and black – were seated in rows around the courtyard. The midday meal was being served to them.

Hari Goshain and Ma Goshain, Nirmala, spiritual father and mother to many of the Bauls present, looked like characters out of old epics. He was tall and lean, with fiery eyes behind his glasses. It was hard to believe he was eighty-two years old. There was not a single white hair on his head. The guru mother, or guruma, was small, plump and merry, with bright black eyes which missed nothing. Both Hari Goshain and Ma Goshain were clad in saffron.

The couple paced down the rows of guests seated for their midday meal, chanting dohas, couplets invoking the gathering to communion. Some ascetics and disciples served the meal, carrying buckets of rice and dal and vegetables which were sloshed onto plates made of teak leaves. My eyes, unaccustomed to the shade, fell on a familiar face – that of Chinmoy, whom I had first met on the top of the bus when catfish had splashed beside us. It had been almost two years ago and what I'd faintly apprehended then was now my reality: I was caught in the Baul net. He raised his hand in a salute, lowered his eyes, dropped his head and returned to his meal.

The meal took place in absolute silence except for the dohas, which spread spontaneously from one Baul to another: 'Jai Radhe! Jai Radhe!' Victory to Radha! Victory to Radha! Invocations rebounded around me.

Ei mahaprasad paiya shobe badaney bolo Hari!
Jahan jahan sadhuguru tahan Vrindabana Puri!
Koiya ei sadhur bani madhur rashey

Bir abodhoot! Kanai abodhoot!
GURUM GURUM GURUM!

(Receiving this great offering,
Take the name of Hari on your lips!
Wherever there are sages and gurus
It's paradise on earth.

With these words of wisdom,
Savour the honeyed rasa
Bir is divine! Kanai is divine!
GURUM GURUM GURUM!)

These last three expletives I had heard from my parents as a child; every Bengali child has heard this at least once in their lives. It was the sound of the fisticuffs which would fall on my back if I did not do what I was told; Bauls use these sounds of remonstration to describe explosions of cosmic energy.

Dazed by the speed at which I was swallowed into this sphere of chanting, ritual and improvised poetry, I turned to Paban to find him spread-eagled on the floor, in prostration at the feet of Hari Goshain, who stretched out his arms, lifted him up, and then placed his hands on our heads. His palm felt cool on my burning scalp.

'Pagli, you are on fire and we must drench you with water!'

'The river is dry!' I retorted as sagely as I could, hoping to dodge his meaning.

'Well, there's always water underground and we'll just have to dig a passage to the water for you to bathe in.'

I liked this man. I was going to get along with him.

Hari drew me away from the courtyard up to the veranda, where the guru mother, thinly clad, smiling, now sprawled luxuriously under an opulent scarlet and saffron canopy. A group of young village women surrounded her. One oiled her scalp, another massaged her feet, and a third fed her. She smiled at Paban, who embraced her tenderly, and she blessed him. She pulled me up to her chest and ran her fingers through my hair.

Paban, in a fresh spurt of energy, reassured by the kindness and the warmth of our reception, threw off his tunic and wound a cotton towel around his hips. Holding me by the hand, he led me to a well next to the kitchen. Two women sanyasins, or ascetics, stick figures clad in fading saffron, stood by the well. One of them rubbed coconut oil onto my scalp while the other popped a cube of sweet, pale green almond fudge into my mouth. I felt foolish, all knotted nerves, but allowed them to pull me down so I was crouching on the ground. This was not a place to shower standing up. Every posture was coded here.

Paban threw a bucket into the well, and its rope slithered snakily into the depths, falling on the water with a thunk! He drew up the bucket and poured it over me. At once, I felt an intense coldness and was seized with trembling, feeling plastered down in my wet clothes. I looked up to see a crowd of Bauls standing around me, waiting to wash their hands at the well after their meal, and obviously enjoying the spectacle of my folly being calmed.

> 'O flute of Shyam!
> Don't sing Radha's name any more!'

Bimal, a Baul, bent his fakir face close to mine and gyrated sinuously around me, his face draped on both sides by straight locks of hair, a red bandana tied to his head, his mouth red with betel juice. Paban took his turn to bathe; the two women sanyasins poured water over him, and a crowd of village men and women gathered around him to watch, laughing and joking with him.

It was only just beginning to dawn on me that we were here to join in the playing of Baul games. Whether I wanted to or not, I had to play the role of Radha to Paban's Krishna. The Baul sages and singers wanted me to act as women in their world did. I was being initiated into a very rich and complex world of theatre.

I resisted, reluctant to be drawn into any kind of religious initiation. I wanted to run and hide. I was not religious, and in any case came from a lay world which lived by postmodern time. But the green fudge, made of bhang, was having its psychotropic effects.

I retreated in my wet clothes to the shed next to the kitchen, where we'd left our bags. Ma Goshain, who was now sitting in the kitchen, had not missed a single thing. She smiled at me reassuringly, pinched my cheeks and shouted loudly into the ears of an old Vaishnavi sitting next to her: 'Take her to my room and give her a sari!'

The old Vaishnavi rose slowly to her feet. She was bent and curved with age. I walked across the courtyard, following her. The disciples of Hari Goshain were sweeping the remains of the meal and preparing for the next round. I followed her into a cool, dark, musty room. In it was a high wooden bed, on which lay piles of bound exercise books and sacks full of cereals and dried herbs. There was a very thick smell here, an odour from some other century. The old woman tugged at a cotton sari of faded saffron, which was hanging on a line suspended across the room, among other clothes coloured saffron, orange and white.

'Put this on, this is the right colour for you.'

Evidently there was no escape.

'Mix your colours with the colours of sages!' was the dictum. The ashram was a magnetic field and as long as I was here, I was its prisoner. I wrapped the sari around me and emerged to find Paban waiting outside. Side by side we hung up our wet clothes to dry.

'You look beautiful. Saffron suits you!'

'All colours are mine!' I responded a little shortly, feeling things slipping out of my grasp.

Paban only looked bewildered at my coldness. He took me by the hand and led me to the kitchen to Ma Goshain. The guruma embraced me and put a clay tilak on my forehead. The women ululated again. We were seated on square rush mats and served food in the kitchen. I was starving.

After a copious meal of rice, dal, vegetables, fish curry, chutney and rice pudding, payesh – bitter, salty, hot, sour and sweet in succession – we retreated, sated, to a shelter in the shade of a peepul tree. Paban spread a mat on the ground. We knelt silently for a while in a traditional yogic posture, vajrasana, just like everybody else.

There were many familiar faces around us, Baul singers whom

we'd met over and over again in the last few months of Baul festivals: Subal, Viswanath, Chinmoy and Durga, Gour Das and his khepi, Phoolmala, and Nimai of course. Each of them was in his or her own pool of silence and reverie. The burning afternoon sun filtered through the canopy of leaves above us. It was still stiflingly hot.

Paban told me that when the festival was over and the crowds had emptied, we were to be given a diksha mantram by Hari Goshain. This was an initiatory mantram, which was the first step to becoming a full-fledged Baul and being taught the sexo-yogic four moons practice Jonny Sitar had sought to learn from Paban; the famous diksha mantram which my aunt had once warned me about, which had driven my great-great-aunt Borthakurma crazy. It meant tying an invisible knot with a guru.

I was apprehensive. Paban and I fulfilled each other sexually, and neither of us had any intention of taking our intimate life to these old gurus. I reminded him of Deepak's drawing in his paper on the Baul monks of Bengal, which he had made me read when we first met in Paris, and I made a rough sketch with a stick in the earth. The male guru prepares the male Baul for initiation; the female guru prepares the female Baul for initiation; the male guru initiates the female Baul; the female guru initiates the male Baul. A perfect wheel, representing the extra-human, with spokes radiating from the centre to the circumference, arrows which cross and interconnect: linking the intra-human to the inter-human.

'Chak a chak! Dhak a dhak!' I said to Paban, remembering the monkey man in Jhautalla.

Paban scoffed at my sketch; he added a tower to the circle, transforming it into an ektara, with eyes and a nose and mouth peeking from behind the string, and told me he was a Baul singer, not a sage, and that no one expected us to follow any kind of regime as we were constantly on the move. The old Vaishnavi came and sat next to us, and fanned us with tressed palm leaves.

Reassured that I would not have to take religious vows – I was an inveterate believer in autonomy and independence – I sank into a deep sleep, in the shade of one of the many trees of the ashram.

I awoke to a breathtaking vista: in the west, the sky displayed a magnificent palette of iridescent colours, magenta, rose, orange and, of course, fading saffron. There really was no escape. Even nature seemed to be colluding with the Bauls of Bengal to mix my colours with theirs. The ashram was a dark vault suspended in space and time; like a giant cocoon awaiting the moment of a mega chrysalis. I realised that Hari Goshain was leaning over me, smiling. He dropped a soft bundle into my lap as I scrambled to sit up, alert at once.

I was still dazed from the sun and felt heavy from my siesta. Both Paban, and the old Vaishnavi, who had been sitting by my side when I went to sleep, had disappeared. Although I didn't want to be bull-dozed into an initiation, I could not disrespect this venerable sage. Apprehensively, I opened the knots of a thick square of sackcloth the size of a large handkerchief. Inside was a pair of baby brown hares.

'For you!' It was a love gift.

The old man disappeared into the darkness. I lifted the hares off my lap and placed them on the ground. The tiny animals could barely walk, and crawled around awkwardly, kicking their hind legs up in the air. The old Vaishnavi reappeared just then with a bowl of milk. Paban arrived behind her, holding a glass of tea. I sipped my tea while Paban fed milk to the animals, cupping the milk in a thick green leaf which he shaped like a spoon, into their mouths. I suddenly missed my children, who were so far away from me, though I knew they were safe with Father.

What on earth was I doing here? Our reason for being here was to seek solace from Hari Goshain for the loss of Swapan, which seemed to be haunting Paban, not to integrate into Baul religious life. Yet it seemed that we could not do one without the other. I had begun to be aware, too, that Paban was deeply religious, an aspect of him which was new to me. He was a believer in spite of all his irrev-erence and the pranks he played on the sadhus around him. (He'd told me how he'd helped Gour Khepa attach the erect penis of a sleeping tantric sadhu to the branch of a tree, much to the delight and laughter of all those around.) My rational, sceptical, twentieth-century mind could not share Paban's blind faith. I had faith in him though, and decided that I had to accompany him into the world in which he could truly find solace.

When evening came, Paban and I joined a crowd at the feet of Hari Goshain. Thick fumes of frankincense drifted in all directions from the centre of the courtyard. The sadhus, seated in the distance in clusters like chorus figures, blew their conch shells to greet the twilight. In the centre of the courtyard, the guru mother Nirmala lay sprawled on a rope cot just behind Hari Goshain, exhausted by her day in the kitchen. A group of women sanyasins and village women, their disciples, surrounded her. Some pressed her feet, others massaged coconut oil into her head, whilst others waved fans over her head to bring her a little breeze on this hot April evening.

A marvellous interplay of forces was forever enacted in this charmed world. Hari was the primeval king father and Nirmala the primeval queen mother. Behind this royal couple was a small doll's house, a temple with clay statues of Radha and Krishna dressed in gaudy colours. For a while, I was only conscious of the forms and colours which floated around me like galaxies in mutation. Figures of old monks in flowing jubbas made of a patchwork of many-coloured cloths, others robed in saffron and still others naked except for their dor kopin, the sacred thread and loincloth denoting their status as sanyasins.

Hari Goshain told me that the people gathered around, sages and villagers, would all become our guru bhais and guru bon – brothers and sisters of the same religious fraternity – once we were initiated. The lineage of gurus to whom Hari Goshain was affiliated went back to the sixteenth century, to Sri Advaitya, one of the six goswamis, along with Sri Chaitanya Mahaprabhu, through whom the Baul tradition was perpetuated. Advaita was the supreme guru and his lineage had been perpetuated through Guru Madhyam Acharya, his disciple, and through the House of Chintamoni. Hari Goshain told me that once we were initiated we would enter a new family: that of Lalitha Sakhi, companion of the mythical Radha.

Lalitha Sakhi was Radha's confidante, and as the guru mother Nirmala played the role of Radha; we were, as her disciples, to play the role of her trusted companions in whom she could confide. I found this piquant, subtle way of transmitting knowledge quite fascinating and told myself I had to shed the notions which had been inculcated in me all my life. It was time to take a fresh look at myself, and at the world, through these multicoloured glasses. The world of fact had ended and we were now in the realm of religious theatre.

Hari Goshain was in fact giving me an imaginary grid on which to live a new life. This was to be the moment of the long awaited meeting with the Master, Krishnakatha; transmissions of teachings – when the guru, personifying Krishna, the male principle, would reveal the theory of the subtle body to his disciples: the very base of prem sadhana, the discipline of love. He would recount the beej mantram, the seed words or mystic syllables indispensable in the practices of hatha yoga. The mystery of the seed mantram was its power of transformation over the senses. For the Bauls, Shabda or Sound was Brahma, the divine element which could make a body an active agent, able to draw from within an everlasting store of dancing energy transformed into song and dance and a play of love.

We all waited for the session to begin. Hari Goshain was holding court: reclining, he leant sideways, resting on his elbow, leg wound up behind him like a contortionist. 'I'm the human armchair!' he told me laughingly, as though to break the extreme formality of the congregation, and then asked me if I had a cigarette for him. The crowd broke into uproarious laughter when I offered him one and he tucked it behind his ear. A second later, he unwound his limbs and leapt up, raising his right hand to the sky. A communal initiation now began to be addressed to all those present.

Hari Goshain's posture was that of an oracle. His hands were raised to the sky. The session began. His intense energy drew all attention to him. He was lyrical, enigmatic, emotional and full of humour.

'You fools! Do you really believe that the *Mahabharata* actually took place? It was an allegory of human life written by sages. The battle of Kurukshetra takes place in the human body.

Dharmakshetra and Kurukshetra are identical. It's your body which is the battlefield. It's your body which is a glade of peace! It's your body which causes all your problems! And it's within your body that you'll find the most exquisite solutions!'

Everyone was listening carefully now. Some around us were weeping. At first, I found it hard to understand his mode of speech. But then I grew rapt, just as intent as the others. His raucous voice raised in gaiety, Hari Goshain began a monumental deconstruction of the beej mantram, which he now pronounced publicly, breaking up each word into consonant and vowel, associating each sound with the subtle shifts of sensual mood of that exemplary pair of lovers, Radha and Krishna, when they were joined together in ecstasy. 'I will now reveal to you the meaning of beej mantram,' he declared.

> KLING: Ka... La... Nng... Chandra Bindu!
> Ka is Krishna,
> La is Radha,
> NG is Alhadini [she who desires to be caressed],
> Chandra is the divine beauty of lovers,
> Bindu is Vrindavana ... the garden of love.
> In the Baul Kama Gayatri are five characters and five
> forms:
> Kling, Sling, Kama, Devaya, Bidaha, Pushpa, Binaya,
> Dhimohi, Tanna, Tanga Prochodayang!
> Ka, from this sound is born the seed of Knowledge.
> Know for certain that Madana is the origin of Ma,
> He who sings Do in Dohas, tames Krishna, surrendering
> his body, drinks rasa ...
> Ra, lift up your arms, embrace at the sound of Ra, kiss
> the intangible, couple again and again,
> Aw, Radhika's soul opens at this sound
> Radha knows what Krishna desires,
> Bi, at this sound awakens the sensuous incantative
> body, which none can apprehend but through the
> eyes of Srirupa,
> Dmmm, at this sound take pride and drink the rasa,

He who is always steeped in rasa attains knowledge,

Hey, at this sound, the golden love of Radha awakens

Krishna savours it, nurturing this love,

Pu, at this sound, he whose body flowers in the
luxury of union as with an arrogant prostitute, is a
great man,

Sp, at this sound, in the heart of Radhika, full of flowers,
blooms the blossom with the flavour of Krishna,

Ba, at this sound the Bhava Krishna, whose love is
unchanging, judges the space of good and evil,

Na, at this sound the actor becomes the Rasa Krishna,
nurturing and tasting the goddess Radha,

Aw, a strange sound, the essence of the knowledge of
the material world,

Tasting the feminine, Krishna becomes marvellous,

Rhi, at this sound, slowly and steadily, the two fluids
rise to two orifices and are tasted in the body,

Ma, at this sound, the great element is interiorised
within the body at the moment of sexual union,

Hi, at this sound, the cinnamon-coloured ancient rasa
will rise and the actress will mercifully reveal her
secret to the actor,

Tta, at this sound, the actress becomes conscious, if she
can hold herself, she becomes enlightened,

Nna, at this sound the new Radha is imbued with new
knowledge,

With new rasa, new love and so a new body,

La, at this sound, the two bodies become pliant and
soft

If they are disciplined, the couple will encounter the
light,

Nga, at this sound, he who masters the body will attain
the results desired in all his pilgrimages,

Pra, at this sound, he whose heart is happy will attain
the priceless element,

Cha, at this sound the devoted waits like a chataka
bird waits for rain, calling the name night and day
one-mindedly,

Ddha, at this sound, address yourself to the element
   desired. He who is one-minded can attain it,
Aw, at this sound, the mysterious element is the essence
   of all mankind. He who can master it, conquers death,
Tha, at this sound, the half-moon of the mysterious element
   is mastered. Look! Shiva has it on his forehead!

As quickly as he had risen, the old man dropped back into his previous position. His face was drawn from the intensity of his incantation. He picked up the end of the Nirmala's sari and wiped his face with it. In a complete change of tone, he turned around to Paban and other disciples sitting around him in a thrall, and said, in an ordinary voice, with a slight smile on his face, 'Go make sure that the box mikes have been installed on the stage.'

The assembly broke. Paban set off immediately, leaving me alone with the old man. Hari Goshain took the cigarette from behind his ear and asked me for a light with the familiarity of a lover. I was confounded by what I'd just heard, unable to make sense of where I was, or register precisely what I was witnessing. Then, I looked around me to see that everyone else was also transfigured by his invocations.

The loud blast of a high-pitched buffalo horn rent the air, announcing the night. Unknown to us, the bhairavasthan – the altar dedicated to Lord Shiva, sages and sanyasins – had been lit with sacrificial fires. A sudden gust of wind carried the smoke to where we were seated. I coughed and sputtered as the smoke rushed in through my nostrils. Hari Goshain leapt up from his asana in the flash of a second and rushed in the direction of the smoke.

The lighting of the sacrificial fire and the invocations to Kali were anathema to the old Baul guru, who had achieved his status of a great master through rigorous spiritual and physical discipline, and not through macabre tantric practices. I jumped to my feet and followed him, curious and apprehensive. People fell back as he advanced towards the miscreant who'd lit the fire: Subal.

Subal cringed slightly but looked fixedly at the flames of his fire, a sardonic smile on his face, refusing to meet the old man's eyes.

Hari Goshain was now towering over him like an avenging angel. Although they were both immobile, they seemed to be circling around each other. Hari Goshain's posture was attacking, that of a hissing snake, while Subal's was that of a snarling, cornered mongoose. Flames poured out of Hari Goshain's eyes.

'Prejudice! Useless ritual!' cried out Hari Goshain, who seemed to be in great pain. 'A Baul does not need a sacrificial fire! Your ruse will only serve to confound humanity! Your tricks are those of magicians who would throw mankind into perdition. Your ploy will only make ashes of love!'

Fearing that he would now deal one of those famous blows – Jaya Khepa had received a blow for coming into the ashram drunk; Nakshatra had been made to drag his nose across twenty-one arm lengths on the ground for having made a pass at a young girl; Gour Khepa had been slapped for his arrogance – I put my arms around Subal in protection.

Hari Goshain withdrew abruptly, leaving me with Subal in my arms. Subal turned his wizened, shrunken old head to me slowly, and I noticed a malicious twinkle in his eyes. He lit his chillum, drew upon it pensively and shouted: 'Jai Tara! Jai Tara!'

He was evoking the dark forces of the mother goddess. Chinmoy, Benimadhav and Swapan from Tribeni, all Subal's disciples, collected around us like a three-headed god. Cries rent the air: 'Shombhu! Bhootnath!', invoking the primeval phantom father.

They sucked greedily on the pipe and frolicked around me like ghosts and goblins of the night. It seemed that Subal had scored some kind of victory over Hari Goshain but I couldn't quite figure out what it was. Only later did I realise that he had been deliberately provocative. 'Killing' the guru; overcoming or crossing swords with him was a condition for a Baul to maintain autonomy.

Bewildered, I detached myself from Subal's circle. Luckily for me, Paban, who had disappeared to monitor the installation of the mikes, was back again, and led me away. He explained to me the reason for Hari Goshain's hostility. Subal was known to be influenced by the Chintamoni Sampraday, one of the Baul fraternities which ruled the roost in the district of Nadia and for whom sexual promiscuity is a condition of enlightenment. I began to realise that Hari Goshain was anxious that Subal would exert his influence on me. I realised then that even the greatest of Baul gurus craved disciples, as the French crave red meat.

Paban took me to see Bhasha Baba, whose name means Floating Father and who was a sadhu who was over a hundred years old, with a saintly face and beautiful eyes with cataracts which floated like ice on blue lakes of water in the perfect circle of his face. His years of sadhana had prolonged his life and indeed many of the sages here, including Hari Goshain, were very old indeed.

Paban pulled me to his chest and told him: 'This is my khepi! Do you want her? I will give her to you.'

The old man smiled and cupped his palms around my chin. 'Bless you, for making my khepa happy!'

Hand in hand, Paban and I explored the ashram. Behind the festivities, sheltered by a grove of trees, was the bhairavasthan. Under the canopy of a peepul tree intertwined with a banyan, the altar was encircled by the thick roots of the peepul, which ran bumpily across the earth in all directions for the length of seven to ten metres. The roots, we soon found, harboured a deadly nest of snakes.

Looking more closely, I noticed two layers of stone shelves which surrounded a square trough on three sides, on which were placed many clay figures of horses and elephants. They were intricately sculpted, pasted with oil and vermilion, heads covered with red hibiscus flowers. Against the shadows that flickered over the sanctuary, the figures stood in rapt attention, their ears erect, their pose that of bodies stretched to receive communion. There was a sunken figure in the central square; from our height, for we were standing in front of it, the figure which half emerged from the central trough looked like a giant kidney bean, a strange protruberance, like some forgotten deity rising slowly out of the earth. Slowly, we deciphered the shape.

It was the back of a clay elephant, half buried in the earth. It was an altar to Dharmaraj, the aspect of Shiva that is Lord of Nature, representing divine life, the twilight zone between the light and dark, between earth and air, between secret and revelation, between song and silence, between action and immobility. We sat there a long time together, silently looking at this ancient amphitheatre.

'These are the hundred and eight spirits who guard the altar of Baba Bhairava!' Hari Goshain said, appearing unexpectedly in front of us. 'I came here thirty years ago and found the altar.'

'Where did you come from, Baba?' I was curious to fathom his mysterious personality.

'From Nadia. The Vaishnava Goshains of Nadia, especially the Chintamoni Sampraday, who indulge in sexual promiscuity, were unable to stand the rigour of my discipline and my challenge of their orthodoxy, and became hostile towards me.

'When I first came to Nabasana, people in the village warned me of dire consequences if I tried to live here. They said that Kalbhairava himself – Dark Shiva, the Lord of Time – inhabited the place and that I would meet certain death here. I installed myself in meditation under this peepul tree. Its roots go deep into the soil and house a nest of dangerous chandrabora snakes. Have you ever seen a chandrabora? No? Well, I'll show you one soon enough. Suffice it to say that this snake has a long, muscular form, just like you and me, containing a respiratory tract enclosed inside the intestines which have a terrific power of suction. This particular snake has no venom, but it swallows its prey through the force of its power of breath. Every night, a strange terrifying presence seemed to haunt the place and the snakes, sensitive to its nightly visit, would emerge out of their nests and swarm around me. But I refused to weaken and held my ground, evoking the protection of the divine mother and breathed evenly, in and out, like the hissing snakes, till slowly, as though recognising me as one of their own, they slid back into the shelter, and Kalbhairava, daunted by my determination, diffused day by day until at last the place was in my power! Come along now, let's go to the stage, the public is waiting to hear you!'

Hari Goshain's life remains shrouded in some mystery. A Brahmin from the highest clan of goswamis of Barisal, he left home – in Barisal, East Bengal – at the age of eleven, as an apprentice sanyasin with the legendary Dharmadas Naga, roaming the

Himalayas with the great Naga baba and a group of sadhus. Dharmadas Naga was the sage who had treated and sheltered the Raja of Bhawal, a victim of palace intrigue, in the early twentieth century. As a child, my mother had told me the story.

The raja had been poisoned by his wife and younger brother. When he was placed on the funeral pyre, a terrific storm broke out and those who came to burn him ran for shelter, thwarted. The rain put the flames out. Dharmadas Naga and his companions, who were travelling through the region and had taken refuge in the nearby Kali temple, discovered the unburnt body of the raja.

Tantrics, my ma had explained to me, practised meditation on the bodies of the dead to overcome feelings of fear and disgust, and were known to visit crematoriums to sit and meditate on dead bodies. Examining the nails of the man on the pyre, Dharmadas realised he was still alive and that he had been poisoned. The raja was carried to a shelter where the Naga sadhu took care of him and revived him. When the raja regained consciousness, he had lost his memory. So, he became a sanyasin. Fourteen years later he returned to his kingdom. The question of whether or not the man who returned was an impostor has haunted generations ever since.

I reflected that Goshain's life spanned practically all of the twentieth century. Once he had accomplished mastery of hatha yoga at the age of thirty, he decided to wander on his own in the garb of a madman to test his own powers. He recounts being hungry at this time and standing in front of a sweet shop, gazing at a small yellow hill of fresh glowing mihidana, a Bengali delicacy of tiny syrupy balls of chickpea flour.

'Bhoy korleyi bhoy, hat bhorey dilei hoy!' (If you fear, life is fearful, may as well plunge an arm in it!)

So saying, he plunged his right arm in the mihidana and stuffed his face with it. The owner of the sweet shop cried out and began to beat him with a stick. He was rescued by a passer-by who recognised the great sadhu.

At the age of thirty-six, when he'd had enough of this kind of experimentation, he realised that all his knowledge of Baul philosophy and tantric practices would be of no avail if he did not find a female partner. It is at this point that he miraculously found Nirmala, a beautiful woman with a strong physique and an accomplished Baul singer, who lived in the East Pakistan Displaced Persons refugee camp. She was a widow with two small daughters in tow, already famous for her sharp wit, and even the army officers who ran the camp were terrified of her virulent tongue. After their courtship, Hari Goshain took her back to his guru, Sri Krishna Das of Vrindavana, and left her with him. He also took charge of her girls and gave them an education. She matured slowly, learning yoga and meditation.

We picked up our instruments and walked to the middle of the grove, where a stage had been set up for the Baul singers. On the way, we passed Subal, who now lay immobile, shrouded as usual in a cocoon of rugs and cloth, his feet towards the flames. Paban poked and prodded him but he waved us off, his eyes firmly shut. 'Later, later,' he murmured, waving his little finger in acknowledgement.

Holding my hand, Paban drew me firmly onto the stage. The singers were sitting around in a semicircle, facing the public, and we joined the ranks already seated there. The mood swung to an ecstatic, frenetic pitch the minute Paban entered the ring. His curls danced and his eyes gleamed with delight. I followed his gestures as he swept some dust off the ground and rubbed it on his forehead. The Bauls and sages sitting on stage folded their hands in pranama and saluted us. Hemanta Das, a Baul singer from the town of Bankura, was alone upstage at the microphone, singing praises to the guru.

> We are puppets in the hands of an unknown master,
> Joined to him by an invisible thread,
> He tugs at the thread,
> We rise from the dead,
> To dance together,
> For his pleasure! [2]

A couple of young Baul singers rose to play with Hemanta. Although their dancing began spontaneously, it seemed rather choreographed. Dressed and robed in alkhalla robes and turbans, they spun like mechanical tops. Paban leapt up as Hemanta's song ended. Hammering on his tambourine, he took over the stage.

The mikes were switched off to conserve the battery of the hired generator, much to our relief. Subal Das Baul emerged from his cocoon of blankets and walked onto the stage, tuning his ektara, and lifted his voice in a slow, lilting morning raga: a prayer to Radha.

> Awake, Radha, awake, charmer of the heart of Shyam!
> Fertile Radha, awake and look, the night disappears.
> Hail, Radha!
> You sleep, Rai, with Shyam's limbs around you,
> Have you no fear of scandal and of limits?
> Awake, Radha, charmer of the heart of Krishna.

The first night's singing session ended as a radiant dawn broke over the ashram.

> Cast the withered flower to water,
> Pluck the fresh blossoms of Shyam.
> Make these flowers into a garland
> To adorn the united form.
> Awake, Radha, awake, charmer of the heart of Krishna! 3

Paban had chosen a veranda where we could rest, now at the end of our first day here. We shared it with many others. Paban fell dead asleep the minute his head touched the makeshift pillow he had made with his bag. But I couldn't sleep, as there was an infernal noise in the courtyard and it was now broad daylight. Hari Goshain crouched on a side of the courtyard, and served tea from an aluminium kettle to a group of villagers. He beckoned to me and poured me tea in a clay cup. The liquor was strong, with a flavour of citronella. Sip by sip, my tiredness slipped away. The old man and the villagers discussed his plans for the day, for the irrigation of the fields around the ashram. He was Father Nature for them, and even the local electrician, attending to their needs. The crowd dispersed. Soon after, a new crowd collected around him. Hari Goshain had opened a pharmacy recently, and numerous patients from near and far came to be treated by him with modern and traditional ayurvedic medicines.

Paban woke after a couple of hours and, after his cup of tea, we took off for a long walk down the riverbed. We found some water downstream which we shared with a troop of buffaloes, and got back just in time for the midday meal, which we savoured seated side by side in the courtyard.

There was no doubt about who called the tune at the ashram. Hari Goshain ceded to Nirmala's every whim like an indulgent royal lover. Capricious, lusty, full of humour and possessed with a gargantuan appetite, the guru mother Nirmala monitored events in the courtyard from her position in the kitchen. She ruled a roost of sanyasinis and women disciples whilst sitting on her little wooden stool, presiding over giant pots and karahis, wiping off the cascades of perspiration from her forehead and surrounded by mountains of provisions; cans of mustard oil, gunny sacks of cereals, fruit and vegetables.

Waving her magic spatula in the air with her right hand, she rose exuberantly from time to time, holding on to a bamboo post with her left hand for support. She improvised lines, humming, droning a thin melody first and then belting out lyrics which were funny, dirty and poetic all at once. Her quick wit, vivacious spirit and loud voice, which she often raised in a roar of song, gave the festivities in the ashram an added dimension of musicality, levity and theatre. She was forever spying on everyone, including the great Hari Goshain, sending the younger women off to tour around the ashram compound and report back to her how the Baul singers and sages were behaving. An astute tactician, she planned and plotted with her disciples all day long, untiringly; punctuating Hari Goshain's teachings with lively games to make novices aware of their bodies. She was especially kind and polite to me; I wondered when it was going to be my turn to face her music.

By our second day at the festival, I was beginning to get used to the rhythm of the ashram and starting to relax and enjoy myself. Almost as if she'd sensed this, Nirmala appeared suddenly in front of us. Wrapped in her sari from head to foot, city fashion, she wore dark glasses and high heels, swinging her hips provocatively from side to side, the figure of a bossy memsaab, while Radharomon, their disciple and a leading kirtan singer who led the morning session of kirtans, sported tight trousers and an afro wig, possibly taken off the head of the Nandi or Bhringi clay statues which adorned the altar. He strutted about, thrusting his hips out, the figure of a blackguard and a heel. The Dasnami sadhus, Bauls, fakirs and Vaishnavas who were gathered around all shouted with laughter. I was hiding my true self under layers of cloth, and Paban was being shown to us in the lewd posture of a lout who prized his pelvis above all!

The Baul gurus and their disciples were playing games with us. But I resisted stubbornly, wary of being drawn into archaic practices. Though, to them, what other reason could I have for coming here with Paban, other than to learn the practice of the perfect science of prem sadhana? Paban told me again that we were to be given the diksha mantram once the festival was over, in a couple of days.

Heavy after our afternoon meal, I fell asleep the minute we stretched out on our mats under a small grove of trees and bushes next to the cowshed and the warren. Bats swung and chuckled on a tall tree behind us, and the repetitive trill of turtle doves punctuated the silence.

Three days later, once the crowds had dispersed, the generator sent off and all the disciples and Bauls dismissed with small amounts of money, we set off with the Baul gurus for Mana on the banks of the Damodar River where Lakhan and Jagannath, Hari Goshain's disciples, were holding a mahotsava. Hari Goshain's mahotsava was part of the second chain of Baul festivals, the ones hosted by the gurus; this was a part of the third chain, where disciples held gatherings in their homes.

We took a bus from Beliator, four kilometres from Nabasana, to Sonamukhi, about twenty-five kilometres east, and walked Indian file once again over fields that led to Mana. Nirmala was carried on a chair by Lakhan and Jagannath. At one point, she had to get off because the path was over ridges and gullies.

Lakhan and Jagannath walked ahead of Ma Goshain, who was puffing and panting. 'Come! Come!' they encouraged her, signalling with their hands.

'Yes!' she answered in a flash. 'I've written my name in the book of whores! I have to go with anyone who calls me.' Even in the most tiresome situations, she never lost her wit!

Hari Goshain wielded a staff and helped me cross creeks and gullies through which water flows into the fields. To my relief, the river was full, this time; the rains from the night before had filled the fields, and the river as well. Paban and I planned to go for a swim once we arrived at our destination.

Hari Goshain regaled us with stories through our journey – and his stories always had a purpose. In Mana, he told us a tale that revealed the ancient philosophical polemic between the Baul and the Vaishnava. The Baul was direct. He sought the active, the innate, the spontaneous. He embodied divinity and light in his own person. The Vaishnava was passive. He wept for Krishna, sought the divine but never achieved divinity as he thought of the divine as an entity outside of himself.

A fight had existed since time immemorial between the cult of the tulsi, that of the Vaishnavas, anuman panthis, who only conjecture about what is divine, and that of the bamboo, of the Bauls who create divine life themselves. The Indian basil, called tulsi, with its magical power of healing, had a central place in any Baul courtyard, and its seeds were strung into fine necklaces, which were worn by Vaishnava ascetics.

'I was invited to a mahotsava by one of my disciples, along with many other venerable Baul and Dasnami sadhus of the region of Birbhum and Bankura. We were invited by the host to partake of the midday meal. As is customary, the sadhus washed themselves in the river and sprinkled water on the tulsi, chanting: "Aum tulsi tor bansher briddhi hok!" Om tulsi, may you breed profusely!

'I told myself that I would not do what everyone else was doing. I had to find a way of doing something different! I sprinkled water on a cluster of bamboos, chanting: "Aum bashom! Tor bansher briddhi hok!" Om bamboo, may you breed profusely!

'The sadhus, who were already seated for their meal, led by Rautara's Khepa Baba, were incensed by the obvious slight, sprang up, picked up their bags and prepared to leave, refusing to touch the food offered to them. There was pandemonium. The host, petrified, fell at my feet: "Father, do something to stop them from leaving."

'Nothing could be more inauspicious than a refusal of a food offering!

'I called the young men of the village immediately and instructed them to take sticks, block the exits and administer severe blows to anyone who attempted to leave! Then turning to the sadhus, I challenged them to a duel.

'"You may go on one condition, that you give a satisfactory answer to my question," I told them.

'The sadhus were obliged to cooperate. The host was, after all, my disciple, and they could under no circumstances leave without answering me.

'"Of what use is the tulsi?" I questioned them.

'Nonplussed by the strangeness of my question, they searched for words, but before they could answer, I uprooted the tulsi from the ground and handed it to one of the sadhus. "Hit me," I said to him. No one advanced.

'"You see," I said, "the tulsi is of no use – if you hit me with it, it will not hurt!"

'Then, tearing a pole from the cluster of bamboos, I said, "Now, I will hit you with this, and you will see whether it hurts or not!"

'Slowly, recognition dawned in their eyes.

'"Now I will tell you of what use is a bamboo," I told them. "A wedge of bamboo is used to cut the cord which ties a baby to its mother. It is on a bed of bamboo that we are carried to the funeral pyre, the bamboo is also the flute of Krishna."

'The sadhus, now mollified by my unassailable logic, burst into laughter and merriment, and the festival transformed miraculously into joyous celebration.'

We were sitting in the courtyard of Jagannath's house. The landscape reminded me of my grandfather's house in the fifties in Bangladesh. There were cottages of thatch and straw on all four sides of a square. Each cottage had an inner veranda, which was crowded with disciples of the holy couple, villagers who'd walked here from the surrounding villages. They were all related to each other through their guru father and mother.

Hari Goshain and Ma Goshain sat next to each other, facing south in the centre of the square, on a pair of high wooden chairs. Ma Goshain laughed and joked with the young women and girls who surrounded them. Some of them knelt and washed the feet of their gurus in basins of water, and dried them with their hair.

Paban pulled me up from my seat in front of the great Baul guru. 'Come! Let's go to the river!'

Eagerly, we walked fast down a small lane behind the house. After we had turned and rounded a couple of bends, we passed by a duck pond and a stable full of white milking cows. A fresh pungent odour of clay, straw, dung and urine assailed our nostrils. Then I heard the swishing and hissing of the waters of the great Damodar River.

The water shimmered and blazed in the April light. We walked into the river hand in hand; I let myself go and the current took me floating downstream. Paban dived and swam around me, circling. We noticed a shining green raft made of the trunks of banana trees, tied with a rope to a post on the river bank. Paban clambered onto it, detached the rope and stretched out a hand to lift me onto the raft.

We lay together on the raft and floated downstream, blissful and happy for some respite before the impending initiation. We'd managed to get away from those baleful old gurus and their slavish disciples! No one had noticed our absence yet but there would be a real hullah-gullah once they found out that we birds had flown.

We laughed uproariously like children who'd given their parents the slip. Villagers, men and women, came up to the river bank and shouted to us.

'Who are you, dears? Where are you going?' asked an old couple.

Paban shouted back: 'We are Behula and Lakhindar searching for the gods!' I was soon to find out who they were.

'Is that so? Come and eat in our home and then be off where your hearts desire.'

We decided to avail ourselves of this generous invitation. Paban jumped off the raft and pulled it to the shore. The elderly couple who had called to us were waiting for us on the river bank. They led us to their home. When we arrived they handed us bowls of mustard oil and coconut oil and gamchhas, and invited us to bathe at their tubewell. They handed me a fresh cotton sari and Paban a thin white dhoti for us to change into, while our own clothes, which were sopping wet, dried in the sun. Later, the old lady served us a simple meal: rice, dal, curried cabbage and panchmishali, a dish made of five kinds of little fish which the old man had caught in a basket in the rice field. After an enjoyable lunch together, they spread out a mat on the veranda for us to rest on.

We were loath to return to Mana, where the old gurus and their disciples waited for us, as we lay on the veranda of this cottage on the banks of the river, listening to the flow of the water.

As we lay, Paban told me the story of Behula and Lakhindar. Shonar Boron Lokhai was a gold-skinned prince whose skin turned blue-black when he was bitten by Manasha, the cantankerous serpent goddess who lived wound around Shiva's locks. His wife Behula took his comatose, poisoned body on a raft and floated down the Ganga in the hope of saving him. Behula danced like a sky nymph and sang like an angel. Now Brahma, Vishnu and Maheshwara sat on the bend of the river playing a game of dice. Enchanted by the spell of her music, and at the request of Vishnu and Shiva, Brahma breathed life into her husband Lakhindar, as well as his six brothers whom Manasha had killed earlier.

Like Behula, the principal characters of Bengali folk tales are often personifications of Shakti, strong women who do all that is possible to save their men. Baul singers and sages uphold feminine liberty as the key to Baul sadhana and have often been on the run because they incited such women to rebel against orthodox village society; and do so even today. They also actively remarried widows and welcomed women who were cast out by society into their fraternities, as they continue to do.

> I had to fly from my country
> Bitten by a mosquito of lust.
> The mosquito flies around
> And sings in my ear.
> I had to fly from my country
> Bitten by a mosquito of lust;
> That mosquito's song is so sweet
> I'm breathless listening to his song ... 4

Sri Chaitanya Mahaprabhu had fled from Sylhet to Nadia in the sixteenth century, possibly to escape death at the hands of local orthodoxy. In Nadia, he found an ingenious way of dealing with the massive local conversion to Islam by inventing the Hari Nama Sankirtana. It was a marriage of styles. Instead of repeating 'Ali Ali Ali' like the Sufis, the Vaishnavas repeated 'Hare Krishna, Hare Krishna'. And Hare represented the feminine principle in the Baul cosmogony, Krishna the male principle.

Four centuries later, Hari Goswami, who came from the highest-born clan of Goswamis, fled from his native land in Barisal, now in Bangladesh, to Nadia. Some Hindu farmers, who were his disciples, followed him there. Once in Nadia, he opposed the Vaishnava orthodoxy, and had to migrate again, this time to Bankura, where some of his disciples had followed him to settle here in Mana. His story of the basil and the bamboo recalled these polemics.

We returned to our base to find that Hari Goshain and Ma Goshain had disappeared into one of the cottages. Lakhan and Jagannath led us to a small hut which had been temporarily built for us on the bank of the river, of reeds and rushes. This was to be our shelter during our initiation. The night was full of stars and the riverside glimmered with fireflies. Paban stretched out and fell asleep but I lay awake for a long time.

When Hari Goshain and Ma Goshain finally appeared, it was practically dawn. The light of an oil lamp flickered on their faces. They sat at our heads.

'I don't believe in God,' I said to Hari Goshain.

Paban looked at me, bewildered. Ma Goshain's eyes filled with tears.

Hari Goshain grinned and gave me a reassuring look. 'This has nothing to do with God. Ja dekhibo na nijo nayane ta bishash koribo na guru bachane.' (That which I will not see with my own eyes, I'll not believe even from the words of a guru.)

We had leapt ahead, and were now right in the heart of things. 'Karna joni jibbha ongam. The ear is a yoni, the female sexual organ, and the tongue is the lingam, the male organ. The relation with the guru is conjugal. Shabda Brahman. Sound is Brahma!'

Through the lips of Hari Goshain and Ma Goshain, the sound of a mantram penetrated us. Hari Goshain whispered the beej mantram into my right ear and Ma Goshain into my left; Ma Goshain into Paban's right ear and Hari Goshain into Paban's left. It was an abbreviation of the extended mantram which we'd already heard in the ashram. Hari Goshain told us that his mantram was only for our ears, syllables echoing the crash of the wave of a secret ocean, revealing a cosmos behind shut eyelids, a sound that sent us to a perennial source of energy. To give away the secret of a mantram, Hari Goshain told us, would be like putting an ad in the paper showing the pin number of a credit card.

I had resolved at last the mystery of the missing mantram whispered into the ear of my great-great-aunt Borthakurma. Not only did she forget the first half of the mantram, which drove her crazy; but the second half, had she kept it to herself, would have helped her to survive and to cross over to the world of the wise. I would hear the echo of the mantram often: in the ring of a bicycle bell, in the flutter of birds' wings flying over us, in a clang in the Paris metro. It resonated with the humkara, the dithyrambic chanting hidden deep inside the belly of Baul songs.

Our initiation had a profound impact on both me and Paban – despite my scepticism, it sealed our love in an intangible bond. Paban and I chatted softly as we fell asleep with bats chuckling over our heads and the wind rustling the leaves. We wove a little fantasy around the very real events we were living through: like the characters in the famous Bengali film *Goopy Gain and Bagha Bain*, we were two ordinary people who had been granted three boons from a ghost king. We would travel to unknown kingdoms together in pursuit of adventure. Whenever we joined our hands together in music and song, mountains of food would appear; we'd be transported magically from one country to another, and we'd charm those around us with invisible bonds of music. This was to become true in a way neither of us could have imagined.

Ek! Dui!
Tin!
Ek dui tin!
Bhooter Raja dilo bor!
One! Two! Three!
The King of Ghosts grants three boons! 5

The next morning, before I was fully awake, Paban and I were pulled out of our hut and dragged through a mud trough in the middle of the village square by a gang of giggling, squealing young women.

I struggled to break free, and realised that we were once again in the middle of a Baul ritual game, mud pasting. We were now part of the fraternity and all those around us were now our guru bhais and guru bon, brothers and sisters linked together through the same fraternity. Paban had surrendered to them and was allowing them to cover him with clay. I scrambled up, resisting, and the women held me down as I was pasted with clay from head to foot.

The women now picked us up chang dola, by our arms and legs, and carried us to the sun where Hari Goshain and Ma Goshain were sitting on their armchairs, under a large multicoloured parasol. They seated us, lotus style, in front of them. The hot sun baked the clay which sat on us into a body mask. I couldn't see much without my glasses, which were in the hut, and I was blinded by the mud dripping off my eyelids. I could feel the skin on my face and my hands and feet stretching, my sari weighed a ton. We were being transformed into clay statues.

The women served us water from green coconuts and built a screen around us with old saris tied to bamboo posts. White cotton drapes flew in the wind and the river sent flashes of scintillating light up to us. We were doused with buckets of water and scraped and cleaned. They offered us two simple strips of cotton to change into, out of our mud-baked clothes. We lay down side by side on a mat woven from the bark of bamboos.

They pasted us with neem, herbs, turmeric and oils from the scalp to the tips of our toes. We were bathed and changed into fresh cotton clothes, and they painted tilaks on our foreheads with sandalwood paste.

They untied the screen finally, and around us there was a surge of human voices lifted in ecstatic incantation. Drums were beaten, bells jingled and the women ululated. They covered us with garlands of flowers: marigolds, jasmines and water hyacinths. Some wept with emotion.

Hari Goshain and Ma Goshain came to embrace us. They handed us two strings of tulsi beads, and Paban tied one around my neck and asked me to do the same for him. Ma Goshain kissed Paban on the forehead. Hari Goshain grinned and, touching me lightly on my head, asked: 'What do people in France eat every day?'

'Go mangsho,' I replied, meaning beef. I was getting really hungry now. He laughed and clapped his palm across my lips.

'Chup ... don't let them hear you say that word!' The Bauls were mainly vegetarians.

The women brought us platters full of prasad, cereals, fruit, yogurt and molasses. Then the crowds disappeared and only the inner circle of disciples remained. Hari Goshain and Ma Goshain now gave us a demonstration of their knowledge of sexo–yogic skills. They were master magicians and their craft of body techniques had been acquired through a lifetime of practice.

Ma Goshain climbed on top of Hari Goshain in the position sixty-nine, and the holy couple rolled around the courtyard in a circle. Chak a chak! Dhak a dhak! I couldn't help remembering the monkey man who had come to my father's house in Jhautalla once again. Behind the smallest, most routine gesture in Bengal is hidden the wondrous, ancient knowledge of the Baul gurus.

I began to laugh helplessly in relief and amusement. I was laughing at my own fears and also at the sheer, joyful simplicity of these old gurus. Hari Goshain and Ma Goshain were fully clothed and they were demonstrating their abilities of sexual yoga like two simple village acrobats. The entire assembly rolled with laughter along with me, and, at last, Paban began to laugh too.

The next few days were spent in close company with the gurus. I chatted with Hari Goshain, sitting face to face on the veranda. He asked me who I was, where I came from and where I thought I was going. I told him about my parents, about my mother, who had been a devotee of Sri Ramakrishna, about the Roman Catholic nuns in the convent where I had studied. I talked of our migration to Kolkata from Shillong in the sixties, my trip to Europe crossing through the Middle East, my sympathy with the left in Kolkata, my days in Presidency Jail and my subsequent departure for Paris. Finally I explained about my life with Terai and Katoun and the children, my meeting with Paban and the Bauls, my return to my origins.

He listened with great interest and finally told me: 'From what I hear, you don't need me at all. There're many ways of getting to the same place. I myself have practised all kinds of sadhana. Hatha yoga is just one of these techniques. It's a body craft but can be misused. After the diksha mantram, which I've given you, I could eventually give you and Paban the shiksha mantram so that you get to the core of the practice of prem sadhana. There's a long period of training and realisation which requires complete isolation and a special diet and a very close observation of the movement of fluids in the body. Char chandra sadhana, the four moons practice, requires you to feed on your own body fluids and matter. To do this, and to overcome all sense of repulsion, your diet must be sacralised: you can only eat grains, roots, sprouts, fruit, milk and whey. Now, from what you've told me, you could be ready for these practices, the aim of which is longevity and a fulfilled life. This is the only life we have and it's a short one. You are already a sensitive woman and understand the value of economy and balance in lovemaking. However, there's another side to this. You can go forward only as far as Paban can go, and it's the same the other way around because you are now together.

'For Paban, there's a different issue. He's told me about his family and about the death of Swapan. Suicide is an apakarma, a negative act, and has long repercussions on those who live. His family is dependent on him now, having lost that precious link in their family chain, and this is something he cannot avoid or relinquish as they are poor people in need. So he seems unable to renounce society and hovers between anuman and bartaman, between conjecture and comprehension. You will have to help him and be his guide. His eyes are still raw while your eyes are ripe.'

Hari Goshain's definition of Paban's eyes as still being green had to do with Paban's own lack of awareness about himself. It was also to do with the fact that he came from a scheduled caste. I was pucca because of my detachment, which was also linked to my own high caste origins. Hari Goshain's entire knowledge was limited by his own experience of life and society, and so I decided not to judge him too severely.

Our initiation was cathartic for Paban. He was exuberant and wildly happy now, unaware of these decisions being made for him by his guru. The spirit of Swapan, which had been haunting him for the last few months, was now exorcised. He helped the women in the kitchen, went fishing with the men, returning with a bucketload of catfish and bringing it to Ma Goshain and the women thronging in the kitchen. They were scolding him like fishwives because it was quite obvious he had had a drink of toddy. Most of all, he took over the music from the kirtaniya Radha Romon and his disciples.

Spending time with Hari Goshain and Ma Goshain had helped me to appreciate once again the rewards and pleasures that lay in following the Baul path, despite its difficulties. There was a place for us together, in their world, a way for us to pursue what we were personally attracted to most; we'd staked ourselves in the poetry and songs more than the physical practices, which are optional, though of course we know and admire Bauls who have mastered char chandra sadhana. My time with them had helped to deepen my love and understanding of this world. An idea began to cohere in my mind as I watched Paban organise the music in the ashram: to start our own Baul mahotsava some day.

It was time to make plans for the next phase of our life. Our year of wandering had made me realise that it was time to leave Shantiniketan, with its moribund atmosphere. I told Paban I wanted to go to France for a while. Krishna and Duniya missed Terai and needed to spend some time with him, and Terai had expressed his need to be with them. Moreover, Paban and I had been invited to participate in a festival in Toulouse dedicated to the human voice, organised by Guy Bertrand, a French musical programme director linked to the Conservatory of Toulouse. Georges Luneau's film was to be shown there and Georges sent me a message through Terai on the phone. I felt that this change would do Paban good, helping him to assert himself as a Baul singer at the forefront of the French music scene.

'Take me to France,' Hari Goshain told me ruefully, though with a twinkle in his eye, as we bid him goodbye. 'I'll show them a thing or two.'

He was sad to see us leave.

VII

PARIS TO KOLKATA: HOME, DREAMS AND AN ELEPHANT'S FALL

Illustration overleaf: Man with a ray going from his head to the ground. This image symbolises the power of projection attained by yogis.

A COUPLE of weeks after our days on the banks of the Damodar with Hari Goshain and his disciples, we picked up the children from Jhautalla, where they were having a riotous time with their cousins, closed down our house in Shantiniketan, and went to Paris, with Father's blessing.

I had to be careful now as I led Paban back into the Western world once again. Our initiation with Hari Goshain had recharged our batteries. I was keen to find a way for us to take our burgeoning new life in tandem into the future, to work along the lines which had already been brilliantly laid out by Deepak Majumdar in Kolkata, collecting Baul songs and learning to sing them.

Paban and I were also beginning to discuss seriously the possibility of recording and producing his own music as a way for his songs and music, and indeed the voices of the other Baul singers, to be made known to the world. Most Bauls were not ready to come around to Paban's way, with his one foot in the modern world. Early in life, Paban had understood the importance of using the media and of recording albums and making documentary films. Baul recordings so far, however authentic, simply scratched the surface of an immensely rich and complex living culture and lifestyle, the core of which is spontaneity and improvisation. Much of the sheer poetry and inexorable rhythms of Baul songs were lost in translation, and even more in recording.

Yet like Hansabati, the legendary Buddhist bird, we had to drink the milk and leave the water behind. Baul songs, in order to live, had to be sung and also to be heard worldwide. I was certain that France, my adopted country, which had provided the magic space that had led to my meeting Paban, would be the right place in which to achieve this. After all, it had been the yearnings of the passionately philosophical French soul which had first drawn Paban to the country in 1980. The French motto of *Liberté, Egalité, Fraternité* and the French spirit of egalitarianism was what would provide the ground under our feet in the future, enabling us to love each other and to live together as equals.

Georges Luneau's 1979 TV documentary about the Baul singers had already established them as accomplished artists and possible participants in the European cultural scene. In the film, the singers were portrayed through the innocent eyes of a vagrant boy, Kartick, and over the years Kartick was to develop into an accomplished Baul singer himself. He came to participate in many other documentary films and is known today as 'Production Das Baul' by his peers.

Taking part in the film also had an amazing effect on the lives of many of the adult Baul singers, who praised the miraculous generative powers of cinema and joked: 'Jai Ma! Cinema!' Victory to the Mother! To Mother Cinema! Partly as a result of the film, Paban, Debdas, Gour Khepa, Subal and many other Baul singers had been invited to Paris to sing for Radio France and at the Alliance Française where I'd first met Paban. Baul songs had crossed over definitively into the Western world from their place of origin. The Baul mist net had spread vertically and the Baul singers had been cast along with it into a global circuit.

Leaving behind us the deeply religious, archaic and holistic village world of India, we would be returning to the rational post-modern world, aiming to nail our round pegs into square holes, so to speak! As I looked out of the plane down at a sea of clouds covering the Transcaucasian Mountains, pondering these considerations, a story I had heard on the Baul itinerary came back to me.

A sage lived a life of austere meditation in a shrine near a crematorium. He acquired occult powers and learnt to transform himself. One day, while sitting in meditation, his soul took the form of a bird – his earthly body remained by the shrine – and he flew away to visit a disciple, who was calling his name desperately in a faraway country.

The disciple was ill, and the sage had to stay on with him longer than he had expected. In the meantime, the sage's disciples in the neighbouring village visited the shrine, bringing him their usual offerings. When they saw him sitting like a dead man, bereft of his soul, they thought he had died. After much lamentation, they carried him to the pyre and burnt his body. The soul of the sage, in the form of the bird he had become to travel to his disciple, eventually flew back after several days. Too late! His body had been burnt to ashes. The soul of the sage, forever a bird without a body, flitted back and forth eternally. The moral of this enigmatic story was surely that it was better to travel body and soul in one place, like migratory birds. Being a nomad had its dangers.

In Terai's absence, his colleague, Jean Louis, a computer engineer, invited us to stay in a spare room in his apartment on Boulevard Saint Germain, wanting to reciprocate our hospitality; in the summer, he had spent his holidays with us in Shantiniketan. Memorably, Jean Louis had hit his forehead on the low wooden door of our clay cottage, receiving a nasty blow – the Bauls, loving his simple face, had told him this accident had opened his third eye. Indeed, quickly seduced by the beauty of the Baul language and sensibility, Jean Louis was to prove altered for ever by his experience in Baul country; it was later to make a Roman Catholic priest out of him!

Soon, Terai called and invited us to shift to his new apartment in Chinatown. We were still the best of friends, in spite of my sudden departure with the children three years earlier. Katoun had left him too, soon after, and since then he'd developed a very Parisian lifestyle with new women friends every so often, but never a serious relationship. After what he'd lived through with me and with Katoun, he wasn't ready at this point to get into a serious relationship again and preferred to focus on the children.

I began to pack our bags, but Paban and Jean Louis looked dismayed. Exalted by Paban's songs, the company of the children and possibly my way of cooking dal, Jean Louis insisted we stay with him.

I warned Jean Louis that Paban had no concept of privacy. He didn't get the mores of apartment life; they expressed a human geography unknown to him. Firstly, they were designed for each person to have their own room, whereas Paban was one of a vast Indian population living on the other side of the railway lines. And secondly, for him the lavatory was not a single room at the end of a shared corridor; it could exist on any track or behind any bush.

But Jean Louis was adamant. He wanted us to stay. Paban agreed, feeling uncomfortable with the idea of being Terai's guest. Terai, who had accepted our relationship with good grace, and was friendly and extremely generous with Paban, possibly seemed too much like Ayan Ghosh, the cuckolded husband of Krishna's love, Radha, to Paban's Bengali village mind. It was two against one: I relented, although I knew that Jean Louis had no idea what he was letting himself in for; whereas Terai, who'd spent his entire childhood in India, understood Paban well, appreciated his music immensely and cheered us on, encouraging us to explore the possibilities of all the musical adventures that awaited us in Paris.

Spring was cold and dark. Jean Louis's flat was at the back of a Haussman-style building and gave on to a silent inner courtyard. There, for the first couple of months, Paban slumbered like Kumbhakarna, the ogre brother of Ravana, who slept half the year and stayed awake the other half. The silence and the lack of light contributed to Paban's somnolent state. He needed to recuperate from the efforts he'd made to sustain his family in Durgapur after the death of Swapan. He needed to rest after our marathon of singing and dancing, which had lasted all winter, ending with the Baul mahotsava and our initiation by Hari Goshain. And a body which gives itself to song, dance and music is endowed with self-regenerating qualities, sleep being essential to this regeneration. I make a point of never disturbing Paban when he is asleep.

When he woke up, he would read for hours in Bengali, which he'd learnt to read over our past three years together, completely absorbed in discovering the history of the world through the wondrous eyes of Rahul Sankritayana, a Buddhist scholar and historian whose complete works we'd bought in Kolkata before we boarded the plane. Soon, perhaps under the effect of the famous light of France which inspired the greatest creations of Van Gogh and Cézanne, he also began to draw and paint, ethereal magical sprites and creatures whose ears turned into knobs on instruments, whose noses became reeds and horns, their bodies wearing strings, and heads full of fish.

Jean Louis was at the office all day, Paban was occupied, the children at school; I had each day to myself, and began a regeneration of my own. I worked on translations at a television and press agency to fill the fridge, and learnt to use a computer, scribbling and dipping into my journals and diaries, which had accompanied us these last couple of years: my first attempts at writing it all down.

No matter how late we went to sleep, the light of day always woke me. It was the legacy of my childhood in the hills of Shillong. Now, I learnt to straddle two rhythms, the diurnal eight to four, while the children were at school, ploughing through the papers, bills and administrative documents which formed the basis of daily life in France; and the nocturnal nine to five, normal working hours among musicians and theatre people in Paris. In between, I took a nap of a couple of hours every afternoon, which made it possible for me to manage these two worlds.

It was summer when Paban finally adjusted to this new city, and the days were long and full of light. He opened like a flower to life on the Rive Gauche: he began to go out on his own and busk in front of the Centre Pompidou, Les Deux Magots and Notre Dame. Here was a Paris which was just opening its heart to the music of Africa, Asia and Latin America. Terai bought us tickets to concerts by Fela Kuti and Pierre Akendenge, to Mori Kante and Salif Keita. As we hopped, skipped and jumped from palaces to gardens, we hummed and sang. The Paris metro resonated with flutes from Peru, throbbed to the djembe drums of the Ivory Coast, swung to the cora, the glorious African harp and the ngoni from Mali. Paban stopped to listen to each group of musicians, rapped and played with them, and indeed would have stayed on for ever if I had not walked off when I'd had enough. He was a man of the street.

He also brought home new friends, who often hovered between life and death on the banks of the Seine. He had no notion that he and his new-found companions were eating Jean Louis out of house and home.

When I tried to explain, Paban patiently heard me out but inevitably brought back more lost souls for dinner. When I threw them out, Paban and the children looked at me in horror; a Baul sings for his supper in order to share it with those who gather round him. I explained this to Jean Louis, who hung his head in guilt. He knew the Baul lifestyle well and had shared in Baul communality with us in Shantiniketan. In Paris, though, he lived in the normal, modern way, in which each man and woman is a sovereign island. After a while, he no longer joined us for dinner. Late at night we heard him turn the key discreetly in the lock, tiptoeing across the corridor to his room.

I urgently needed to find a place for all of us to stay. We could not return to Terai's apartment and wreak havoc on his life again. But who in Paris would have time to listen to our problems? I decided to call Peter Brook's theatre. His production of the *Mahabharata* was now in full swing, and we'd met him during his production of *Carmen*. Peter Brook's office suggested that we call the Théâtre du Soleil, and I was put in touch with the celebrated director of the theatre, Ariane Mnouchkine, the great lady of French theatre. On my second call, her warm, feminine voice answered the phone. She offered us the keys to an apartment situated inside her theatre, telling us we were welcome to stay here whenever we needed to: a promise she's still keeping.

Mitterrand's Paris was exciting in the mid-eighties and we made the most of it. There was a fever of interest in India thanks to the festival of India. President Mitterrand lived on a street just near Jean Louis's apartment and we would sometimes bump into him walking to his favourite restaurant, on our way home. Paban was amazed to see that politicians could live like ordinary people, and was charmed by the deeply egalitarian spirit of French society.

And African music and rhythms were rocking Paris now. At the Théâtre du Soleil, we met Thom Diakite, a singer and a cora player from Mali, and in his turn he introduced us to the great mandingue musician Cheick-Tidiane Seck. Cheick embraced Paban, recognising him as one of his own, and introduced Paban to musicians from all over the world. Cheick's own trajectory was pretty miraculous: he had started off as an art teacher in Mali and switched to music later in life.

He had taken the mandingue musicians of Mali, mystics and

nomads whose traditions were a little similar to the Bengali bards', towards the jazz musicians of New York. He'd composed and produced albums with Salif Keita, for Jimmy Cliff, Hank Jones and for Dee Dee Bridgewater. He created an Afro-jazz band around Paban's songs, and we did a couple of concerts in venues of world music together. I joined in all these activities as the keeper of Paban's tempo, making sure that these powerful musicians did not tamper with the innate and complex rhythms which Paban played. For Paban, besides being a great singer, was of course a master percussionist as well. After accompanying him for hours on end, I learnt to master the ektara and cymbals, and took my place beside him as his muse and Shakti.

In order to work in France, we formed a non-profit association to take Baul songs forward, calling it Luna as a homage to the lunar calendar followed by the Bauls. Paban drew a little woman with her hand stretched up, holding a crescent moon in her hand, as our logo. Francis Bonfanti, the sound engineer of Luneau's film *Le Chant des Fous*, made a recording and we produced a cassette and sold it during Paban's concerts. Paban had recorded three albums earlier: one which was released by the Musée de l'Homme, produced by Georges Luneau; the second released by Prithwindranath Mukherjee under the label Sonodisc; and a third produced in France by Georges Luneau again, under the label of Arion. He hadn't earned a penny from these recordings, and now at last, he was his own producer. Paban began to find out how difficult it was to get Europeans to listen to Baul songs. He realised that he'd earned nothing from his early recordings as his music was new to and unknown in the West. At first only a handful of people were committed to promoting Baul music and the Baul way of life. The late Deben Bhattacharya's book and records, Georges Luneau's film and Prithwindra Mukherjee's broadcasts on Radio France had led to Paban's first European tour and brought Baul singers to the West in the eighties. It was a challenge for us to sustain and develop this initial interest, but now we could get by without falling into debt; we had been constantly tightrope-walking on a shoestring budget. We were both delighted. (Many years and albums later, when Real World Records published *Real Sugar*, Paban's album with Sam Mills in the nineties, Guy

Hayden of Virgin EMI explained to Paban and me how hard it was to sell Baul music in the commercial mainstream in the West. 'You're not the Spice Girls, you know,' he told us ruefully.)

Dark clouds were gathering over our heads. I received an enigmatic telegram from India: it was Father. 'When an elephant falls in a hole, even a frog can piss on him.' It was a call for help. He had suffered a heart attack. I knew I could cheer him up as no one else could.

When I called Terai to give him the news, he suggested I return to Kolkata to devote some time to my father. He offered to keep Krishna and Duniya with him in Paris for the school year. But my heart ached at this separation from the children; we decided I'd take the children with me to Kolkata and send them back after the Christmas holidays.

Summer was over and the light was fading. Paban looked depressed. He was a fish out of water, a dark pool of silence in front of the television screen, whereas I was a sea of words, chafing and fretting under the weight of my responsibility. I realised that his lack of education handicapped him sorely and that he was not yet ready to live in the West. His street habits and Baul manners died hard in Paris. Although he was picking up English quickly (partly because so many English words had already crept into Bengali), the French language, discursive and logical, was beyond him. This inability to communicate made him completely dependent on me. Friends commented that I was the planet he lived on. We decided to return home, to India. I knew I now had to build a home with foundations in the air, a halfway house, to bridge the gap between his world and mine.

My father laughed when I recounted our adventures in France. We were sipping Darjeeling tea. It was dawn and everyone was still asleep: these were our precious moments together. He was dying, and wanted me near him. I'd rebelled against him all my life; now I realised I was losing my very best friend and ally. It was fighting him that had made me strong and resistant, and also Indian to the core of my being.

Paban and I installed ourselves in the room I had once shared with my mother, and we moved now between Jhautalla and a family home in Boral, a small village near Kolkata where we had stored our possessions from Shantiniketan. My brother did not look too happy about this but these days he looked unhappy about most things: Father was cantankerous and gave Gautam a hard time, although he was liberal with me.

From mid-January to April, Paban and I moved between Baul fairs and festivals and our two camps. The idea of holding a Baul mahotsava was slowly taking shape through our conversations with Deepak. Boral felt increasingly like the right spot. Local poets Shoubhik Chakravarty and Bimal Deb and many other friends of the Baul singers rallied around.

We formed an association here too, which we named Sahajiya, in homage to the origins of the Baul way of life, which we hoped to revive and reinvent in a modern context. The word 'sahaj', after which the society was called, implied surrender to the innate and the spontaneous, and evoked the path established by the ancient tantric Buddhist Sahajiya masters. For some Buddhists, enlightenment is said to come step by step through ascetic discipline, through a progression of chakras or wheels of time. For others, like the Zen Buddhists of Japan, illumination hits the seeker like a streak of lightning. The Sahajiya tradition amalgamates these two schools of thought by placing the human body centre stage: the chakras are to be found within the human body. Baul singers, practitioners of the sahaj path, are called vanaprastha – struck as if by lightning by the arrows of self-knowledge, drawing liquid cosmic honey from within themselves to pour it over their auditors. And so the process continues, from mouth to ear, and from ear to mouth again, the Baul singers tranmitting sweet knowledge of divine life in a spiral, an autotelic flight, without borders.

The Baul singers had heroically resisted being appropriated by patriarchal village society for centuries. Gour Khepa, exemplary in his aloofness and rage against any kind of recuperation in his soul, had turned now into one of those blazing mythical sages of the sacred epics, who had the power to reduce you to ashes with a single glance. He was frequently and violently attacked during fairs and

festivals, when he let his vitriolic humour loose against the orthodoxy around him. He exercised this power too frequently though,
which often simply reduced him to a small-town hood.

Now, we began to talk, tentatively, about my idea of creating our
own festival, which would become part of the third chain of festivals
in the Baul itinerary. The only way to bridge the abyss which yawned
between Paban's world and mine, indeed to save our relationship
in this newly uprooted situation of ours, was to inspire and uplift
the people around us by celebrating Baul songs and wisdom. It was
through the magical institution of the mahotsava, literally a grand
feast, a gathering of sages and mystic minstrels and holy men with
ordinary people, that the gurus transmitted their ancient, esoteric
knowledge.

I believed in Paban's miraculous powers of regeneration and in
those of Hari Goshain and Ma Goshain. Tongues wagged around
me, trying to discredit Paban and to discourage me in my utopic
enterprise. I did not listen to them.

One day, Subal came to visit us in Jhautalla along with an assortment of Bauls and vagrant characters attached to his temporary
akhra, all humming and droning, the bells on their feet jingling.
They'd got wind of our plans for the Boral mahotsava.

Chitto Sadhu, a youngish tantric sadhu from the Nadia district,
dressed in red robes with tantric paraphernalia, rudrakhsa seed necklaces, fat and knobbly, and dreadlocks, led in a goat on a leash by the
name of Shoni Thakur, or His Holiness, Saturn. Shoni Thakur was a
failed sacrifice and was considered to have been saved by the goddesss
Kali herself; therefore he had a privileged status and was allowed to
roam freely. Confused by his urban surroundings, the noise of the
generator and Tootsy, my brother's pet sausage dog, he hid under the
Queen Anne dining table and dropped a line of little turds on the
floor, stalling and stiffening as Chitto Sadhu, embarrassed, tried to
pull him out, much to our amusement and to the horror of the maids.

My father called me to his room. 'I want you and Paban to stay
here with me. But please avoid bringing your Baul festivals into my
house! You are preposterous!'

I dispatched Subal and company to Boral, where the local boys, Shiraz, Biltu and others who worked in our garden there, would take care of them. Although Jhautalla was only about a dozen kilometres away from Boral, centuries separated village from megapolis. The Baul lifestyle and tradition of hospitality were still understood in Boral. The village was mainly inhabited by a suburban Muslim population of farmers and market gardeners who grew cereals, vegetables and fruit, and who were familiar with Bauls and fakirs as Ghutiarisharif was close by – the southernmost tip of the Baul itinerary.

Subal left, asking us to meet him the next evening at Shastri Baba's akhra in Kalighat.

The next evening we took a crowded, clattering tram to Kalighat. The Kalighat temple already existed in the fifteenth century, and it is said that the right foot of the goddess fell here.

The principal dome of the temple, with four corresponding domes on each side, was barely visible behind the buildings and the trees. Modern chaos covered old symmetry. Kali was represented here with a prominent third eye and a tongue dripping with blood. Hundreds of pilgrims thronged the temple. A goat was being sacrificed in an inner courtyard, legs all tied up, neck thrust into a small guillotine.

The temple lay on one side of the Buri Ganga, and was surrounded by a tiny city of its own with labyrinthine streets, bordered by a red light area. On the other side lay Alipur, the city built by the British, with its mansions and lawns, its courts and jails and barracks.

Thousands of birds chirped in the great banyans and the peepul trees, which formed the grove behind the temple which sheltered the crematorium. Debdas Baul of Suripara, sublime and saintly, and blind Kanai Das Baul of Tarapith, were already at Shastri Baba's akhra behind the funeral grounds and greeted us with great gusto.

Shastri Baba was an old tantric sage, clad in a red cloth, with a kind face and bright, bird-like eyes. He spoke fluent English and had once been an officer in the merchant navy, travelling all over the world.

When he retired, he left home and joined the itinerant path of the sadhus. He had no connection with his family any more, but said he had a son and a daughter probably somewhere in Kolkata. He lived in Kalighat, in the ashram of Bete Baba – a tantric sage of the nineteenth century who was a dwarf and very popular with the prostitutes of Kalighat – with his faithful follower, Tiger, a vivacious dog who constantly jumped at the crows that hovered about. Devotees sat around him, making elaborate preparations of a chillum of ganja.

'Ki re! Tui badam bechti ekhon sadhu sejechis?' (Hey, you used to sell peanuts, now you're posing as a saint, are you?) Paban prodded Debdas, whom he called Debu and who instantly went red with rage. Soon the two friends were quarrelling, Blind Kanai smilingly enjoying the exchange.

Chatting among themselves and looking on, a crowd of women in colourful saris clustered around them. By now, I was familiar enough with the secret world of the mystics and sages to know that they were probably sex workers, here for their evening devotions before a night of streetwalking.

The akhra was a ramshackle sort of place, covered with layers of plastic sheets and caked with soot and grime. In the middle of the room was an altar to Kali, covered with a sheet of white cloth. Hundreds of crows cawed in the banyan trees above our heads as we entered.

Shastri Baba greeted us casually and invited me affectionately to sit next to him. The difference between sadhus and ordinary men is that sadhus never interrogate women; they usually treat them with respect and devotion, and do everything they can to empower them. Naga sadhus and tantric sadhus can sometimes even be very violent in protecting women. I'd seen a curious bystander in a Naga akhra in Tarapith have his fingers smashed with iron tongs by a Naga sadhu, because he dared asked me who I was and where I came from, while Paban was singing!

Shastri Baba was relatively mild. I told him about my dream early that morning. After years of not dreaming about my mother, I had dreamt that I'd met her in a red double decker bus at the crossing of Chowringhee and Park Street. She looked pleased to see me, but a little shy.

'Ma!' I cried out, my heart pounding with joy as I tried to draw her into my arms. The ticket collector interrupted us, clicking his punching machine under our noses. I paid for her ticket and mine. She said with a kind of finality that I could not visit her. The dream evaporated, leaving me unsatisfied. I tried to go back to sleep, hoping to catch her again, but she was gone for good.

Blind Kanai listened in, perking his ears up in a way that only blind men can, and began to sing in a nasal, aerophonic, resonant voice, twanging his ektara made from an empty tin can.

> Arriving in this bazaar of Gour Lila
> I'm amazed,
> A needle hole is a funny thing
> When an elephant crosses through.
> A pair of mangoes grow on a drumstick tree,
> Inside the mango is a sapling of jamun
> With fruit ripening
> And witnessing this, a dead man laughs,
> Shouts Ha Gouranga
> And love drips in a river of poison ... love drips.
> Arriving in this bazaar of Gour Lila
> I'm amazed ... [1]

Paban jumped in, thundering on the dubki, Kanai's blind face shone, ecstatic, and a smile lit up Debu's kind face. The audience of women embraced them and kissed them. Tonight, Shastri Baba would hold the Tin Nath Mela, and many women from the local brothels would come to celebrate with him. They would perform rituals and sing songs to Tin Nath, the male trinity of the three Hindu gods Brahma, Vishnu and Shiva. This was their moment of respite. A secret world lurked behind the visible one in Kalighat, one inhabited by sages and wanderers as well as pimps and dealers of all kinds. The sacred and the profane mingled here as though they belonged to each other.

It would be practically impossible for an undiscerning eye to visualise this world. To my friends in France, I usually describe it by saying: imagine if the hookers of Rue St Denis in Paris spent Saturday night in the local Chartreux monastery celebrating the divine quality of sexuality with the monks, who served them liquor brewed in the monastery. That was exactly the relationship between the Bauls and sadhus and the streetwalkers of Kalighat who come here to pray, to meditate and to cleanse themselves with the blessings of the sages and Bauls, taking with them that little bit of spiritual air and tranquillity which makes their often sordid lives bearable.

Gourima, the old tantric sadhuma we'd met in Ghoshpara, had originally lived in Kalighat. She'd told me that the sex workers of Kalighat were great devotees of Baul songs. Many a prostitute, having done their time, had ultimately moved from profanity to a higher and more spiritual world. According to the Bauls, sex workers in the city fulfilled a role without which the institution of marriage, which was big business in the city, would collapse. They were the drains and canals which dredged out the excess beej, seed or sperm, which had not been ejaculated within the bonds of society. It is this 'arrogant' prostitute Hari Goshain had referred to in his deconstruction of the seed mantram: the woman who was capable of abandoning herself to sexual pleasure was the woman who would find her way to her inner self. It was a unique inversion of traditional middle-class Bengali morality, which venerated marriage and prescribed sexual inhibition outside marriage.

Paban needed to buy some goatskin for his dubki so the two of us wandered off. A maze of streets criss-crossed each other. Everything in Kalighat burst with symbols of an intensely lived religious life: the brightly coloured lithographs of divinities, shining brass pitchers and lamps for ritual use, marriage goods, white cowrie shells which are used symbolically to buy husbands at weddings, white bone bangles to attach them to, vermilion for the forehead. Artisans worked incessantly here. Everywhere Kali danced on her spouse, Shiva. The itinerant potua painters who originally painted the famous Kalighat potua paintings had disappeared from here. They had been replaced by potters, working at their wheels from dawn to dusk. Saraswati Puja was just a week away and rows of voluptuous clay statues of Saraswati, standing on her clay swan with her lute-like veena in her hand, were drying on the pavements. Once the clay dried her swan would be painted white and her sari and crown white and silver, her smile would flush pink under loving brushstrokes, and her eyes would turn black and pointed as the painter gave her sight. Redeemed from blindness, she would look out seductively, play a note on her veena and ensnare her creator in her invisible web of charm.

Two lanes flanked the market: the Boro Goli, the big lane, and the Choto Goli, the little one. Courtesans, who were the painter's models, had inhabited them in the previous century. A painter must have penetrated into the depths of this neighbourhood, perceiving by chance a beautiful woman, her black hair hanging down to the sill, leaning on her balcony with a violin under her chin, playing an exquisite, plaintive melody. Only the painting (a Kalighat one now in the Victoria and Albert Museum) which he must have made sitting up all night with slow brushstrokes in the light of a hurricane lamp, remains now as a witness to his revelation. He gave his muse the costume of a Bengali woman but the expression on her face and her posture are indubitably those of a gypsy playing a bolero, pining for a home she could never return to.

In sombre workshops, craftsmen sat cross-legged on the floor, tuning tablas. A smell of fresh paint and wood pulp pervaded the air and mingled with frankincense. Hammers swung and banged down repeatedly. The entrance at the back led to an inner courtyard where cameos of women could be seen, framed in doorways: sitting, cooking, drying their hair, chatting with each other, draped in clean white cotton.

Day gave way, rapidly, to night. A dense yellow mist mingled with the smoke from chula stoves, shrouded the sacred architecture of Kalighat, protecting its mystery. The women stood in clusters on the street and incantations from the temple flooded the streets through the funnels of microphones.

Gongs reverberated. A group of women walked the maze of streets around the temple. Their ritual functions as yoginis were long gone. Brahmins had long usurped all power over the bodies of women in this world. Clad in white, their shaven heads bearing pigtails in the back, foreheads stained white, they preyed on today's pilgrims in motor cars, windows wound up, coming by to make their offerings to the Mother; to pick up a streetwalker for a night of lust at Keoratala.

Behind the temple were the crematoriums. There was a modern electric incinerator and next to it the older one, where the dead were burnt with firewood. This is where my mother had been placed on the pyre. My aunt and I had dressed her in her hospital room. I'd chosen her favourite sari, white silk with an orange border. It was like dressing a wooden doll. When the undertakers arrived, my aunt held me back with all her strength, standing behind me, putting her arms around me. Girls do not participate in the last rites: I was devastated as I watched my mother disappear into the traffic on a bamboo cot decorated with garlands of white flowers, jasmine and tuberoses, sticks of incense smoking around her. No one had been closer to my mother than I. And yet, at the very end, she was torn from me.

Behind the crematorium was a world unknown to those who come to burn their dead. Under the shelter of a grove of trees, on the banks of the old Ganga, was the samadhisthan – the sacred tomb – of Bete Baba, that popular dwarf sage. It was frequented by the Doms. They burnt the dead with infinite patience, taking a break from time to time from their unremitting labour near the fire, from the churning of wood and flesh, to smoke a pipe of ganja with the sadhus in the ashram. They sang kirtans, songs of painful rupture and of separation. They wept and groaned for those who left the world. They sang hymns to the Mother.

> O Mother, in the form of the image,
> Redeem humanity
> O Mother, in the form of a fish,
> Dominate the waters ...
> O Mother, in the form of a bird,
> Possess the skies.

In June, we were invited to hold a concert in Agartala, Tripura. We were delayed on our flight back home and returned to Jhautalla late at night. My brother Gautam opened the door to us grumpily. Father had been expecting us all day, he explained wearily. We crept into my room and tumbled into bed.

Early next morning, I woke up with a start to find the neon lights on in Father's room. I usually made him tea when I was home as I was up before anyone else.

I found Father making coffee.

'Why are you drinking coffee? Isn't it bad for you?' I scolded him.

'There's no tea.' His voice was heavy. He pushed me away by the shoulders. 'Back to bed, you look sleepy.'

I returned to bed. Paban looked up, bleary-eyed, wound himself around me and fell fast asleep again, and so did I.

A couple of hours later, Gautam woke me up. There was a visitor at the door on a motorbike. He had come from the Calcutta Club. He had been swimming in the club pool with Father, and saw him standing at the edge of the pool. A few minutes later he saw him floating upside down in the pool. When he swam up to him and touched him, his body tipped over. He was unconscious; apparently he had had a massive heart attack. He was now in the Woodland's Nursing Home in Alipur.

Gautam and I rushed there. In the office, they told us that no one by my father's name had been registered here. We walked out apprehensively. A man came up to us. He took us to an Ambassador car in the parking lot and opened the back door. Father was lying there on his side in a foetal position, gone for some time now, his arms crossed over his chest. He looked peaceful.

Jhautalla felt empty and lonely when we returned home. I remembered that Father had often sung a kirtan in the shower.

> O my love
> I'll be as sandalwood,
> With a cool touch,
> I'll play a game of colours.
> I'll jump in the sea of love of Krishna.
> I'll float in the currents of its waters
> I'll touch Krishna's shore with my body. [2]

At the end of that day, Father's last rites were held in the crematorium in Keoratala. I touched his stiff cold feet before he was pushed into the incinerator. This time, I was getting to say goodbye, unlike at the time of Mother's passing, but I ran out to get a breath of fresh air, trying to escape the acrid smell of charred flesh.

If at Mother's death I'd felt as though the land had slid from under my feet, with Father's death I felt as though the sky had fallen on me, that the umbrella which he'd held over my head, protecting me from hail and storm, had suddenly vanished into thin air. There was no longer anyone I could turn to. Father and I had been mortal enemies when I was a teenager, but we'd become the best of friends later. I discovered, much to my surprise, late in life, that in his own way he was deeply philosophical, and I resembled him much more than I'd have liked to admit. But what I would miss most of all now was his sheer integrity and utter devotion to me. Although he was a tyrant to many, to me he had been my closest and most understanding friend. I realised now that no matter how old one is, the loss of a parent is like the undoing of the thread which binds you to life.

Father had left no will, and there was much to be sorted out. I explained the situation to Terai: I needed to remain in Kolkata for a year or so to settle things once and for all with my brother. He was immediately sympathetic to the idea of the children spending a year in the International School in Kolkata.

My brother and his wife, on the other hand, urged me to return to France with the children. After travelling with Paban among the Bauls, I seemed to have been transformed into someone else. No one had quite understood me as my father did, or taken an interest in my journey with Paban. My family in Kolkata was bewildered. Why was I shuttling constantly between France and India? Where was I headed? I didn't understand fully myself. Perhaps, everyone thought, it was best for me to return to France, the country of my adoption and that of my children, who were French citizens. I was stubborn though and insisted on staying on, at least for a year or so. Besides, we still wanted to hold a Baul mahotsava in Boral. Paban and I promised my brother not to bring crowds into Jhautalla but to live as a family with the children in my room. Weekends we would spend in Boral.

'We think destiny is in front of us and we run to her, but destiny laughs as really she's our shadow,' Father had once remarked. Little had I heeded his warnings.

VIII

BORAL: A SINGING GARDEN AND A FESTIVAL'S BIRTH

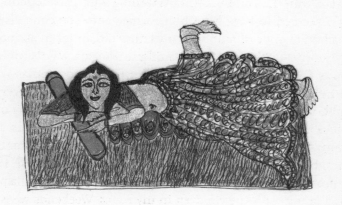

Illustration overleaf: Radha reclining. This image symbolises the eternal feminine in a state of restfulness and dreaming, the source of all creation.

BORAL IS IN the southernmost district of West Bengal, where rich agricultural lands end in the delta of the Ganga. Here the river meets the sea in the intricate patchwork of sands and mangrove swamps that are the Sundarbans. Between Boral and the Sundarbans is Ghutiarisharif, the southern tip of the Baul itinerary, where Sufis and fakirs congregate every August in the holy majaar, the Sufi meditation gathering. This is where Paban had first heard the song 'Dil ki Doya' by an unknown author; a Sufi song which would sweep us up, a decade later, onto a vertiginous flight through the industry of world music and into a new orbit of hackers, stalkers and pirates.

For the moment, we were well grounded. Our place in Boral was adjacent to Saral Dighi, a small lake. Although we were part of the southern swamps of Bengal, the land had dried up considerably owing to the shifting of the Hooghly River, which had changed its course by nine kilometres over the last three centuries, and the mushrooming of innumerable brickfields which serviced the local concrete invasion. The flow of the river continued underground and pipes touched the water table about a hundred metres below the surface of the soil; a table which, we would discover during the tsunami almost two decades later, was linked to that of all of Southeast Asia.

The space in Boral naturally lent itself to festivity: forty-two kathas, about an acre of agricultural land. Father had gifted this land to Mother in 1965, knowing she had dreamt of a mythical Bengal after seeing the 1955 film *Pather Panchali*, while still living in distant Shillong. The land he had found was just next to Saral Dighi, where the director Satyajit Ray had shot the first scene of his famous film. This was my father's ruse to wile my mother down to the plains, away from her homeland in the Khasi and Jaintia Hills. Mother was a movie buff, brought up on dreams from the silver screen, and she fell for it, hook, line and sinker, quite unable to differentiate fact from fiction, her life there from the movie. Now, almost a quarter of a century later, our parcel of land seemed to be the right space for us to settle down for a while. Mother had left us an intangible gift; the perfect scenario to reincarnate the Baul way of life. The trees she'd planted here twenty years ago formed a lofty grove now, a place for respite and wish fulfilment.

We lived in what was basically an outhouse, a small two-storeyed building with a tiled roof and a veranda on each floor. Father had built it with the intention of following it with a beautiful residence for my mother, who felt stifled by life in the city. But the cancer that laid her low ate its way to her heart within five years of her quitting Shillong; Mother had lain down and never got up again, and Father never built the house. He used the outhouse to shelter retired cousins who relocated in Kolkata from Bangladesh and Assam. It became a kind of a home for the dying and the destitutes of our family. Thus, two old uncles lived in the ground floor but the first floor was empty.

This was where we moved in, and began to thrive. The natural beauty of Boral overwhelmed me; glowing, misty winter mornings full of birdsong. A bunch of ripe coconuts hung on one of the two palm trees by the northern wall.

One day, Paban asked Akhram, a local boy, to scale the tree and pick them. A kingfisher's nest on the trunk of the tree crashed to the ground, when Akhram made a false move halfway up the tree. The three peacock-blue and sea-green fledglings in the nest squawked and muttered in surprise, and the mother bird, alarmed, screamed and flitted from tree to tree. Krishna and I watched as Paban made a small cage of spliced bamboo and placed the baby birds, one by one, into them. But just then, Duniya woke up and confronted Paban with a huge, almost oceanic roar, for caging the birds. Paban hung his head, giving in to the whooping war cry from her old sea soul, and Krishna set them free, equally upset.

All morning, we heard the mother bird screaming to the fledglings. Paban scowled horribly, saying that the crows were sure to get the baby birds but at last he demurred, seeing tears splash down

Duniya's face. Finally silence was restored in the afternoon: the kingfisher had built a fresh nest on a jackfruit tree and had carried her family to safety. The children were all smiles. They had proved their point; the ways of birds were not to be interfered with.

And in the meanwhile – *Bakum! Bak bakum!* Pigeons and doves shuffled and cooed between the matted ceiling and the tiled roof of the second floor of our outhouse. Paban cunningly swooped down on them, plucking them and stirring them into a curry under the delighted gaze of the boys from the neighbourhood. My two resident uncles, Moni kaka and Ranga jethu (my father's older cousin), aged sixty-five and seventy-five respectively, were horrified when Paban, after the meal was over, gleefully revealed to them the contents of their dinner.

Moni kaka was in the terminal stages of tuberculosis and stayed locked up in his room so we didn't get to see him much. Ranga jethu, with whom we spent a lot of time, was a magical person. He was sickly too, a thin reed of a man; Krishna renamed him ET. He was little more than a respiratory tract with skin and bones and a little flesh hanging on him. The old man watched the sky constantly with his oversized almond eyes and seemed to know all the whims of nature. Sometimes, before leaving for the city, we peeked into his room to wish him goodbye. He'd be lying there on his bug-infested bed, his mouth wide open, looking as if he'd already died except for a little shaking toe. But the moment the door creaked open, he'd sit up smiling: 'I've been listening to the BBC. It's been snowing in your Paris.'

The villagers liked him too, especially the women, and he knew them all by their first names. Kakuli, Madhabi and Mohua were all Hindu wives who came every morning to collect hibiscus, jasmine, honeysuckle and mango leaves for their morning devotions. Muslim women, Asiya, Noori, Hasina and Zebunessa, who were much poorer, came in a little later to tie their goats and cows so they could graze on the long, wild grass that grew profusely in our neglected garden. They'd created a support system around the two uncles, scrubbing their dishes, cooking their food, washing their clothes for a little money.

Every morning, the old man was up at dawn, uprooting weeds in the garden with a worn-out sickle. He acknowledged my presence on the balcony upstairs with a wave of his sickle and a rasping cough, and carried on his work. When Paban joined him in the gardening one day, he was annoyed. Bouncing with energy as always, Paban started to uproot some plants. The old man tried to stop him but Paban would not listen; he told Ranga jethu that the plants were too many and too thick and would prevent the fruit trees from growing. Ranga jethu, deprived of his monopoly on gardening, sulked for days afterwards. Land settlements were bitter issues in these parts. Paban's presence as my consort was tolerated only if he stuck to his singing. Any attempt to direct his energy towards the land was seen as encroachment, creating a situation that would have been funny if it wasn't painfully real.

In front of Ranga jethu's room stood four cotton trees full of large white tufts. He picked the cotton carefully and piled it in miniature baskets. In the rainy season, he sat inside and carefully spun thread on a tiny spindle – a bonsai Gandhian.

'Your mother planted four cotton trees. If you are lucky, you will plant forty, and Duniya will have four hundred in her lifetime, and maybe her daughter will have four thousand,' he told us.

Everyone laughed at the old man's dreams of grandeur. He reminded them of that famous character of Bengali cinema, Banchharam, who was haunted by the ghost of greed and the miserliness of a zamindar, a landlord. Ranga jethu paid no attention to them. Proudly bound to the vocation of his caste – he was a Baidya – he had planted innumerable medicinal herbs of all kinds: kalomegh, vsalyakarani, mahabhringaraj and kesia leaves. His knowledge of herbs came from fifty years of experience tending my grandfather's herb garden in Sylhet. Unfortunately, there was no one around to develop his practice and take it to the next level. His cousins, including my father, lived in the city, and had no time for him. But in spite of their negligence he was obsessed with them, and with the family tree. He was the proud owner of an album of photographs of four generations of our family, often autographed by the people in them.

There were no traces of this neglected life in the old man's face. The only peculiarity he manifested was a refusal to let us clean his room. Processions of termites ground and climbed in antique pace up the walls of his room. I was sure that we could eradicate them if we could clear the room of the wooden cupboards and the trunks that were stored under his bed, but the old man was adamant. 'You can clear the room once I'm gone for ever,' he insisted, defending his empire.

It was only after his death, years later, that we discovered that his cupboards and trunks were full of old newspapers with remnants of seeds layered between them. I scoured them to see if they had any value as archives but realised that their only purpose had been to give him a sense of property. And if they provided nourishment for the termites, all the better, as he would have said.

The arrival of shoals of Bauls and fakirs, all at once, transformed our little halcyon environment. Till now, Ranga jethu and Moni kaka had lived like forgotten fragments of the world along with pigeons and a solitary tokkhok, a reptile cohabiting with them in the eaves, which Paban believed was auspicious, a promise of plenty. It only revealed itself in the evening through its bizarre call, a cross between a lizard's click and a cock's crow: 'Tok kay! Tok kay! Tok kay!'

But now my uncles were forced out of their solitary lives by our communal lifestyle upon the arrival of the Bauls. It tired them, although they enjoyed the cacophony we created. Slowly, neighbours started dropping in. They were curious to know more about us and stayed on, reassured when Paban began to sing. We soon made many friends.

As spring advanced, Boral became a green, steaming jungle full of creepy-crawlies, pests and flies. The heat was intense; I moved the children from the shade of one tree to another to escape the sun's rays. We spread mats under the trees and spent the daylight hours outdoors, playing and drawing with the children. They adapted to the environment quickly, slipping off at midday with the village kids to bathe and swim in Saral Dighi, and returning to tell me of their latest adventures: a rat snake seen gliding towards them, cupping its hood above the water; a family of mongooses living in holes in the wall of our pond; kingfishers and cuckoos pecking and trilling. Duniya created mermaids with her crayons and Krishna played card games and bagh bandi, a rural game of draughts, on a board drawn by Paban with a stick on the earthen floor. They used dried bean seeds as the pieces. When the sun went down, we sat behind smoke screens which Paban had built with piles of dead leaves and twigs, set alight with twists of old newspapers, to keep out the large black mosquitoes which zoomed in on us the minute it was dark.

We explored the area around Boral. The Oil and Natural Gas Commission had blocked off the road towards Natunhat, near Boral, where it appeared that the soil had broken open. Black oil was oozing out of the earth, and the government had slapped acquisition orders on cabbage patches. We took a walk to look at the oil rig which had been installed. Wild rumours circulated about the plans of the government for the total urbanisation of this area; land here was becoming the most prized commodity. But Paban and I were still too engrossed in the visionary world of the Bauls and in charting out our mahotsava to pay attention to these changes in political economy, as the city devoured its hinterland. Man had always poked and prodded soil, pushed in pipes to bring up oil, projected satellites to mimic the moon, but he had no eyes to see the magnetic energy field which opened up to him during his few moments of intercourse with a woman. But man could remedy this grave error now, instead of joining the rat race for the conquest of energy sources. He could tap into the vast reserves of energy locked up and stifled inside him, if he could only fine-tune himself to the needs of a woman, with a little help perhaps from the lunar core of knowledge of the Baul masters: find the hidden store inside himself.

What treasures lay hidden under Boral? In the kitchen, we used a shil nora, a mortar and a pestle, which had been found buried deep in the earth, and extricated when one of our starving uncles, in his desperation, had the pond dug about five metres deep to sell the clay. The shil was small, the size of an ordinary plate, and the nora was well worn. We were excited to think how it had been used by people hundreds of years ago and how we were using it again now. A statue of Vishnu in black granite, dated by the Asiatic Society as being from the period of Chandragupta Maurya (third century BCE), had been dug out of our neighbour Shaila Ghosh's pond in the sixties. We trooped off now to look at it. Exquisitely carved, the statue had a Grecian head full of curls, and had been reinstalled in a concrete box-like room without windows. Cement, the new god, hiding the old one; the black statue drowned in the darkness of that which would newly shape our world.

Bakr Id was soon to be celebrated in the neighbourhood; boys came around to invite us to their homes to partake of the feast. Paban was nostalgic for the sumptuous biryanis of his childhood in Mohammedpur, those cooked for hours at home by the mothers of his Muslim friends, in huge flat copper dishes, and sealed in with embers from wooden fires.

Paban belonged to a school of thought which firmly believed that breaking taboos around food was an active way of combating religious fundamentalism. Food habits were what separated people all over India. Although Bauls were mainly vegetarian, unlike the Vaishnavas and Brahmins in south India, fish was acceptable to them and as much of an essential to them as it was in all Bengali households.

When Jumman Ali, a local lawyer, dropped in to visit us, Paban extracted an invitation for an Id lunch, to be cooked the next day by Jumman's wife. 'You've been sharing meals with us in our garden for some time now. Isn't it time that you invited us to your home?'

Jumman laughingly agreed. He had stood for elections from the constituency of Shathgachhiya as Jyoti Basu had, three decades ago, and was a Congressman of the older generation, aware of the syncretist colour of Paban's demand. Jumman was very cultivated and had marvellous insights into the lore and beliefs of this region, which lay just north of the Sundarbans. He told us the stories of local Sufi divinities and saints: of Bon Bibi, a local deity, a forest mother who protected the people from the vicious attacks of tigers and crocodiles which proliferated in the region a century ago; Johura Bibi, a Sufi saint who lived in the region in the eighteenth century; Ghazi Khan, a fakir who is still worshipped all over Bengal and for whom the Tazia is celebrated, with fireworks and kite flying; and Satya Pir, another Sufi saint possibly from the seventeenth century. Local lore has it that Gazi Khan met Viswakarma, the Hindu god of artisans, on a visit to Mecca and was illuminated. Hindu and Muslim lore are also inextricably mixed up in the fables of Satya Pir.

Jumman Ali was, moreover, intimately acquainted with local customs as he often defended local people as a civil and criminal lawyer. After living in Boral for a few years I found out that civil issues often spilt into criminal ones here. The violence of social life was no different from suburbs around cities all over the world. Boral too was on that line: the poverty line that separated villages in the southern agricultural region of West Bengal from the city of Kolkata. Recurring traffic jams on the choked bottleneck between Garia, where Jumman Ali lived, and Boral where we were, were symptomatic of the collision between city and village. Kolkata seemed to be suffering from a kind of arterial sclerosis, its tired heart unable to pump the excess fat out of its system as the city turned its back on its hinterland.

On the day of Bakr Id, at midday, there was no news of Jumman. Shiraz, Biltu, Sabir and Zakir had invited us to their homes too, but Paban had refused them all, explaining that we had been invited to Jumman Ali's house. They deferred, and when they dropped by to the garden to see if all was well, Paban snarled at them and vigorously threw himself into weeding the garden and starting a bonfire. Later, he returned to join our group; we were planning a little brochure for our Baul mahotsava. We sat in a circle on a large all-purpose wooden cot, on which I'd spread a white- red- and green-striped thick cotton rug. At night, we slept on the cot, on rainy days we ate our meals from it and, when there was a meeting, it transformed into a conference table.

The door burst open. Jumman stood there looking downcast, framed by the bright light outside. Paban glared, but I hastily invited

Jumman to join us before he could say a word. Sabir, who was keeping us company, poured him a cup of tea. Jumman told us his sad story.

The evening before, Jumman had bought a lamb from the meat market in Kassipur where thirty thousand animals, cows and goats, are sold and slaughtered for Bakr Id every year. The animal had looked sprightly enough in the market but seemed to droop a little when Jumman brought him home. A scream of alarm from his wife awoke him in the dead of night: the lamb seemed to have fallen into a coma. The household was full of foreboding. The local vet, roused from sleep, administered an injection to the lamb but, after a few convulsions, it dropped dead. The women began to weep with distress. It was an ill omen that the sacrificial lamb had died before being slaughtered.

Jumman decided to dispose of the dead animal. He went with his son to dig a hole outside the house to bury it. It was already about four in the morning and an old Hindu widow was doing her ablutions nearby. Seeing the men burying the corpse of the lamb, she set up a hue and a cry. Irate neighbours came forward suspiciously, insisting Jumman had no right to do what he was doing; that is, to bury the lamb on public land. Finally, Jumman managed to bury the lamb in his own back yard.

Paban relented after hearing this unfortunate tale, seeing that Jumman was more than upset; the shadows around his eyes confirmed his sleepless night. Jumman took his leave, inviting us to lunch the next day. Sabir, who had heard the whole story, returned with a bowl of meat for Paban. The Muslim community here still shared meat on the day of Id with the inner circle of family, the outer circle of friends and relatives, and the third circle of the poor, the mendicants and the fakirs. We were lucky to be part of this third circle.

The next morning, we knocked on the door of Jumman Ali's house in Garia. He welcomed us in. His wife served us gleaming, pearly biryani flecked with saffron, tender, succulent wedges of meat hidden beneath its hill of rice, the princely dish accompanied by a finely sliced cucumber, fresh mint salad and tiny shammi kababs which melted in the mouth. Jumman himself fetched a copper jug and poured water for us so we could wash our hands over a copper bowl. The entire event was solemn and ceremonious. Afterwards, we retreated to Jumman's library. Jumman handed Paban a volume of songs of Phulbassuddin, a little-known contemporary of Lallan Fakir, who had lived in the late nineteenth century.

When we returned to the garden, we found Shiraz, Biltu, Sabir and one other friend, Babushona, waiting for us, and stayed outdoors with them till the light faded. Then we retreated to spend the evening browsing through the book of songs, till we found a passage that pleased us.

The text celebrated an amorous couple with humour and tenderness. Written a hundred years ago, the subject of the songs remained contemporary.

> Go, with devotion to the house of happiness.
> Here, there is no sorrow
> But constant pleasure.
> In this open market, bazaar of joy,
> One finds happiness and peace.
> When two souls unite
> Disappears the pain in their heart.
> When you offer a seat
> In the temple of the heart
> All hopes are realised,
> All confusion disappears in a sea of love;
> An amorous couple sits
> On the throne of laughter and pleasure,
> Spending exhausting days and nights
> In daily adoration,
> Says Phulbas, extenuated ... [1]

The life of a couple, Baul or otherwise, was a delicate balance, teetering between conflict and compromise across a continuum of space and time. Our union, sealed with a simple exchange of kanthis, collars made with basil seeds, was a cohabitation by mutual consent. We had to work hard to tolerate each other and to stay together. We both loved solitude and both needed hours of quiet meditation, but were both gregarious and enjoyed the hours spent cooking and feeding people. As we chopped and cut and stirred and fried and confided in each other, we kept learning how to live together, warily observant of the processes that bent and shaped the contours of our life together. We were still two galaxies in mutation, still from disparate worlds.

Sometimes, I was the avid city, he the relenting countryside; sometimes he was the demanding child, and I the generous mother; and often, he was the king, I the fool.

We began gradually to put our plans for the mahotsava into action, and decided to invite Hari Goshain to design the festival. He came to visit us in Jhautalla for an evening, and promised to inaugurate and direct the festival in the true Baul tradition. He blessed us and warned us to hold out against the terrible storm that would unleash itself against us should we dare break the norms of acceptable behaviour in this suburban, puritanical middle-class world.

We were sure of ourselves now because of the friendship we'd received from our neighbours in Boral. We had been shuttling between here and Jhautalla for a year, and we'd also been inspired by the exuberant enthusiasm of young people in Kolkata for our proposed mahotsava: musicians, poets, artists, doctors and lawyers and even corporate executives.

But a week before the event we still had no funds and nothing short of a miracle, we realised, would save us from the fallout of this impulsive, unsponsored event. I had been determined not to plan too much, to be able to take the best of what life would offer us. Perhaps it would be true to say that ours was an act of faith, although we did indulge in the minimum of organisation.

It began. Terai passed through Kolkata to pick up the children and contributed a thousand francs, which converted into two thousand rupees. A Mr Sen, keen to become the patron of the festival, donated another two thousand. Hari Goshain persuaded the film maker Ruchir Joshi to give another two thousand in exchange for the rights to film the festival for his documentary *Eleven Miles*, for Channel Four – the film would later win the Joris Ivans Prize at a film festival at the Pompidou Centre. He and his gifted film crew, Ranjan Palit and Mahadev Shi, accompanied us as far as they could through the lens of a camera and a tape recorder, and continue to accompany us to this day.

We persisted. Under the banner of our association, Sahajiya, we produced a small, low-cost brochure with pieces written by Deepak Majumdar, Shakti Chattopadhyay, Sunil Gangopadhyay and the artist Paritosh Sen, in the tradition of the 'little magazines' which were so popular in this city. Hiran Mitra, a modern painter who lived nearby, took charge of the artwork and the publishing, and we asked people for donations and advertisements for humble amounts of money. In the local tradition, we printed a low-cost flyer in Bangla and a donation book.

It was the festival of Makar Sankranti, marking the beginning of the harvest season. Paban and I left for Joydeb Kenduli to take a dip in the Ajoy River and returned to Boral a few days later with a group of ten Bauls. Subal and several others, Pakhi, Tinkori and Vishthu, assisted us indefatigably. We visited the town council and the mayor to invite them to our event. Our miracle was taking shape.

The first Baul mahotsava in Boral was held in early February 1988. It was an ephemeral, utterly spiritual pageant in the shade of mango, jackfruit and coconut trees. There was excitement in the air as Paban and I prepared the garden; local villagers, men and women, joined us to prepare the feast. Paban ripped down the tangled golden vines that had trapped the trees and set fire to the wild grass, dead leaves and branches that covered the garden. The women from neighbouring Nischintyapur, who often tied their goats to graze on the wild grass which grew on our plot of land, shouted at him, saying that he was burning up their year's stock of firewood. Paban told them that the smoke would do the mango trees good, and called them in to clean the entire garden. They collaborated with us, suddenly full of hope and wonder as we prepared to share food together.

We piled earth into a little plateau over which we built the traditional aat-chala, an octagonal roof which houses an akhra, in which the old Baul gurus and singers and fakirs would sing and speak – as they would now. We set up a temporary kitchen, and a pot of rice boiled constantly for those who worked with us. We took turns to cook; our old friend Nimai arrived and after the first barrage of insults from Paban took over the cooking. Grinning crookedly as he stirred the khichuri, a dish of boiled rice, lentils and vegetables, he hummed a song popularised in the eighties by the late Goshto Gopal, son of Dinabandhu Das Baul, and arranged by Nilkamal Roy, though its original author was unknown, as was common. The song's quaint catfish metaphor decried the situation of the Sufi and Baul poets who lived deep in the Bengali country-side, among scheduled castes and tribes and disempowered women.

> Tangra fish are easy to cut,
> Magur fish slip and slide,
> Singhi fish prick with their bones,
> O my life is on fire!
> Bheda fish eat mud,
> Puti fish die from lack of water,
> And when it rains, koi fish walk on banks.
> O compassionate one,
> What a fish you've caught in your line!
> Earthworms dig into soft soil,
> Pakal fish tear through hard ground!
> The guru says: it's not a lie
> I've caught about six chang fish
> I'll cook a stew with two brinjals. [2]

Shiraz, Biltu, Sabir and the other boys helped us constantly in the days before the mahotsava. We built temporary shelters for the Baul singers in the grove, constructed lattices and covered them with thatch, made curtains from jute bags and cotton to divide the shelters into plots, leaving a pathway winding around the garden. The base of the trees was paved over with clay to form the spaces for traditional asanas, seats for the Baul singers and sages, held in by brick. The women helped us pave over the entire surface with soil and dung.

One day we set to work on the garden, and by evening, the entire garden had been spruced up, paved over and was shiningly clean. Then, we bought an earthen dhunuchi, a flat clay pot with a handle, on which we burnt incense sticks and lit small lamps all over the garden. The stage was set.

We hired a rickshaw and sent the boys out to announce the news of our festival through a megaphone, in the days preceding our mahot-sava.

'Shobinoy nibedon! Our humble invitation to all! The Baul mahotsava, directed by the celebrated Baul singer Paban Das Baul and his guru, Sri Haripada Goswami of Nabasana Bankura, will commence tomorrow morning in the Sen gardens in Boral. For three days and three nights, Bauls and fakirs from Nadia, from Birbhum, from Murshidabad and from Bankura will sing Baul songs! All are welcome!'

At dawn on the first day, along with a cluster of young Bauls, we toured the local guilds and markets in Garia, Sonarpur, Natunhat and Kali Bazaar, singing to the clash of Subal's kartalas and the drumming of Pakhi's deep bass khol. We were reviving the tradition of collecting alms, madhukuri. We also distributed flyers announc-ing the mahotsava wherever we could. Paban roared the news to the shopkeepers, the fishmongers and the vegetable sellers, villagers from the southern hinterland of the great city, already linked to local networks of Bauls, Vaishnavas, fakirs and Bairagis in the region: the news spread like wildfire. We returned from our early morning exertions to see that the garden had begun to fill up.

Paban and I had formally invited twenty Bauls, but we soon lost count of the number of Bauls, fakirs and kobiyals, folk poets, who began to arrive. They were now seated in the grove of mango and jackfruit trees, their eyes wondrous. The trees planted two decades ago by my mother now formed a lofty canopy. In the centre of the grove, in the shade of two jackfruit trees the trunks of which Paban had bound with clay, dung and bricks, reclined the great sadhu, our guru, Hari Goshain. He was surrounded by his disciples: Baul singers from all over and his village disciples from the Mana area of the Damodar river valley.

Hari Goshain's shining eyes were fixed on Ma Goshain, who directed some Vaishnavis and Bairagis, clad in white and saffron, on the laying of the bricks to build the communal oven. They were from the Samudragarh ashram in Nadia.

Tinkori Chakravarty paved the oven into a hollow in the earth next to what had earlier been a chicken coop, another failed enterprise of my old uncles, who had tried to raise poultry without success. It had now been transformed into a temporary store room, bursting with provisions. Our flyering initiative the evening before had worked wonders. The local market guilds had sent us bags of rice, dal and oil.

To inaugurate the oven, Ma Goshain set green coconut on the mouth of a clay pot in a bed of heart-shaped betel leaves. She covered the coconut with sindoor and sandalwood paste. Calling Paban and me to her, she anointed us with tilaks on our foreheads. We built the oven with a prayer that the pot would always boil in this place. It was a peaceful moment, one of complete symbiosis. The women ululated and we embraced each other. As if on cue, conch shells began to blast out all over the garden and drums began to roll. The sadhus were sounding the horn of plenty.

Early February in Boral was still cold. More and more Bauls arrived and made their asanas under the trees. We tied plastic sheets overhead to protect the heads of our precious visitors from the morning dew. The sounds of nature blended with the sounds of music, song and dance. I left the front gate open, deliberately. People started wandering in, hesitantly at first, and then, when they realised that this was a house without prejudice – rather a grove full of sages and singers – relaxed and collected in small groups around them.

We heard an old lady who was passing by remark: 'I didn't know dharma and karma existed in this garden.'

*

At the end of the day, the day before the mahotsava, when we did a headcount we found that one hundred and eight Baul singers had arrived in the garden. They included Jaya Khepa from Ranaghat in Nadia, Dinabandhu and Visakha from Hooghly, the brothers Chakradhar and Lakhan Das Baul from Sheori, Viswanath Das from Bolpur and Chantal from Paris, Norrotom Das from Kalyani, Subal from Aranghata, Satyananda Das from Bankura, Sanatan Das from Khayerboni in Bankura along with his son Biswa, Madhab Das Baul from Kalna, Chinmoy and Durga, Swapan and Beni from Tribeni, Shoshti Khepa from Kalyani, Krishna Das from Aranghata, Radharani Dasi from Gopalnagar, Nimai from Suripara, Naba and Krishna Dasi from Ghoshpara, Sadhan Bairagya and Maki Kazumi from Hat Gobindapur, Gangtok Babaji, Chintamoni Dasi from Sainthia, Giribala Dasi from Agartala, Nonibala Dasi and her husband Krishna Das Khepa from Nadia district, Debdas Baul from Bolpur and Bhaktadas Baul from Kolkata, Shombu Das from Ilambazaar, Nityagopal Das and Sandhyarani from Bolpur, Tarak and Baka Shyam from Joydeb Kenduli, Dhona Khepa from Ahmedpur, Hemanta Das from Bankura, Gour Khepa and Tinkori Chakraborty, and many others.

Among the fakirs were Halim Fakir and Man Kumari from Rampurhat, Anwar Fakir and Gulam Shah from Bardhaman, Mansoor Fakir and Chand Bibi from Nadia, Mehboob Shah, Mastan Fakir and Gopal Shah from South Twenty-Four Parganas.

The mahotsava was inaugurated the next day with an unexpected flourish of Chhau drums: dhols and dhamshas. The great Chhau guru Gombhir Singh had arrived from Purulia, hearing about our festival, and the Chhau dancers with their gorgeous, glittering masks of Ganesha and Kartik, Shiva and Parvati, leapt out of his black truck, which he backed against the compound wall and – dha dha dha dhinaka dha dha dha dhinaka – the massive drums rolled and thundered, and hundreds of laughing and shouting children swirled into the compound, shouting excitedly, followed by their parents.

It was a massive churning, like the mythical churning of the ocean by Anant Nag, the serpent of eternity, and suddenly it seemed as if ambrosia, the very essence of joy, was being poured on us; the myth had become a reality. The Bauls and fakirs, surprised by this joyous atmosphere, were now in high spirits, and there was singing and dancing and exchanging of embraces and garlands of flowers and much celebration.

Paban and I were worried about how we would feed everyone. On the first day, we made do with our own resources. We had a flourishing vegetable patch with the usual winter vegetables, and we hacked down a banana tree in addition, to make a tasty traditional thor ghonto dish out of the heart of the tree trunk. Paban and I planned the menu with the ashramites from Samudragarh and with the guruma. We spread little hills of vegetables on the ground and began to peel and cut. Meat, eggs, onions and garlic, considered to cause excessive passion, were excluded from the menu. Tinkori was in charge of chai, which we served several times in the morning with molasses, flavoured with home-grown citronella. We served muri and chapattis with vegetables for nashta, breakfast. For lunch, we cooked purple and pale green aubergines, fried in tender neem leaves from our own trees. Kolmi sag, bindweed, which grew in thick clusters in our waterhole-cum-pond, were our greens. We cooked dal and panchmishali tarkari, mixed vegetables.

At midday, to my amazement and to Hari Goshain's triumphant chuckling, alms started pouring in. Anwar Hussain, a local farmer and a daytime taxi driver in Kolkata, sent us a cartload of cabbages. Two cartloads of mixed vegetables arrived: pumpkins, aubergines, potatoes and yams. Alms were being offered up at our mahotsava in exchange for Baul songs. I was excited by the possibilities that might be opened up to us if we successfully revived this ancient tradition; it was when people realised the importance of sharing their resources that a true revolution could take place in such a fractured society. However, this was sooner said than done.

The local village women lagged behind: I had forgotten that they were mostly Muslims. Ma Goshain, along with her disciples from Mana in Bardhman, now flatly refused to let them into the kitchen. As usual, diet was the hub of conflict. No one who had not been initiated could be permitted to enter 'sacred' territory.

Hari Goshain did not intervene; the old sages made their laws explicit. Paban looked at me in awe when I clamoured to point out that the Baul was free from caste or creed. But the Baul belonged to a society conducted by Brahmins. And, in spite of all his singing against caste and religious prejudice, in real life, he often had to give in to the law.

I was reprimanded, and the order prevailed as it always had, to some extent. The Muslim women of Nischintyapur backed out from the conflict without protest and later in the day came back to listen to the songs of the Bauls and fakirs. They put their arms around me, knowing that I was furious, and told me that Paban had been right to smoke out the trees. Blossoms were burgeoning on the mango trees, spring was here. We had time on our side, they told me. Once the festival was over, the Bauls and fakirs would all go away and we'd share the fruit once more in the hot season, which would soon be here.

I was sad for these submissive women and felt isolated, as there was not a single woman friend of mine I could call upon to join me in the enterprise of standing up to what was so evidently ordained in these parts. My left-wing feminist friends back in Paris and in Kolkata looked suspiciously at the mahotsava, in any case, which seemed to them like a religious event. I would have to work very hard over the years to keep these from becoming one. Only after repeated festivals and after Paban had made the album *Real Sugar* with Sam Mills, a guitarist and composer from London, which was produced by Peter Gabriel through Real World Records and seen on European television, did this equation begin to change. We had to switch gods in some senses, to be accepted by middle-class Kolkata society, whose fads and fashions were largely determined in the West.

By twilight, the local decorators had wired up our makeshift stage with bulbs and set up the microphones. The music was about to begin.

Gautam Nag, an excellent sound engineer, provided an impeccable sound system. The folk poets Amulya Sarkar and his nephew Tamal rose up to begin the performance at our request, engaging in a duel on the theme of Sahajiya, the Baul ideal of enlightenment we strove to achieve. Hari Goshain did not come forward but relaxed under his tree, although his eyes and his spies were everywhere, reporting to him.

An old drummer thundered on his drum and a young woman played a few plaintive notes on the harmonium. As the drum began to reverberate, more and more people came into the garden and collected around the stage. Soon there was not a bit of space in which to sit, and we saw people begin to climb trees, and similarly to ascend to the top of the high buildings around us, to get a view of the event. Excitement among the Bauls, who were watching all this from the grove, was at fever pitch now as the public listened, captivated.

Tamal, in the role of a disciple, questioned Amulya, who took on the role of the master.

'O Master, answer this: what is Sahajiya? People talk of the sahaj, the simple way. What lies beyond these words? Pray tell us. Unveil this mystery. I'll not talk further, when water and milk mingle, the swan separates the water and drinks only the milk. You who are congregated here today, audience of swans, hear my words; the master will surely bless us today with an answer.'

To this Amulya Sarkar responded, his voice lifting in incantation: 'I will answer with a story. Now, you've all heard of the saint Trailangaswami. You've seen movies about him, read books, watched performances which reenact his life. When he awoke to spiritual life, he was in two minds: could he find God at home or did he have to renounce everything? He was walking by the side of the river, preoccupied with his thoughts, when a raving madman accosted him in front of a crematorium. "Look at the ashes which I hold in my fist. If I blow on them, they will disappear without a trace. With time, you and I will be reduced to ashes too," he said. Trailangaswami was illuminated. The equation was evident. When you burn in fire, you are reduced to ashes. The old is defeated, the new advances. Look around you. In this very grove, old leaves tremble as they know they will fall to give place to the new leaves pushing their fronds on the trunks of the mango trees.'

Amulya and Tamal's duel and exposition of Sahajiya continued in front of a rapt audience for a couple of hours. Then, the fakirs took over the stage. The mood and the rhythm changed as tambourines and violins took over from the dhol and the harmonium. We were now on the road of the aashiq and the maashuq, the lover and the loved one, the murid and the pir, the child and the father. Paban joined in their drumming, to their delight, transforming like a chameleon from a Baul to a fakir, his Murshidabad origins surfacing through his spiralling rhythms as he played his tambourine.

The noble-faced Halim Fakir began first, plucking a few magical notes on his dotara, swinging into a pacey tune of the Sufis.

> Khoda is at his own place, that's why he's dancing;
> He who cannot perceive the womb of his mother,
> Sees darkness everywhere.

Man Kumari, his wife, sang and danced, playing her ektara. The couple swung around each other, stamping their feet, swinging their hips. Man Kumari was a Brahmin's wife, endowed with the gift of song and dance. She'd run away from her husband and family to become Halim's spiritual partner. Her posture bold, strong and seductive, she sang loud and clear.

> In the invisible city, in the bazaar of existence,
> Live Allah and Rasool.
> The two love each other in secret.
> Who can recognise them?
> Raise your veil, lower your mask,
>   see the altar within you.
> Were you to go to Mecca and Medina,
> Would you find the treasures within you?

Then Ansar Fakir from Bardhwan got up to sing, scraping a repetitive melody on his violin, making of it a snake-charmer's flute.

Who will go to the banks of the river? Be quick!
In the boat of the grand sire: Noor Nabi.
There's no fear of waves,
Says the poet Mansoor:
Those who don't hear his call,
Into the water's depths they fall
Without the boat of Noor Nabi,
They lose their lives.

And Halim Fakir continued.

Give me news of food and water,
Give me the wisdom of the pir.
The Hindus call it by one name,
The Muslims call it by another.
I want that and only that,
Which is common to both,
Give me the wisdom of the pir.

The audience was enchanted now. At midnight, Paban joined the fakirs on stage, followed merrily by Jaya Khepa, who shouted, 'Baul? He within whom blooms flowers is a Baul. And the others are batul [empty talkers].'

When Paban tuned his ektara and handed it to me, a ripple of excitement went through the crowd. Many of them were from our neighbourhood but they had never really heard Paban sing before. And then Paban roared, bel canto, like an ogre raising his hands to the sky, closing his eyes and throwing his head back: 'Manush Manush Manush.' He paused, then:

O Manush, how will you go
To the slippery banks of the curved river?
What will you hold on to?
Odorous Kali sits there, waiting for sacrifice;
If you must go to war with her, shoot arrows at her,
Then, oh my heart, lock the door of your house.

I closed my eyes as I listened to him, hearing his clamour and his rage, his tearful, baffled groans as he expressed the bewilderment of a man faced with his desire for a woman. Primitive now, peeled of all masks and roles, I rose to dance to his compelling rhythm, our bodies soon wet with effort, our eyes interlocking, our spirits soaring in joy. Paban's fingers bled as his drum thundered out, punctuating each cry he uttered with explosions of rhythm, unconscious that the audience around him hung on every beat of his tambourine, waves of energy rolling through them.

After a while, Gour Khepa suddenly manifested himself on stage and began a duel of percussion with Paban. The crowd roared with surprise at this new presence. Gour was renowned through the land for his immense repertoire and his grandiose delivery of epic Baul songs, as well as his rigorous practice of Baul sexual rites. The audience teetered on the brink of the precipice he was leading us up to as he slammed on his khamak, and soon all swung to his slow, crashing, oceanic waves of rhythm.

His song was a challenge and a response to Paban's song.

> Do you imagine you'll cross the ferry without sadhana?
> You'll end up losing your oar and you'll drown in
>   the waves.
> Your father's treasure is what belongs to you, take
>   good care of it,
> Honour it, once a month, in the room of emotion!
> Live in the house of your master, why travel abroad?
> Obey your heart and dedicate yourself to truth.
> Khepachand Baul says:
> If you want to catch the fugitive moon, pay attention.
> That very instant, you'll be summoned and chained.
> And you'll have some fun.

A kalbaisakhi, an anti-cyclonic electric storm, was beginning to rattle and roll like massive drums in the sky. Streaks of lightning zigzagged across the sky. Gour's dithyrambic chanting, his primordial voice many decibels above what was bearable, flashing red danger signs on the sound monitor, had pierced through to the very sky where thunder now crackled like a sub-machine-gun; hot rain poured down, drenching the audience. A high wind blew through the trees and brought a swirling shower of dead leaves to the ground. But Baul magic was too powerful now. No one moved, as though rooted to the earth. Gour grinned and grimaced as if he'd brought down the storm himself, but as suddenly as the storm had subsided, he was becalmed, embracing and kissing Paban.

The mood changed now, Paban danced and sang with great hilarity around Gour Khepa, leaping and kicking. I sat between them with my magic ektara, which resonated in a sphere of widening waves of vibrations as I let myself go. Paban was a jhumuria, a woodland poet, playing the forest jingles of his origins on his tambourine; throwing his head back, he raised his voice high, and Gour stood behind him, backing him up with infallible precision, short, sharp, high notes twanging on his khamak.

'Haaaaariiiiiii! Bandho mon!' he sang, from a contemporary Baul song written by Dhiraj Chakraborty, who had been a failed Naxalite but a lovely poet who drank himself to death at a young age.

> O my spirit,
> Tie a jar to the date palm tree.
> First learn to cut the trunk of the tree,
> Learn to know it,
> If you tie your jar to the tree of truth,
> You will get real sugar.
> So many scallywags try to climb the tree,
> But they fall down and die.
> Only those discerning get to taste the sap,
> The foolish never get to know its savour.
> When the tide flows in the tree,
> Slash its bark cleverly,
> And the sap will flow, drop by sugary drop.
> Don't let the hemp rope tied around you break,
> Or you will fall below,
> O my spirit
> Tie a jar to the date palm tree. 3

Subal now joined Paban and Gour. It was about two in the morning. He took us right back, centuries back, as he sat down to sing his song. The public, which had been roaring in their gaiety while Paban and Gour performed, now slowed down and listened to him in hushed silence. His voice raised in a slow solemn melody, he closed his eyes, his head bent as he tuned his ektara unsuccessfully – at which point Paban snatched the ektara from him and, tuning it, handed it back. Subal twanged on his ektara and sang an epic song, recounting the human condition.

> You've come here, to this life, to play a game of cards,
> Learn first to know the ace of one Brahma, of supreme breath.
> O Gyananana what have you done?
> You came to play cards but you lost,
> Under the spell of five and six,
> You forgot all about the ace. 4

As Subal's song came to an end the sages roared: 'Dih!' An evocative sound, miming the release of energy.

The festival continued at this pace for three days and three nights. All day, the Bauls chanted invocations, told stories and skits with a popular, ribald village humour. Paban and I were so tired and sleepless that we realised only later that our festival was a grand success. In the gloomy, cramped atmosphere of this outpost of suburbia, our festival was an explosion of dynamism and energy. It offered the city of Kolkata the possibility of getting to know the Baul mode of life, of discovering their visionary souls, a chance to probe into the mysteries behind their enigmatic texts, share their spontaneity and their sensitivity to the environment. With its extremes of wealth and poverty and its curious blend of cults of all kinds, both Hindu and Muslim, the area now brought up a variety of colourful characters, sending them into our garden. Weeping, nostalgic pensioners, bewildered young men from the innumerable local clubs, university dropouts, young students hungry for a pop culture of their own, cultural 'guerrillas', political groups from both the extreme left and the extreme right, closet homosexuals looking for midnight company, dealers of illicit liquor and ganja, loonies and junkies; all jumped on our Boral bandwagon.

Baul and Vaishnava sadhus cooked on giant pots and pans for all those who would be nourished. It was a miraculous sharing. Everything multiplied.

On the second day, Shaila Ghosh, our neighbour and the owner of the local sweet and pastry shop, brought us a bucketload of fresh fish from his pond, donated by his family. It was Shaila's family who had found the Vishnu statue in the pond next door and it was Shaila's family who now flocked around Hari Goshain and would become his disciples. We had enough now to feed our hundred-odd guests and more for over three days and three nights. The scene turned biblical.

We cooked fish for the midday meal amidst great hilarity and celebration, and ended the meal with a drop of honey that had come from some young friends of Paban who practised beekeeping in the Sundarbans. Dinner was served late, once the songs were over. We fed everybody on sal leaf plates, and kept the gates stubbornly open so that the public could enter all day and all night to listen to the songs of the Bauls.

Conversations continued between Deepak Majumdar, Hari Goshain, Paban and myself. Deepak suggested that our festival could become a 'tertiary' and permanent festival, of the kind which was celebrated in the homes of disciples.

This Boral mahotsava, which Paban and I held in Boral on twelve occasions over eighteen years, from 1988 to 2000, became our way of bringing singers and sages closer to Kolkata, and of creating a connection between those fakirs and Bauls imbued with a profoundly articulate spiritual culture, between people of all faiths and paths in life. It also reached out to those searching for something missing within the teeming megapolis.

The last Baul mahotsava was held in Boral in the year 2000, against great odds. A mass lynching of villagers had taken place in a village called Bangalpara, barely a kilometre from our garden. Sheikh Binod, a criminal boss from the south of the city, had taken shelter in the village along with his henchmen. When the authorities became aware of their presence, a lynching was organised by the local CPM party bosses. The gang who had masterminded the plan to hide out in the village had mobile phones and escaped, while eighteen innocent local people were slaughtered by an enraged public. The photograph in the newspaper looked like a recent East European massacre.

When we arrived in Boral, we noticed militias guarding every street corner. A young apprentice imam from the madrasa was now in charge of the garden, and an older one emerged from the toilet which he'd obviously been using to tell me that there were 'machines' (a euphemism for guns or arms) now in every house. But our local friends and helpers Shiraz, Sabir, Biltu and the others pleaded with us to ignore these events and hold the mahotsava as we had planned.

Urbanisation and globalisation had set in with a vengeance, and the boys who had helped us with the mahotsavas were now grown men who worked in the local cake factory and who had swollen up like cream puffs. Most of the old Baul gurus had disappeared and in their place newfangled gurus had taken over.

In his usual contradictory way, Deepak Majumdar argued that I was trying to revive a carcass. Perhaps his vision had failed him too. I remain convinced that Baul singers, as true artists, have a great role to play in the world of today. They are not merely singers. It is only when they fail in grappling with the world around them that they are reduced to being solely performers. The Bauls themselves are ignorant of the fact that the world has changed profoundly, and has perhaps been ready for their knowledge and their wisdom for some time. Senses need to be freed, barriers to be broken: we need to reconnect with our deepest selves.

In the morning after the last day of the last mahotsava, while Paban and all the men were still asleep, exhausted by their nights of song and days of festivity, Paban's mother Ulangini and I slipped away to neighbouring Nischintyapur, where Biltu's and Shiraz's wives welcomed us in for a chai. Ulangini had no prejudice against

Muslims, having lived in Murshidabad, and was familiar with their customs and manners.

We entered Biltu's house. I noticed my rosewood cupboard with the warped mirror, which was missing from the outhouse in Boral. Biltu's wife, Rina, noticed me looking at it and told me guiltily that her husband had brought the cupboard here for treatment because it was full of woodworms, that he hadn't had the time to return it. I told her to keep the cupboard as I did not need it any more.

Just then, two very old aunts of Biltu and Shiraz entered the house. They were tall and slim, and had beautiful white hair, their bodies draped with pieces of white cloth. They huddled in front of us on the floor. Rina winked at me: 'Didi, do you want to see some fun?'

She called out to the two old aunts: 'Will you have some chai?' They nodded, smiles breaking out on their wrinkled faces. Rina pointed to the warped mirror where the two old ladies were now reflected, their heads bent out of shape. 'Ask those two ladies if they will have tea too.'

The two old women stood up and beckoned at their own reflections in the mirror. Then, they turned to us sadly. 'They can't hear us. They won't come.'

Rina and Ulangini went into paroxyms of laughter, and the two old women smiled, uncomprehending. I realised now that they'd never seen a mirror in their lives. That looking-glass world was as real to them as life itself; it was just a threshold waiting to be crossed.

EPILOGUE

Illustration overleaf: The Vault of Existence No 2. The second Vault represents a metamorphosed being, one who has mastered his life force. He serenely balances seven pots (representing the seven energy chakras) on his head. The white rat of Day and the black rat of Night walk away from the chequered pillars of time, the serpent falls asleep, the tiger leaves and, on top of the pillar of pots, the joint form of the lovers Radha and Krishna swing on a pole above the man's head and he becomes immortal.

IN 1990, Paban created Antar Jantar, a cooperative society of destitute artisans specialising in making folk musical instruments. Antar Jantar today provides sustenance to twenty-five families of artisans and exports instruments to the four corners of the globe through Sasha, an equitable marketing house, based in Kolkata.

Today, Paban and I shuttle between India, France, the UK and Mexico, as we compose and collaborate with musicians from all over India and all over the world, great and small.

The worldwide releases of Paban's albums *Real Sugar* (1997) and *Tana Tani* (2004) through the Real World/Virgin/EMI family has given him global celebrity. *Real Sugar* has been hugely pirated by the Sylheti diaspora in Brick Lane. Result: Paban is adored in Bangladesh, where his song 'Dil ki Doya' is being sung by the poorest of the poor and the richest of the rich.

> Din duniya'r malik khoda,
> Tomar dil ki doya hoyna?
> Tomal dil ki doya hoyna?
> Katar katar aaghat dao go jar,
> Tar phuler aaghat shoyna.
> Tomar dil ki doya hoyna?
>
> (Khoda, lord of the unfortunate
> Have you no compassion in your heart?
> Have you no compassion in your heart?
> He whom you strike with thorns,
> Cannot bear the blows of flowers.
> Have you no compassion in your heart?)

Paban first heard this song in a majaar, a Sufi gathering, in Ghutiarisharif in the South Twenty-Four Parganas. Only a smattering of people knew it then. Now, a decade after the release of the album *Real Sugar*, the song is globally popular and Paban still earns royalties – in dribbles – for his interpretation of the song. As the song is in the public domain of 'traditional' music, the rights are mainly earned by the Performing Rights Society in London.

Only yesterday, I got an email from Beatrice in the village of Fiac in the Tarn Valley, north of Toulouse. She wants me to transcribe the song phonetically to her so that she can learn it with her music group. The album is out of print now. The other day, Lionel, a didgeridoo player, made us a copy of a copy so that we could, in our turn, copy the copy of a pirate copy to send to her!

Let's hope there's some truth to the Baul adage: nakal korey pabi ashal! (Being false, you'll get to the real!)

In Kolkata today, although massively popular Bangla rock bands like Cactus and Bhoomi revere Paban, and many young urban and rural musicians emulate his songs and his style, Paban is little known and hardly solicited. Occasionally Gour, Subal and Paban are invited to sing at concerts in the city. These events are usually managed by well intentioned men steeped in alcohol and sentimentalism. They would do better to hand the management to the Bauls, though; let them take care of designing the environment.

Instead of drawing our disparate worlds closer together, globalisation seems to have had the opposite effect on our lives. Paban's fellow Bauls and his family in Durgapur, who live in a state of perpetual debt, imagine that Paban has reaped fortunes; quite unaware that we live on a shoestring budget, balancing precariously on a tightrope between East and West.

Every day, Paban and I need to think about how we can hold on to each other, how we can continue taking care of our extended tribe of family and friends spread over several continents. Every new day, we need to think about how to get out of the blind alleys we stray into, artistic, musical, temporal and spiritual and financial.

Should we bend our rhythms to hip-hop and break-dance tracks? Continue to explore Mandingue melodies from Mali and jazz rhythms? Take our musical encounters with the fabulous desert musicians of Rajasthan towards an album? How do we cross over through the grid of rules and regulations, laws and by-laws which govern copyright, and, in fact, existence itself in Europe?

In France, we rent a small, old worker's house in Montreuil with a garden in which Paban's green fingers make flowers burst into blossom. In Kolkata, we rent a flat in Salt Lake so that I can write and do all the administrative work which is related to our global journeying. The minute I've finished, we take to the Baul road. To Bolpur and to Lohagarh. To Kenduli and to Tarapith. Nights are dedicated to song, under the eyes of the Saptarishi Mandala, the constellation of stars under which we began our journey.

Wild Paban flings his arms out and swirls around me in gestures of total abandon. Yet he controls every gesture. I sit like a rock and keep time to him, with the kartalas, that little high-pitched tinkle floating and pulsating, giving him that tightrope he seeks.

We're on the move, constantly pitching camp everywhere.

As we hop, trip and jump into buses, trains and planes, we hum and sing and play with each other, and tell each other stories. When we get to our destinations, we shop, cook, clean, rest and write new songs.

Should we drop all this and return to Boral and build a house on our land, which has now been divided between my brother and me? Should we go to Baul country in Birbhum and create a Baul mahotsava on our newly acquired land in the village of Lohagarh near the teak forests which border the Kopai River? Do we abandon our fantastic shuttle between Europe and India? Can we do both?

If songs can define territory, in the manner of migratory birds, then the map that describes the journey of the Baul singers today goes well beyond the borders of present-day West Bengal and Bangladesh. It follows vertical directions into mystic spheres and travels horizontally around the globe, via the new networks of world music.

As we cross these borders now, I try to help Paban take into account this shifting taxonomy. In today's climate we seek the reincarnation of Baul art and its mode of life; a quest that has never seemed so salient, so necessary and so urgent.

Hari Goshain disappeared for good in April 2008, ten days after his annual mahatsava in Nabasana. He would have lived a few years more had he not insisted on riding a motorbike at the age of one hundred, over fields lying fallow. A fall gave him a nosebleed that never left him. Then, even as he lay dying in Ma Goshain's arms, the villagers descended on the ashram in a pack, tearing and ripping open the mattresses and pillows to see if he had hidden wealth inside them, helping themselves to the few objects which he had acquired during his travels to Paris: a Swiss cuckoo clock, a plastic torch in the shape of a cancan girl and his mobile phone. In spite of all the years Hari Goshain had served the village, they had passed his profound intelligence by, missed the point of the intangible heritage he offered and carried on. It is still true to say that a prophet is never recognised in his own country.

According to the Baul gurus, rebirth can take place within this very life. Four vaults characterise human existence. The first vault is the womb of the mother, the very first encasing in which we come into existence. The second vault is the parental one in which we are cherished and nurtured. The third vault is the samsara we create around ourselves, and the fourth vault is the final one, the vault of the sky which waits to encircle us as we prepare to die.

It is dawn. Paban is still fast asleep as I write these lines. The light is changing here as we get to the end of the winter equinox, and the birds chirrup and coo in the laurel tree at my window, which they'd abandoned for a while. The camellia tree will soon burst into a galaxy of blazing white blossoms, and the blackbird will nest in it. And by that time, we will have flown away, in a southeasterly direction.

Notes

I. Beginnings: a life on two continents

1. Bhaba Pagla, twentieth century
2. Author unknown, nineteenth century
3. Traditional, author unknown, late nineteenth century. Gour (as in 'the thorn of Gour') is another name for Sri Chaitanya Mahaprabhu, a Vaishnava monk and social reformer of the fifteenth and sixteenth centuries who was part of the Bhakti movement which preached love and devotion to God as the highest goal. Baul gurus trace their spiritual lineage back to Chaitanya and his six main disciples, the six goswamis
4. Ram Chandra, nineteenth century
5. Author unknown, nineteenth century
6. Vaishnavites (or Vaishnavas) are those Hindus who worship Vishnu, the second god within the triumvirate of Brahman, Vishnu and Shiva; while Shiva worshippers are Shaivites. Most Hindu families are either Vaishnavites or Shaivites. Vaishnavas such as Paban's family are mendicant worshippers of Vishnu. They often dress in white and saffron, and collect alms and food and live off them. Their dharma is to live their lives in service to humanity.
7. Traditional, popularised by Abdul Halim, 1950s

II. Durgapur: campfires, witches and shantytowns

1. Collected from Mastan Fakir, Bardhaman, 1970s
2. Popular folk couplet, author unknown
3. Aal Kaap, a tradition of musical folk theatre in Murshidabad, and part of a traditional repertory of Shuhankar Das
4. Author unknown, nineteenth century

III. Kenduli: festivals, stars and a singing heart

1. Lallan Shah Fakir, nineteenth century. Rabindranath Tagore would quote this song in his first speech to a Western audience at the Musée Guimet in Paris in 1916. This translation has been adapted from Prithvindranath Mukherjee's book *Les Fous de l'Absolu*

2. Haore Goshain, late nineteenth century
3. Author unknown, collected by Paban Das Baul from Gour Khepa
4. Lallan Fakir, nineteenth century

IV. Shantiniketan: secret arts of love and initiation

1. Nabani Khepa, early twentieth century
2. Poddolochan, nineteenth century
3. Poddolochan, nineteenth century
4. Bhaba Pagla, 1970
5. Author unknown, folk song, nineteenth century

V. Ghoshpara to Agrodwip: music, women and sorrow

1. Lallan Fakir, nineteenth century
2. A parivar is a group who follow a particular course of teachings or study
3. Bhaba Pagla, 1970s. Sung by Paban on the album *Inner Knowledge*, UK: Real World 1997
4. Collected by Paban Das Baul from Rana Pratap Mukherjee, 1981

VI. Nabasana: hidden altars and holy games

1. Shivananda Goswami, twentieth century
2. Duddu Shah, nineteenth century
3. Traditional devotional kirtan, author unknown
4. Ananto Goswami, nineteenth century
5. Satyajit Ray, twentieth century

VII. Paris to Kolkata: home, dreams and an elephant's fall

1. Goshain Ambika, nineteenth century
2. Part of a traditional repertoire of Padabali kirtans, author unknown

VIII. Boral: a singing garden and a festival's birth

1. Phulbassuddin, nineteenth century
2. Nimai Chand, twentieth century
3. Dhiraj Chakraborty, twentieth century
4. Gyananda Goswami, nineteenth century

Baul sources and resources

Selected by Rangan Momen

There has been a steadily rising interest in the music and spiritual practices of the Bauls and fakirs of Bengal over the past few decades. The disciplines of anthropology, religious studies and ethnomusicology have produced numerous studies and field recordings in this area. These have been supplemented by a large number of studio recordings and film documentaries. Recently, there has also been a growing Baul presence on the internet in various forms. Here is a selection of written, recorded, visual and electronic material related to the Bauls. Most of the books and recordings are available either new or used over the internet.

i. Books

Bhattacharya, Bhaskar. 1993. *The Path of the Mystic Lover, Baul Songs of Passion and Ecstasy*. Rochester: Destiny Books.

Bhattacharya, Upendranath. 2000/1957. *Banglar Baul o Baul Gan*. Calcutta: Orient Book Co.

Capwell, Charles. 1986. *The Music of the Bauls of Bengal*. Kent, Ohio: Kent State University Press.

Chakrabarti, Sudhir. 2001. *Baul Phakir Katha*. Calcutta: Loksamskriti o Adibasi Samskriti Kendra, Ministry of Information and Culture, Government of West Bengal.

Dimock, Jr, Edward C. 1966. *The Place of the Hidden Moon: Erotic Mysticism in the Vaisnava-Sahajiya Cult of Bengal*. Chicago: University of Chicago Press.

Fakir, Rudrani. 2005. *The Goddess and the Slave; the Fakir, the Mother and Maldevelopment*. Varanasi: Indica Books.

Jha, Shaktinath. 1995. 'Cari-candra Bhed, Use of the Four Moons', in Rajat Kanta Ray, ed., *Mind, Body and Society*. Calcutta: Oxford University Press.

Jha, Shaktinath. 1999. *Bastubadi Baul: Udbhab Samaj Samskriti o Darshan*. Calcutta: Loksamskriti o Adibasi Samskriti Kendra, Ministry of Information and Culture, Government of West Bengal.

Mukherjee, Prithwindra. 1985. *Les Fous de l'Absolu: Chant Baûl*. Paris: Editions Findakly. With the participation of the Ministère de la Culture (France).

Openshaw, Jeanne. 2002. *Seeking Bauls of Bengal*. Cambridge: Cambridge University Press, Oriental Series.

Openshaw, Jeanne. 2009. *Writing the Self: the Life and Philosophy of a Bengali Baul Guru*. Oxford: Oxford University Press.

Salomon, Carol. 1991. 'The Cosmogonic Riddles of Lalan Fakir', in Arjun Appadurai, Korom and Mills, eds., *Gender, Genre and Power in South Asian Expressive Traditions*. Philadelphia: University of Pennsylvania Press.

ii. Records

Bauls Des Fous de l'Absolu, 1989, France: Studio SM.

Bengale: Chants des Fous, 1979, France: Chants du Monde.

Bengali Bauls at Big Pink, 1968, USA: Buddah.

Indian Street Music, 1971, USA: Nonesuch Explorer Series.

Le Chant Mystique des Bauls, 1982, France: Sonodisc ESP.

Les Musiciens Bauls 'Fous de Dieu' du Bengale, 1983, France: Disques Arion.

Religious Songs from Bengal: Songs of the Bauls and Poems of Chandidas, c. 1957, France: Disques BAM.

The Bauls of Bengal, 1968, USA: Elektra.

The Bengal Minstrel, 1975, USA: Nonesuch Explorer Series.

iii. CDs

Din Doyal Das Troupe, c. 2004, *Om Nama Shiva: Bauls of Bengal*, USA: Folktribe Records.

Paban Das Baul, Gour Khepa, Nimai Goswani and Mimlu Sen, 2002, *Manuche o Rautan*, Brussels: Fontimusicali.

Paban Das Baul and Haripada Goswami, 1993, *Inde: Chants d'Initiation des Bauls du Bengale*, Paris: Buda Musique.

Paban Das Baul, Subal Das Baul and Nitya Gopal Das, 1997, *Inner Knowledge*, UK: Real World.

Parvathy Baul, 2002, *Radha Bhava*, Paris: Ethnomad.

Satyananda Das, 2008, *Baul Songs*, Korea: Satyahori Records.

Shahjahan Miah, 1992, *Chants Mystiques Bauls du Bangladesh*, Paris: Maison des Cultures du Monde.

Subol Das Baul, Nitya Gopal Das and Kalipoda Adhikary, 1996, *A Man of Heart*, Rome: Amiata Records.

Various Artists, 1998, *The Mirror of the Sky, Songs of the Bauls of Bengal*, USA: Hohm Press.

Various Artists, 1999, *Inde: Kobiyals, Fakirs & Bauls, Oral Traditions of Bengal*, Paris: Buda Musique.

Various Artists, c. 2004, *Joya Dev Mela, Spiritual Love Festival*, USA: Folktribe Records.

Various Artists, 2005, *Bauls of Bengal: Mystic Songs from India*, UK: Arc Music.

Viswanath Das, Anando Das and Nitya Gopal Das, 1998, *Bauls du Bengale*, France: Daqui.

iv. Films and documentaries

Abak Jaye Here, 1997, Ranjan Palit.

Achin Pakhi – The Unknown Bard, 1996, Tanvir Mokammel.

Bauls of Bengal: Luxman Baul's Movie, 1975, Howard Alk.

Bishar Blues, 2008, Amitabh Chakraborty.

Egaro Mile, 1992, Ruchir Joshi.

Lalon, 2004, Tanvir Mokammel.

Le Chant des Fous, 1979, Georges Luneau.

Looking for Deb Das Baul, 2007, Charlie Stanier.

Waves of Joy: Anandalahari, 1974, Deben Bhattacharya.

v. Internet

baularchive.org

Yet to go live, but promises to be a major portal for music, video and information on West Bengal's Baul singers.

baulfakirsahajsai.blogspot.com

Abhishek Basu's new and promising discussion forum on all things Baul/fakir. Includes some great film clips and Fakir Mela recordings.

bauliana.blogspot.com

Maqsoodul Haque's Baul blog from Bangladesh. Highlights include Bauliana, an online book on the Baul path and a highly informative article on Lalon Fakir by Farhad Mazar.

Baul.it

Artist website for master dotara-player and Baul singer, Naryan Chandra Adhikari.

ektara.net

Soumya Chakravarti's excellent but seldom updated site offers field recordings of the traditional folk music of India. Highlights include a Lalon song by the late Khoda Baks Shah from Kushtiar.

lalon.org

Sudipto Chatterjee's website on his performance, *Man of Heart,* on the life and times of Lalon Fakir. This website also includes photographs, video and sound recordings from the extensive field research behind the play, as well as archival documents.

myspace.com/pabandasBaul

Artist web page that includes sound and film clips including a rare footage of Paban Das Baul in action from 1979 in the German documentary *Vagabunden Karawane.*

parvathyBaul.mimemo.net

Artist website for Kerala-based Parvathy Baul.

thestatesman.net

Type in 'Mimlu Sen' in the search field for her regular column on the Baulsphere.

youtube.com

Type in 'Baul' or 'Bauls' for a wide range of homemade clips of Baul songs and related videos.

Acknowledgements

To Georges Luneau, whose film *Le Chant des Fous* was the beginning of this journey.

To the late Deepak Majumdar, who set me off on the journey although he got off halfway down the line.

To the late Laetitia Comba, whose invitation to hold a seminar on my travels with Paban for Diotima, a group of women philosophers in Verona, led to the initial idea of this book. 'Could you describe to us how you shifted from social activism to a deeper, more feminine démarche?' she asked me. The seminar was never held as Laetitia died in a car crash on the highway one morning, on her way to the University of Verona a few days after her mail. But the seed she planted in my head sprouted, in spite of myself.

To the late Bhaskar Bhattacharya, his wife Rohini and his son Bhuva for welcoming me into their fold when I began to write my very first sketches in their home in Gurgaon, providing me with the soil that my new sprouts craved for.

To Chitralekha Basu and Mike Flannery of *The Statesman*, for whom I wrote a column on my travels with Paban, which provided the bedrock from which this book emerged.

To William Dalrymple and his wife Olivia, for their friendship and lending us their homes in Pages Yard, London and in Mehrauli in New Dehli during the crucial moments of writing and editing this book; for their unfailing enthusiasm for Paban's songs and my projects and for leading me to Chiki Sarkar.

To Santanu Mitra, who accompanied us through the most joyous and painful moments of this journey, providing us with tender loving care and unconditional support. To Ratan Khanna, who followed us intrepidly though somewhat blindly with his camera into the depths of the Baul world, providing me with another angle of vision.

To Chiki Sarkar, whose short, sharp and subtle questions and snappy emails worked wonders in helping me get to the deeper groove of my story, without which I would have been like Pessoa's sheep: my thoughts are like flocks of sheep. I spend my time running after them, the poet said somewhere.

To Simon Godwin, who helped me see that my story had a beginning, a middle and an end, and to his father David Godwin, who was brave enough to risk his career with me.

To Rajni George, whose tenderness and patience saw me over the bumpy road I'd built for myself.

To Prithwindranath Mukherjee, whose translations of Baul songs in French and English nourished me during the writing of this book.

To Partho Das and Akhila Krishnan, for the map.

To Joy Panatil, for his help in accessing the Chitrabani archives.

To Judith Kendra and Sue Lascelles for their delicacy, precision, constant enthusiasm and support in helping me find my way to a Western reading public.

To Caroline Newbury, Alex Young and the staff at Ebury Publishing. It's been a pleasure working with all of you.

To Margo Sagov, to John Macmillan (MAC) and to Ilana Pearlman for providing us with a support system during our forays into London with the madmen of Bengal over the past two decades.

To Francis Bonfanti for his constant support in recording Paban's music without reverbs and for providing me with a shoulder to cry on, for his marvellous Corsican cuisine and hospitality in Paris over the past three decades.

To Simon Broughton, who kindly led us to World Music Networks and made it possible for us to realise our dream of publishing a book and an album.

To Phil Stanton and Brad Haynes of World Music Networks who realised the importance of creating an album of Paban unplugged, *Music of the Honey Gatherers*, to accompany my book, thus making it possible for Paban and myself, and the oral and written tradition, to remain in tandem.

To Chili Hawes of October Gallery for her enthusiasm and interest in our quest to represent the Baul songs and way of life.

To my brother, Gautam Sen, for his tenderness, humour, constant vigilance for my well being and equilibrium during the past quarter of a century – in spite of being in the awkward position of my Big Brother – and for teaching me the science of neti, which has kept me well on our erratic and often acarian-ridden shuttle.

To Gopa Sen, my sister-in-law, for keeping me stocked with saris and for reminding me that I am a woman and an Indian.

To Duniya, Krishna, Paban and Patrice for taking care of me, filling the fridge and paying my unpaid bills, printing my copies and running my errands so that I could write in peace.

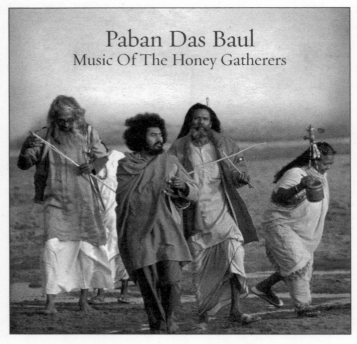